Lexical-Functional Grammar

An Introduction

A clear introduction to Lexical-Functional Grammar (LFG), this outstanding textbook sets out a formal approach to the study of language using a step-by-step approach and rich language data.

Data from English and a range of other languages are used to illustrate the main concepts, allowing those students not accustomed to working with cross-linguistic data to familiarise themselves with the theory while also enabling those interested in how the theory can account for more challenging data sets to extend their learning.

Exercises ranging from simple technical questions to analyses of a data set, as well as a further resources section with a literature review, complete each chapter. The book aims to equip readers with the skills to analyse new data sets and to begin to engage with the primary LFG literature.

KERSTI BÖRJARS is Professor of Linguistics at the University of Manchester and Professor (II) of Nordic Languages at Oslo University. Her current research focuses on syntactic description and analysis and on linguistic change. She has taught courses at undergraduate and postgraduate levels on English grammar, syntactic theory and diachronic linguistics. She has held grants to study linguistic change in Pennsylvania German (ESRC) and for a study of the English possessive (AHRC). She is editor of the *Journal of Linguistics* and co-author (with Kate Burridge) of *Introducing English Grammar*.

RACHEL NORDLINGER is Professor of Linguistics at the University of Melbourne, Director of the Research Unit for Indigenous Language and a Chief Investigator in the ARC Centre of Excellence for the Dynamics of Language. She completed her PhD in Linguistics at Stanford University, USA in 1997. Rachel's research centres around the description and documentation of Australia's Indigenous languages, and their implications for syntactic and morphological theory, working within the framework of LFG.

LOUISA SADLER is Professor of Linguistics at the University of Essex, where she has taught courses at graduate and undergraduate levels on syntactic theory (LFG and HPSG), the description of English, semantics, argument structure, morphology, PROLOG and computational linguistics. She has been involved in a number of research projects using LFG with a number of languages, including Welsh, Archi and Portuguese. Her current research interests centre on LFG, syntax and its interfaces with morphology and semantics and the grammatical description of the Arabic vernaculars, including Maltese. She currently holds a Leverhulme Major Research Fellowship for research on Arabic syntax.

‘This lucid and entertainingly written textbook is an excellent introduction to the theory of Lexical Functional Grammar. It presents the fundamentals of the theory in a way that is both accessible for beginners and engaging for linguists who are familiar with other frameworks.’

Mary Dalrymple,
University of Oxford

‘ … a clear and comprehensive introduction both to syntax and to the LFG framework, covering many core phenomena that have been central to syntactic analysis. Readers are skilfully guided through an impressive range of data reflecting the wide spectrum of languages.’

Peter Sells,
University of York

‘Developed by three notable linguists who are also gifted teachers, the book distinguishes itself by its accessibility, its rich coverage of morphology and f-structure, and its up-to-date references to current research in LFG.’

Joan Bresnan,
Stanford University

‘This is an ideal introduction to formal syntax and can also be used by practising syntacticians to familiarise themselves with the research developed within the framework of LFG.’

Alex Alsina,
University Pompeu Fabra, Barcelona

Lexical-Functional Grammar

An Introduction

KERSTI BÖRJARS

University of Manchester

RACHEL NORDLINGER

University of Melbourne

LOUISA SADLER

University of Essex

CAMBRIDGE
UNIVERSITY PRESS

University Printing House, Cambridge CB2 8BS, United Kingdom

One Liberty Plaza, 20th Floor, New York, NY 10006, USA

477 Williamstown Road, Port Melbourne, VIC 3207, Australia

314–321, 3rd Floor, Plot 3, Splendor Forum, Jasola District Centre, New Delhi – 110025, India

79 Anson Road, #06–04/06, Singapore 079906

Cambridge University Press is part of the University of Cambridge.

It furthers the University's mission by disseminating knowledge in the pursuit of education, learning and research at the highest international levels of excellence.

www.cambridge.org
Information on this title: www.cambridge.org/9781107170568
DOI: 10.1017/9781316756584

First published 2019

Printed in the United Kingdom by TJ International Ltd, Padstow Cornwall, 2019

A catalogue record for this publication is available from the British Library.

Library of Congress Cataloguing-in-Publication data
Names: Börjars, Kersti, author. | Nordlinger, Rachel, 1969- author. | Sadler, Louisa, author.
Title: Lexical-functional grammar : an introduction / Kersti Börjars, Rachel Nordlinger, Louisa Sadler.
Description: Cambridge, United Kingdom ; New York, NY : Cambridge University Press, 2019. | Includes bibliographical references and index.
Identifiers: LCCN 2018041300 | ISBN 9781107170568 (hardback : alk. paper) | ISBN 9781316621653 (paperback : alk. paper)
Subjects: LCSH: Lexical-functional grammar.
Classification: LCC P158.25 .B67 2019 | DDC 415.01/8234–dc23
LC record available at https://lccn.loc.gov/2018041300

ISBN 978-1-107-17056-8 Hardback
ISBN 978-1-316-62165-3 Paperback

Brief Contents

Contents

Tables

Tables

Preface

The aim of this book is to introduce the reader to Lexical-Functional Grammar (LFG), a formal system for analysing language.

Our aim is to ensure that this book is understandable to someone with some basic knowledge of linguistics, but with no previous experience of grammatical theories. We will assume that you know how to identify categories such as NOUN, VERB, ADJECTIVE, ADVERB and PREPOSITION. We will expect you to know that there are arguments for assuming that sentences have a hierarchical structure, that you know how to identify the constituents that make up this hierarchical structure, and that you understand how these can be represented as tree structures. We will also assume that you have a basic understanding of grammatical functions such as SUBJECT and OBJECT. Furthermore, we will assume that you know something about the difference between syntax and morphology and that you have some idea of what semantics is. We will have a lot to say in detail about categories, constituents, grammatical functions and morphology, but we will not go back to basics. If you feel you need to remind yourself of this, we suggest you look at Börjars and Burridge (2019) or Payne (2010) if you would like concepts explained through English examples, or Kroeger (2005) if you prefer a broader range of data. Radford et al. (2009) provide an introduction to a broader range of topics in linguistics.

This book will also be suitable for those already familiar with some other theoretical framework. However, even though it is interesting to compare how different frameworks analyse particular linguistic structures, we will have nothing to say in this book about other frameworks.

For most topics, we will use both English and other languages to explain the concepts of LFG. English will be used since this is a language that all readers of this book have in common. However, the languages of the world show a tremendous variety, for instance when it comes to the importance of hierarchical structure or morphology, and any theoretical framework worth its salt should be able to account not just for English, but also equally well for languages that work with radically different principles of organisation from those of English.

It is important to point out that we don't intend to try to provide a detailed LFG analysis of any particular language, but to use the different languages to introduce the tools of LFG and how to use them, so that readers are able to apply them to whatever language data they have. Indeed a reader may find evidence for a different analysis of a language that we have considered in this book. After all, we would not claim to have explored each language in full detail, but we hope to have given the reader the tools they require to formulate an alternative analysis.

Of course we will not be able to provide a complete picture of the work that has been done within LFG in a book like this, but we suggest further reading at the end of each chapter, and, at the end of the book, we provide reading on some areas of linguistics where LFG is used that we have not dealt with in the book.

In order to keep the text as simple as possible, we keep references to the literature out of the main text, except to provide the source of examples, but at the end of each chapter we provide references to the issues discussed in the chapter as well as suggestions for reading beyond the material presented.

We owe thanks to many people:

- to Koen Bostoen, Anna Hannesdóttir, Henri Kauhanen, Christin Schätzle and Christina Sevdali for help with data from a range of languages;
- to Shatha Alruwaili, Doug Arnold, Abdullah Almalky, Maris Camilleri, Paloma Careterro Garcia, Shaimaa ElSadek, Tibor Laczkó, Helge Lødrup, Louise Mycock and Nigel Vincent for comments and discussion;
- to John Payne and Chris Hicks, who have taught LELA20021 with KEB at the University of Manchester, to all students of LELA2002 and to Xianjie Zhang, who was good at spotting typos;
- to Maia Andréasson, Hannah Booth, Peter Hurst, Victoria Rosén and two anonymous referees, who read an earlier draft and provided valuable comments;
- to our editors at Cambridge University Press: initially Rosemary Crawley, and then Lisa Pinto and Nicola Chapman; and to Andrew Winnard, who commissioned the book in the first place.

Abbreviations

For the abbreviations of glosses of examples, we have used the *Leipzig glossing rules* (www.eva.mpg.de/lingua/resources/glossing-rules.php) as far as possible, but some of the glosses we need are not included there.

1	first person, or noun class 1 for data from the Bantu language Mbuun
2	second person, or noun class 2 for data from the Bantu language Mbuun
3	third person
I	noun class I
ABS	absolutive case
ACC	accusative case
ADJ	adjunct
AOR	aorist (used for Greek)
AUX	auxiliary
BEN	benefactive marking
C	complementiser
CAUS	causative
CoargD	co-argument domain, a domain for binding, the nucleus that contains the anaphor
COM	common gender
COMP	closed clausal complement
CONJ	conjunction
DAT	dative case
DEF	definite
ERG	ergative case
F	feminine gender
FIN	finite verb form
FOBJ	future object, for languages that mark tense on noun phrases
FUT	future tense
GEN	genitive case
GF	grammatical function
ILL	illative case
IMP	imperative

IND	indicative
INDF	indefinite
INF	infinitive verb form
LOC	locative case or locative θ-role
M	masculine gender
MinCompN	minimal complete nucleus, a domain for binding, the smallest f-structure that contains a reflexive and a SUBJ function
MinFinD	minimal finite domain, a domain for binding, the smallest f-structure that contains a tense feature
N	neuter gender
NEG	negation
NCLASS	noun class
NFOBJ	non-future object, for languages that mark tense on noun phrases
NFUT	non-future tense
NOM	nominative case
NPL	non-plural, for languages where singular is not the only alternative to plural
NPST	non-past tense
NUCLEUS	the smallest f-structure that contains a PRED feature and the arguments required by it
OBJ	object
OBJ_θ	(second) object, usually restricted to Theme
OBL_θ	oblique argument, θ may be instantiated by a θ-role, e.g. $OBL_{Location}$
OCOMP	object control element, used for Warlpiri
PASS	passive voice
PRF	perfect tense
PL	plural
POSS	possessor
PPTCP	past participle
PRS	present tense
PST	past tense
PTCP	participle
PTV	partitive case
Q	question particle
REFL	reflexive
RootD	root domain, a domain for binding, the complete f-structure of the utterance
SELF	gloss used for the Swedish *själv* that forms part of the reflexive *sig själv*
SG	singular

SM	subject marker
SUBJ	subject
SUP	supine, used here for the verb form that occurs with the perfect tense auxiliary in Swedish
VM	verbal modifier, used here for Hungarian
XADJ	open adjunct, an adjunct without an overt subject
XCOMP	open clausal complement, a complement without an overt subject

1 Introduction

1.1 Dimensions of Linguistic Information

Any natural language is a seriously complex system – in fact, learning your native language(s) could be considered your all-time most amazing intellectual achievement, even though you did not have to put much effort into it. The aim of any theory of grammar is to build an abstract model that can account for this complexity, that can predict what is and what isn't a grammatical sentence and that can, in some sense, explain why. What else is included in a model of grammar varies between theories; meaning may be included, and in some cases the pragmatic circumstances under which the particular linguistic element would be used. Some models are also committed to a particular explicit view of how children acquire language. The framework we will describe in this book – Lexical-Functional Grammar (LFG) – does not commit to any specific assumptions about language acquisition. However, when the ideas that led to the formal system that is LFG were first developed, this was in part a reaction against other approaches at the time that were perceived to be unrealistic as representations of how humans 'do' language. One of the founders of LFG, Joan Bresnan, wrote, 'If a given model of grammar cannot be successfully realized within a model of language use, it may be because it is psychologically unrealistic in significant respects and therefore inadequate in those respects as an empirical theory of the human faculty of language' (Bresnan, 1978, 2). In a similar vein, the first major work on LFG was entitled *The mental representation of grammatical relations* (Bresnan, 1982c).

LFG then aims to model the linguistic information that a native speaker has of their language; this information is complex and multifaceted, especially keeping in mind the variety that we find across the world's 6,500 or so languages. If you take a sentence like the one in (1), there are a lot of things we can say about it linguistically; there are many types of linguistic information associated with it.

(1) The cats devoured their breakfast.

Assuming that the sentence was spoken, there would be sounds, probably something like (2).

(2) / ðə kæts dɪvaʊəd ðeə brekfəst /

There may also have been emphasis on some part of the sentence to indicate what the speaker thought was the most important information. If there was emphasis on *their*, this would probably be because the speaker was contrasting *the cats' breakfast* with someone else's breakfast that the cats did not devour, so they might have added ... *not the rats' breakfast*. In this case, the speaker would have used stress or intonation – together referred to as PROSODY – to indicate which information is new to the conversation and which is assumed to be known already. These distinctions with respect to the INFORMATION STATUS of constituents is yet another type of information about linguistic items. Many languages can use word order to indicate the information status of constituents, and when they do there is a tendency to organise sentences so that old information precedes new. However, English offers relatively little scope for changing the word order and so prosody is frequently used instead.

Different CATEGORIES of words can be identified; *cat* and *breakfast* are NOUNS and *devoured* is a VERB. The reason for saying that *cat* and *breakfast* belong to the same category is that they behave in similar ways formally. For instance, words like *cat* and *breakfast* can have a plural ending and can combine with *the*, whereas *devour* cannot. A word like *devour*, on the other hand, can occur in present or past tense – *devour* vs *devoured* – and can take a third person singular *-s* in present tense. The words *the* and *their* behave in similar ways and we will refer to such elements as DETERMINERS. Like many concepts we will use in our analysis, categories are idealisations; not all nouns have all the noun properties we can identify – they are not all equally "noun-y" – and the morphosyntactic properties of nouns vary across the languages of the world. The number of categories that can be recognised by formal criteria varies between languages; some languages may not, for instance, make a formal distinction between verbs and adjectives.

(1) is not just a flat string of words: some words belong more closely together, so *their* and *breakfast* form a unit, which in turn combines with *devour*. This yields the hierarchical structure that we refer to as CONSTITUENT STRUCTURE. The word-level categories form phrases, so that the NOUN *breakfast* forms a NOUN PHRASE with *their* and the VERB *devour* in turn forms a VERB PHRASE with that noun phrase. As we will soon see, the degree of structure that can be identified varies greatly across languages, with English being a particularly highly structured language. We will also have more to say about English clause structure specifically in Section 2.3.2.

Though *the cat* and *their breakfast* are both noun phrases, they take on different GRAMMATICAL FUNCTIONS – or GRAMMATICAL RELATIONS – within the sentence. The function of *the cat* in (1) is referred to as the SUBJECT and *their breakfast* is the OBJECT. Grammatical relations are central to LFG and we will introduce them more thoroughly in Section 2.2.

There is also information about the internal structure of words to be captured. A complete description of (1) will have something to say about how the words are built up and the role the different parts play in the sentence. There is MORPHOLOGICAL information which tells us that the words *cats* and *devoured* both consist of two parts, the main meaning part – *cat* and *devour*, respectively – and an inflectional morpheme indicating plural (*-s*) and past tense (*-ed*).

We also know things about the meaning of words – about the SEMANTICS – and how the meaning of individual words is combined to form the meaning of phrases and sentences. The meaning of *cat* is intuitively clear in that we agree pretty much on which entities in the world can be referred to appropriately by using *cat*. We also have ways of describing the semantics of words like *the*; we use it roughly speaking when we think the entity referred to by the noun following it is known to the hearer. The semantics of a verb such as *devour* is a bit more complex in that knowing about its meaning also means knowing that it needs to combine with other elements; you cannot get any devouring going unless you have someone to do the devouring and something (or someone) to be devoured. We will refer to this as the verb requiring ARGUMENTS. The arguments have different roles with respect to the semantics of the verb; for instance, in (3a) the roles of *the dog* and *the postman* are different – *the dog* carries out an action whereas *the postman* undergoes the action. The role of each of the noun phrases is also different between the sentences in (3a) and (3b) – *the dog* no longer carries out an action in (3b) but experiences an emotion, and *the postman* may not even be aware of the feelings, whereas he would be aware of the biting in (3a). These roles are referred to as THEMATIC ROLES or θ-ROLES, and when we record information about the number of arguments a predicate takes, we also need to include the θ-roles of those arguments.

(3) a. The dog bit the postman.
b. The dog loves the postman.

As we have seen, there are many types of information that a full description of a language would need to refer to. **How** different models do this varies a fair bit. Some models assume that certain types of linguistic information should not be included in the model of grammar itself, but should be dealt with outside the actual grammar. LFG includes all these dimensions of linguistic information in the model. The different dimensions capture the information in different ways, so whereas a hierarchical tree is a natural way of representing constituent structure, this is not the best way of representing information about functions. The dimensions are then linked by mapping rules. The fact that dimensions of information are represented separately, but are linked, is a fundamental characteristic of LFG, and for this reason it is referred to as a PARALLEL CORRESPONDENCE ARCHITECTURE. LFG is formally explicit, which means that analyses can be tested computationally.

1.2 The Architecture of LFG

We have established that we need information about different aspects of linguistic elements and that this information may take different shapes. The LFG architecture contains the following dimensions:

- argument structure and thematic roles: A-STRUCTURE (for argument structure)
- syntactic categories and constituency: C-STRUCTURE (for constituent or category structure)
- grammatical functions and other functional features: F-STRUCTURE (for functional structure)
- morphological properties: M-STRUCTURE
- prosody: P-STRUCTURE
- semantics: S-STRUCTURE (usually modelled using 'glue semantics' as the theory of the syntax–semantics interface)
- information structure (or discourse structure): I-STRUCTURE (or D-STRUCTURE)

These different dimensions of information need to be linked – or in LFG terms MAPPED. The mapping will make explicit how a particular c-structure is linked to an f-structure, or how a p-structure is linked to an i-structure etc. If this linking was not part of a language user's knowledge, we would not be able to connect the correct semantic interpretation to a particular string of sounds. To take a simple example, a native speaker (or anyone who has learned English to even a basic level) knows that the sentence in (3a) involves *the dog* and not the *the postman* doing the biting. In LFG terms, this means that the c-structure of (3a) must be mapped to an f-structure in which *the dog* is the subject and *the postman* the object.

The dimensions that will be central in this book are a-structure, f-structure and c-structure, and we will briefly outline them here. Much more will be said about them in Chapters 2, 3 and 8. These are the most well-established components of LFG. For some of the other dimensions there are alternative ways of representing them within LFG, but we will not go into the details here; instead, we will provide useful references at the end of the chapter.

C-structure is represented as category-labelled trees. This means that the trees capture both category and constituent structure. We'll consider English first. Take the sentence in (4).

(4) The dog did bite the boy.

As referred to in Section 1.1, there is a hierarchical structure to a sentence like this in English. The two instances of *the* form constituents with *dog* and *boy*, respectively. Similarly *bite* forms a constituent with *the boy* and *did* with *bite the boy*. We can apply constituency tests to show that these strings function as units structurally. The resulting structure for (4) can be represented as in (5).

(5)

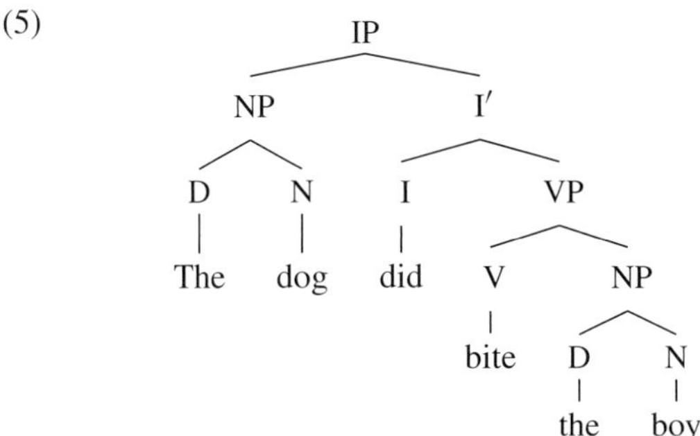

There are some things about this tree that may appear odd at this stage: the fact that *did* heads the phrase *did bite the boy*, that this involves a category I and that there is a category I′, for instance. We will explain these choices in some detail in Section 2.3, where we will also take another look at the NPs. At this point all we want to do is illustrate the fact that the hierarchical structure is represented as a tree, and that the constituents in the tree are assigned a category label. The tree in (5) consists exclusively of ENDOCENTRIC constituents, that is, all constituents have a head, the IP has a head I, the NP a head N etc. This is quite a striking fact about English; it is highly CONFIGURATIONAL. This means that the hierarchical structure plays an important role in expressing linguistic information. We will show how this is captured in LFG in Section 3.2. It is also the case in (5) that each node has at most two daughters – the tree in (5) is BINARY BRANCHING. This is quite common in English, but it is not exclusively so; some nodes may have only one daughter, or three or more, and in other languages, non-binary branching is the norm.

Not all languages rely as heavily on syntactic structure as English does. Consider the data from Latin in (6), for instance. (Since we will be using a range of languages in this book, it is important that the reader gets used to using the glossing to understand examples: see the List of Abbreviations at the beginning of the book.)

(6) a. Caesar suas copias in
Caesar.NOM REFL.ACC.F.PL troop.ACC.F.PL in
proximum collem subducit
nearest.ACC.M.SG hill.ACC.M.SG withdraw.PRS.3SG
'Caesar withdraws his (own) forces to the nearest hill.' [*De bello Gallico* 1.22]

b. copias suas Caesar in
troop.ACC.F.PL REFL.ACC.F.PL Caesar.NOM in
proximum collem subducit
nearest.ACC.M.SG hill.ACC.M.SG withdraw.PRS.3SG
[*De bello Gallico* 1.24]

c. copias suas in proximum
troop.ACC.F.PL REFL.ACC.F.PL in nearest.ACC.M.SG
collem subducit Caesar
hill.ACC.M.SG withdraw.PRS.3SG Caesar.NOM
[constructed]

d. non respuit condicionem Caesar
NEG reject.PRS.3SG proposal.ACC.F.SG Caesar.NOM
'Caesar did not reject the proposal.' [*De bello Gallico* 1.42]

There are some similarities with English here. For instance, notice that *in proximum collem* is not separated in any of the first three sentences and occurs in that order, just like English *to the nearest hill* would, so Latin appears to have a prepositional phrase here much like English does. On the other hand, though *suas* 'his own' and *copias* 'troops' occur together, both orders *suas copias* and *copias suas* are possible, and we can conclude that Latin has noun phrases, just like English, but that the order within them is somewhat freer. These conclusions are based on the assumption that the data in (6) is representative, obviously; we would need a lot more data to confirm this initial assessment. The big difference between English and Latin lies in the order of the major constituents. If we consider the verb, the subject 'Caesar' and the object 'his own troops' in (6a)–(6c) or 'the proposal' in (6d), then the order is [Subject Object V] in (6a), [Object Subject V] in (6b), [Object V Subject] in (6c) and [V Object Subject] in (6d). Though (6c) is constructed, there is good evidence that this order existed under the right pragmatic circumstances. Since the verb and the object do not have a fixed position with respect to each other-indeed they do not even have to be adjacent-there is no reason to include a VP in our c-structure for Latin. A language that lacks evidence for a VP is often described as NON-CONFIGURATIONAL. There are also no arguments in Latin for assuming that there is an I and an IP, but we will get back to the issue of what motivates the use of IP for a clause in Section 2.3.2. This means that trees like those in (7) to (10) are more appropriate for the Latin sentences in (6) (to keep the trees simple, we have ignored the adverbial). The key differences compared to the tree for English in (5) are that there is no VP, that the sentences are of the EXOCENTRIC – that is non-headed – category S and that different orders are possible. We end up with a flat tree at clausal level. Unlike in English, it is not the position that identifies the subject and the object, but case markers on the noun phrases – NOMinative for subject and ACCusative for object – and the agreement on the verb – here third person singular. Both these means identify *Caesar* as the subject in this example. We will see how this works in more detail in Chapter 4.

(7)

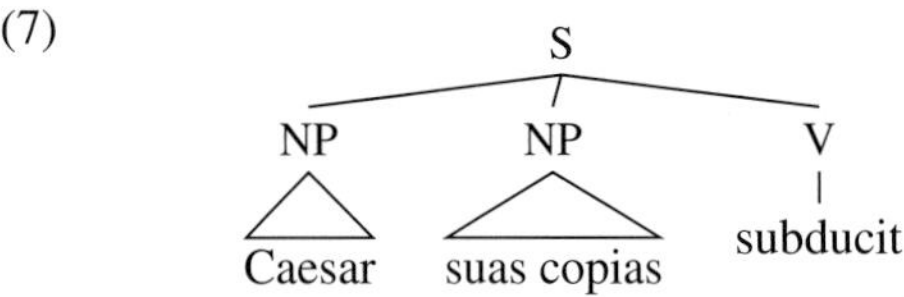

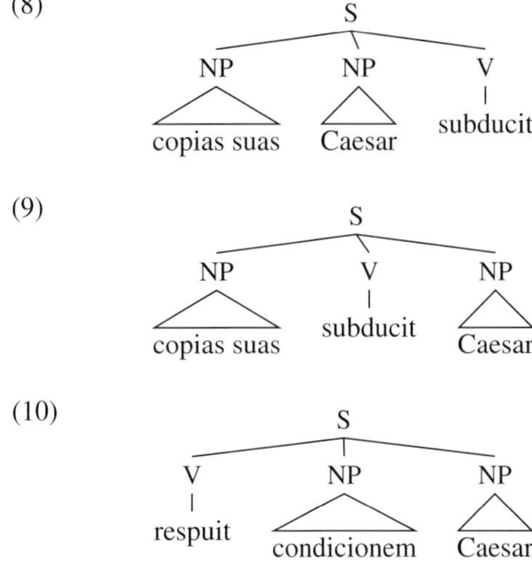

We have shown here that the extent to which a language relies on structure to identify functions varies and that this variation is represented as different c-structures in LFG. We will see more c-structure variation in Section 2.3.4.

If we turn to arguments and θ-roles, we find a different picture. Take *bite* in (4): if you know what this means, you know that it involves two participants. As we said in Section 1.1, one argument carries out an action and the other one suffers from that action. This is all part of the meaning of *bite*, and indeed of any other word meaning the same, whether it is Latin *mordeo* or Dutch *bijten* or indeed a verb meaning the same thing in any language. It is common to generalise over θ-roles, so rather than refer to them as "biter" and "bitten one", we use AGENT and PATIENT for any verb where there is some participant acting on another participant. We will return to θ-roles briefly in Section 2.1 and more extensively in Chapter 8. The a-structure for the word meaning 'bite' in any of these languages is then as in (11).

(11) < Agent, Patient >

Similarly with f-structure; whatever means a language uses to identify what is the subject and what is the object, the Agent will be identified as the subject and the Patient as the object in the translation of (4). This means that the f-structure for any of the sentences in (4) or (12) will be as in (13), in spite of the obvious difference even between these three relatively closely related languages (ignoring details such as definiteness and number, as well as the presence of *did* in (4), it will be clear in Section 2.3.2 why we included it in this example). We hope that the ideas behind (13) are clear to the reader, though PRED might require some explanation; it can be said to capture the semantic form of the predicate and the respective roles of the SUBJ and OBJ within it. SUBJ and OBJ are features with the respective values [PRED 'DOG'] and [PRED 'BOY']. We will have more to say about PRED and f-structure in Section 2.2.

(12) a. De hond heeft de jongen gebeten. (Dutch)
the dog have.PRS.3SG the boy bite.PPTCP

b. Canis puerum momordit. (Latin)
dog.NOM.M.SG boy.ACC.M.SG bite.PRF.3SG

(13)

[PRED 'BITE <SUBJ,OBJ>'
SUBJ [PRED 'DOG']
OBJ [PRED 'BOY']]

1.3 Mapping between Dimensions

In the chapters that follow, we will have a lot more to say about the mapping between the dimensions of information. However, at this point, we would like to give you a rough idea of how it will work, at least in a language like English that relies on structure for the identification of grammatical relations and contrast it with a language like Latin that relies less on structure. Take the c-structure for *The dog did bite the boy*, which was provided in (5). Because *the dog* is in the structural position it is in the tree; we know it is the subject. Hence the mapping function must provide a link between that position and the value of SUBJ in the f-structure. Once a speaker has identified that *the dog* is the subject, she also knows that it is the Agent of the verb in this example; this is how a speaker of English can tell who is biting whom. This means there must also be a mapping (or correspondence) between the SUBJ in the f-structure and the a-structure Agent of *bite*. Similarly, the position of *the boy* in the tree must be mapped to the value of OBJ in the f-structure, which corresponds to the Patient in the a-structure. Considering the Latin sentence in (12b), we know from the discussion around the examples in (6) that the word order could have been different in (12b), so that it is not the position of *canis* that tells the hearer that it is the subject. Instead it is the NOMinative case marker that provides the crucial clue and hence the mapping to SUBJ must link to the case-marked noun. English and Latin thus share the same associations, or mapping, between a-structure and f-structure, as shown in (14), but have quite different c-structures, as shown in (15).

(14)

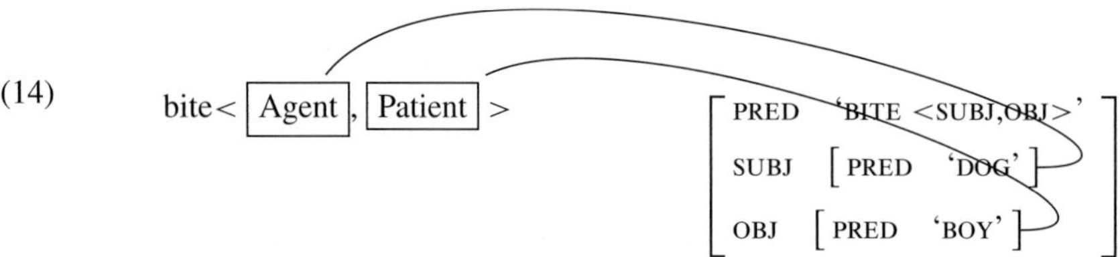

(15)

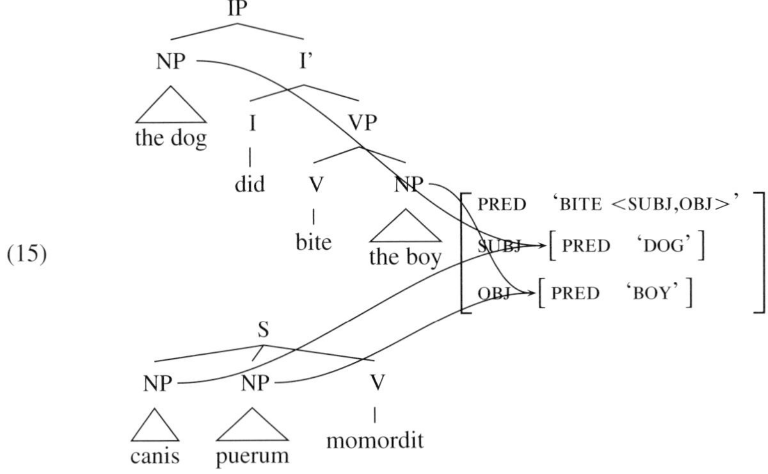

1.4 Why Different Dimensions?

We have shown here that the linking between categories, functions and arguments varies between languages so that there is cross-linguistic evidence for the need to distinguish the different dimensions of linguistic information; there are arguments in favour of a parallel correspondence architecture. In fact, data internal to English also supports this distinction.

Let's consider category first and compare the COMPLEMENTS of some verbs. We use 'complements' as a cover term for all elements required by the verb apart from the subject. The examples in (16) show that the verb *believe* can take a clausal complement or a noun phrase complement, either a pronoun or a full noun phrase. We have labelled the clause here as '*that*-clause'; this is just informal, we will come back to details about the category of clauses in Section 2.3.2 and Chapter 6. Do note that *the fact that there are fairies at the bottom of the garden* is a noun phrase built up around the noun *fact*, which takes as its complement the clause *that there are fairies at the bottom of the garden*. The verb *smile*, on the other hand, cannot take any complement, as shown by the ungrammaticality of the examples in (17).

(16)
a. Oscar believes [that there are fairies at the bottom of the garden]$_{\textit{that}-\text{clause}}$
b. Oscar believes [it]$_{\text{NP}}$
c. Oscar believes [the fact that there are fairies at the bottom of the garden]$_{\text{NP}}$

(17)
a. *Oscar smiles [that there are fairies at the bottom of the garden] $_{\text{that}-\textit{clause}}$
b. *Oscar smiles [it]$_{\text{NP}}$
c. *Oscar smiles [the fact that there are fairies at the bottom of the garden]$_{\text{NP}}$

This correlation is not remarkable; the distribution of complement types appears to be predictable from argument structure. If you *believe*, you have to believe some sort of proposition and it may be represented by a clause or a noun phrase. It only takes one entity to *smile*, so no complement is required.

However, things are not as straightforward as this. Most verbs are particular about what category their complement is: *enjoy* in (18) can take an NP, but not a *that*-clause; *hope*, on the other hand, can take a *that*-clause but not an NP, as (19) shows. Still, in semantic terms, the complement of both verbs describes a situation that you *enjoy* or *hope* for.

(18) a. *Oscar enjoys [that there are fairies at the bottom of the garden]$_{that\text{–clause}}$
b. Oscar enjoys [the fact that there are fairies at the bottom of the gardens]$_{\text{NP}}$
c. Oscar enjoys [it]$_{\text{NP}}$

(19) a. Oscar hopes [that there are fairies at the bottom of the garden]$_{that\text{–clause}}$
b. *Oscar hopes [the fact that there are fairies at the bottom of the garden]$_{\text{NP}}$
c. *Oscar hopes [it]$_{\text{NP}}$

More generally, an element like a verb can determine not just how many complements there can be, but also the category of these complements. We cannot derive information about category from our knowledge of how many arguments there are; we need information separately about arguments and categories.

Turning now to the relation between category and function, so far all subjects we have seen have been noun phrases. If a particular function is always filled by a particular category, then we might think we only need to have one of the two types of information specified. However, subjects can be of categories other than noun phrase as in (20).

(20) a. [The young man]$_{\text{NP}}$ surprised his mother.
b. [On the beach]$_{\text{PP}}$ is a great place to be.
c. [That Oscar had finally found a girlfriend]$_{that\text{–clause}}$ surprised his friends.

The subjects in (20b) and (20c) may have some unusual properties in comparison to noun phrase subjects, but in many respects they do behave like subjects.

It is maybe more obvious, but also worth pointing out, that noun phrases can bear functions other than subject, as in (21). We use traditional labels for the functions here, but we will return to LFG terminology in Section 2.2.

(21) a. Oscar saw [the film]$_{\text{Object}}$
b. Oscar gave [his sister]$_{\text{Object}_{ind}}$ [a present]$_{\text{Object}_{dir}}$
c. Oscar left [the day before yesterday]$_{\text{Adverbial}}$

This is an indication that we need to specify category and function separately.

How about grammatical functions and θ-roles, do we need both? Often it is the subject which is the Agent, but in (18b) and (18c) the subject of *enjoys* can be described as an EXPERIENCER. In fact, subjects can have any number of other roles as the examples in (22) show.

(22) a. [Oscar]$_{Recipient}$ received the present from his sister.
b. [The hammer]$_{Instrument}$ drove the nail into the wood.
c. [On the beach]$_{Location}$ is a great place to be.

There are certain syntactic processes which reorganise sentences so that the same function can be linked to different θ-roles in different versions. One such process is passivisation. The subject of a passive sentence has the θ-role that is associated with the object in a corresponding active sentence, so that a Patient noun phrase can also be a subject, as in (23), or indeed any other θ-role that can occur as an object.

(23) [Sarah]$_{Patient}$ was tickled by Oscar.

In some cases, the same verb, in the same form, can also have subjects with different θ-roles; one such example in English is *break* as in (24).

(24) a. [The boy]$_{Agent}$ broke the window with a stone.
b. [The stone]$_{Instrument}$ broke the window.
c. [The window]$_{Patient}$ broke.

There is then evidence that the relation between categories, functions and θ-roles is not a one-to-one relation and that as a consequence we need to keep information about categories, functions and θ-roles separate. The different types of information are connected by mapping rules which do not necessarily predict a one-to-one relation between the dimensions. This realisation is crucial to the architecture of LFG.

Reading

If you are interested in the earliest formulations of LFG, then you might want to look at Bresnan (1978) or the articles in Bresnan (1982c), but keep in mind that the approach has developed since then, so some aspects of the formal notation may be outdated and some analyses may have been updated in more recent publications.

In Section 1.2, we introduced seven dimensions of information. In this book, we shall have a lot to say about three of these: a-structure, f-structure and c-structure. In Chapter 9, we say a little more about p-structure, m-structure, s-structure and i-structure, but, most importantly, there we provide further references to the literature for you to follow up if you are particularly interested in one of these dimensions.

A summary of issues that arise around non-configurationality can be found in Nordlinger (1998); we will return to how to analyse such languages in Chapter 4. If you are interested in the Latin data, you can find an LFG analysis of aspects of Latin in Jøhndal (2012).

2 Dimensions of Information

2.1 A-structure

In this chapter, we will introduce the three dimensions that we will focus on in this book in more detail, starting with the basic concepts of a-structure. We referred to Agents, Patients and Experiencers without much explanation in Chapter 1, but we will take a step back here and talk a little about where they come from. The argument structure of a word is closely associated with its semantics: *smile* takes one argument because it only takes one participant to get some smiling going, *give* takes three arguments because giving involves a giver, a receiver and something to be given. The verbs *tickle* and *love* both take two arguments, but the roles of those arguments are different; the argument that has been tickled will know it has, whereas an argument that is loved may not be aware of it. It is not just verbs that have argument structure, any PREDICATE does. For instance, the adjective *proud* requires someone to be proud and something or someone to be proud of.

We will want to do more than just state how many arguments an element takes; we will want to categorise arguments into different types. This is an area where there is quite a lot of variation between linguists. In principle, we could have very few categories, say, a category referring to the entity doing whatever the verb means – the "doer" – and one referring to the "undergoer" of the verb's action (if there is one). The danger with this is that we would not be able to capture all the distinctions we need to describe the data properly. On the other hand, you could argue that the semantic roles of the subject of the verbs *eat*, *kick* and *tickle* are all different so that we need semantic roles like "eater", "kicker" and "tickler". However, this would actually fail to capture some of the generalisations that languages make, for instance that all arguments which perform an action by free will and cause an effect on some other entity are treated in the same way. This means that we want to generalise over "eaters", "kickers" and "ticklers". It is common to recognise somewhere around ten SEMANTIC ROLES – usually referred to as θ-ROLES, or THEMATIC ROLES. There is, however, no absolute agreement as to exactly how many θ-roles there are or how to define them. For our purposes, the following nine roles will suffice, though it should be noted that there are many variations on this, for example Stimulus and Theme may be merged into one role.

AGENT	causer or initiator of an action
EXPERIENCER	animate entity which experiences a sensation or emotion or perceives a stimulus
PATIENT	entity which is affected by an action
THEME	entity which undergoes a change of state, location or possession or whose location is specified
STIMULUS	object of perception or cognition or entity that prompts an emotion
LOCATION	spatial reference point of event or entity
RECIPIENT	entity which receives something
BENEFACTIVE	entity that benefits from an action or an event
INSTRUMENT	inanimate entity used by some participant to perform an action

Some illustrative examples can be found in (1).

(1) a. **Oscar** kicked **the ball**.
Agent Patient

b. **The boy** likes **the dog**.
Experiencer Stimulus

c. **Oscar** cut **the cake** with **a knife**.
Agent Patient Instrument

d. **Oscar** put **the cat's breakfast** on **the floor**.
Agent Theme Location

We will have more to say about θ-roles and the mapping between a-structure and f-structure in Chapter 8.

2.2 F-structure

We have already seen through the examples in Chapter 1 that f-structure represents syntactic predicate–argument structure in terms of grammatical functions such as subject and object. We represent information about this dimension of linguistic structure by means of an ATTRIBUTE–VALUE MATRIX (AVM), which is a collection of attributes and their values. We will often use the term 'feature' instead of 'attribute'. An AVM is an unordered set of features and their respective values. Three types of feature can be distinguished, and we will look more closely at each below: (i) PRED, (ii) grammatical functions (or grammatical relations) and (iii) features with atomic values.

The PRED feature is special among the features in that it takes a SEMANTIC FORM as its value. The semantic form really is a pointer into the semantics, but we will not go into detail when it comes to lexical semantics. Notice that the semantic form (such as 'OSCAR' in PRED = 'OSCAR') appears within single quotes; this is because the semantic form is instantiated to a unique value for each use of the word it is associated with. Although we will not discuss this at any length, you can see what is at issue by thinking about a sentence such as *John saw John*. Outside of special contexts, this can only mean that there are two different people named John and one of them saw the other; that is, this means 'John$_i$ saw John$_j$', where we use indices to indicate that the two instances of *John* have separate referents, and hence the two PRED values ('JOHN') are distinct. The uniqueness of the PRED value could also be indicated by adding indices to the PRED values in the f-structures, but it is standard practice in LFG to rely on the use of single quotes around PRED values to indicate the uniqueness. As we proceed, we will see that the uniqueness of PRED values plays an important role.

We will also see that for predicates that must combine with grammatical functions in order to form a complete and coherent phrase, these are also indicated as part of the PRED value (we will define 'complete' and 'coherent' below). For instance, the verb *devour* requires a subject and an object and hence it is specified as PRED = 'DEVOUR<SUBJ, OBJ>'. You can think of this as indicating that any event of devouring involves two participants. How the grammatical functions in the PRED feature are linked to the θ-roles in the a-structure is something we will return to in Chapter 8.

Throughout, we use the English word for the semantic form: 'DEVOUR' appears in the PRED value for *devour*, *devours*, *devoured* and *devouring*, and indeed also for the Swedish equivalent *sluka* and elements with the same meaning from other languages. However, remember that this is just a label; we could easily have used the Swedish word or the Latin word or something completely different.

A fundamental property of LFG is that grammatical functions (GFS) are key concepts. They are not quite primitives; as we will see in Chapter 8, they are derived from the a-structure, so from the semantics of the predicate, but importantly they are not derived from their structural position, as they are in some other approaches to syntactic analysis. Grammatical functions are features that take as their value another f-structure, hence we get f-structures within f-structures. We return now to the example we considered in Chapter 1, repeated here in (2a), with the associated f-structure in (2b) (ignoring *did* in the original sentence).

(2) a. The dog bit the boy.

b.
$$\begin{bmatrix} \text{PRED} & \text{`BITE <SUBJ, OBJ>'} \\ \text{SUBJ} & \begin{bmatrix} \text{PRED} & \text{`DOG'} \end{bmatrix} \\ \text{OBJ} & \begin{bmatrix} \text{PRED} & \text{`BOY'} \end{bmatrix} \end{bmatrix}$$

In (2b), the value of the feature SUBJ is itself an f-structure containing the feature–value pair: PRED = 'DOG' (we are ignoring properties such as number, gender and definiteness for the moment, but if we did the full f-structure, these would also be features of both SUBJ and OBJ). Simplifying somewhat, we can say that this indicates that the subject has the meaning 'dog' and the object the meaning 'boy'. In (2b), PRED, SUBJ and OBJ form an unordered set of features; (2b) could equally well have been written as in (3), or indeed any other order.

(3)

OBJ	[PRED 'BOY']
SUBJ	[PRED 'DOG']
PRED	'BITE <SUBJ, OBJ >'

The f-structure in (2b) (or indeed the one in (3)) is also the appropriate f-structure for the Dutch and Latin sentences in (12) in Chapter 1. The fact that the c-structure is rather different in English, Dutch and Latin does not matter for the f-structure. F-structure is then relatively invariant, unlike c-structure, which can vary quite substantially between languages; we will see more of this in Section 2.3. It follows from this that the mapping between c- and f-structure will also need to be different between English, Dutch and Latin in order to map from three different c-structures to one f-structure.

The f-structure in (2b) is only PARTIAL; there is more f-structure information associated with the sentence in (2a). Most of the f-structure representations we will give in this book will be partial, as we will often abstract away from information which is specified, and belongs in the f-structure, but which is not relevant to the point under discussion. However, it is not uncommon to be more detailed than (2b), and (4) is an example of a more detailed representation of (2a), though there is still more information we could provide about the f-structure of this sentence, for instance GENDER.

(4)

PRED	'BITE <SUBJ, OBJ>'
TENSE	PAST
SUBJ	[PRED 'DOG' NUM SG PERS 3 DEF +]
OBJ	[PRED 'BOY' NUM SG PERS 3 DEF +]

In (4), we have introduced four new features: TENSE, NUM (for number), PERS (for person) and DEF (for definiteness). These features take a simple value, in this case PAST, SG (for singular), 3 (for third person) and + (to indicate a positive value for definiteness). These are referred to as ATOMIC values. There are many features with atomic values and any such feature can have two or more values. DEF is a binary feature; it can have two values: + or – whereas a feature like TENSE can have several potential values, depending on the language, for instance, PRESENT, PAST and FUTURE. The feature NUM in English can have the values SG or PL, but other languages have more subtle systems for marking number and may also have values such as DUAL (for exactly two) and PAUCAL (for 'a few'). PERS has three values: 1 (for *I*, *we* and related forms), 2 (for *you* and related forms) and 3 (for *she*, *he*, *it*, *they* and related forms as well as most regular noun phrases).

In Section 3.2, we will look in detail at how the different features in (4) come to be in the f-structure for the sentence in (2a), but we will just say a brief word here about the relation between the features associated with individual words. The feature–value pair DEF = + is contributed by *the*. Obviously, the feature PRED = 'BOY' is contributed by the word *boy*, but so is NUM = SG, it couldn't come from *the* since this has the same form for both singular and plural noun phrases; *the boy*, *the boys*. Similarly *bit* contributes both PRED = 'BITE <SUBJ, OBJ>' and TENSE = PAST. One word can then contribute more than one feature. One feature can also be contributed by more than one word. Take the noun phrase *these boys*. It has the feature NUM = PL and the value PL is associated both with *these* and *boys*. Two (or more) items being associated with the same feature is a common property of language and it is fine as long as the values contributed are the same. This ability to deal with MANY-TO-ONE MAPPING between c-structure and f-structure is a crucial property of LFG. The f-structure associated with the NP *these boys* must contain all the pieces of f-structure information associated with *these* and all the pieces of f-structure information associated with *boys*, so there is no problem provided the information contributed by each element is compatible. Another way of saying this is that the f-structure associated with *these boys* must satisfy all the constraints associated with *these* and *boys*. On the other hand, if two elements provide incompatible values for the same feature in an f-structure, as would be the case with **this boys*, then there will be no f-structure which can contain all the information associated with the two elements. This is captured by a well-formedness condition in LFG, the UNIQUENESS CONDITION (also referred to as the CONSISTENCY REQUIREMENT):

Uniqueness: every attribute must have exactly one value in a given f-structure

The f-structure of a sentence contains information contributed by its parts; f-structures for phrases are built up from the f-structures of its component parts and – as we will see in later chapters – from mapping principles associated with the way in which the words are put together. It is a crucial and general principle of LFG that when information is combined in this way, information can only be added, it cannot be removed. This is referred to as MONOTONICITY. The fact that information is preserved and never lost is particularly important for the computational robustness of the model since it means that all the information of the parts is preserved in the bigger whole.

We can then sum up what we have said about the types of f-structure features and values as in Table 2.1.

The only examples we have provided of grammatical functions so far have been SUBJ and OBJ. Both can be selected by a verb (or other predicate), and such functions are referred to as GOVERNABLE GRAMMATICAL FUNCTIONS. We should point out that a function can be selected by a verb without being obligatory. A sentence like *Oscar has eaten* is perfectly fine without the OBJ, but we still say that *eat* selects an OBJ because it assigns a θ-role to the object; it is just that this is optionally expressed.

Table 2.1 *Feature types and their values*

Feature	Value type	Example
PRED	semantic form	PRED = 'SMILE <SUBJ>', PRED = 'RAT'
Grammatical functions	f-structure	$\left[\text{SUBJ} \left[\begin{array}{ll}\text{PRED} & \text{'MOUSE'} \\ \text{NUM} & \text{PL}\end{array}\right]\right]$
Simple features	atomic	NUM = SG, TENSE = PRES

SUBJ and OBJ are not the only governable functions. Consider the two sentences in (5).

(5) a. Fred posted his mother **a birthday card**.
 b. Oscar put the cat's breakfast **on the floor**.

In these sentences, *his mother* and *the cat's breakfast* behave like OBJs. However, as the ungrammaticality of the sentences in (6) shows, the bold phrases in (5) are also obligatorily selected by the verb and are therefore governable functions. (You might argue that if you imagine Fred having put his mother in a giant envelope and having pushed her into a letterbox, then (6a) may be just fine, like *Fred posted the letter*, but if we think of it as *his mother* still being a Recipient, then it is not good.)

(6) a. *Fred posted his mother.
 b. *Oscar put the cat's breakfast.

A birthday card in (5a) behaves in some ways like an object, but in some ways not. It cannot for most speakers be the subject of a corresponding passive, and it is restricted to the θ-role it has; it is always a Theme, that is, an element in this function is always something that changes location or possession. Because of its restricted θ-role, *a birthday card* in (5a) will be referred to as an OBJ$_{\theta}$. *On the floor* in (5b) is quite different from an OBJ, most strikingly in English because it is a Prepositional Phrase, a PP. In languages that would use case rather than prepositions for a phrase with this function, such a phrase would be a noun phrase, but would occur in an OBLIQUE case, such as LOCATIVE. We will return to this when we consider prepositional phrases in more detail in Section 3.3. The preposition or the case indicates the θ-role of the element, in this case 'location on top of'. The grammatical function of *on the floor* is then referred to as OBL$_{\theta}$. In both OBJ$_{\theta}$ and OBL$_{\theta}$ the subscript θ indicates that the grammatical function is specified as to what semantic role it can have within the clause. In the case of *on the floor* in (5b), the thematic role is that of a *Location*, so in fact we have an OBL$_{Loc}$. In the case of *a birthday card* in (5a) we have an OBJ$_{Theme}$. Notationally, it is common practice to omit reference to the specific θ-role and just use the labels OBJ$_{\theta}$ and OBL$_{\theta}$. We will return to the relation between grammatical functions and θ-roles in Section 8.3.

Of the grammatical functions we have looked at so far, it turns out that SUBJ, OBJ and OBJ_θ have special properties in a range of languages. We will refer to them as the TERM FUNCTIONS (they are also described as CORE FUNCTIONS).

We have seen examples of verbs selecting noun phrases and prepositional phrases, but verbs can also take clauses as their complements, as illustrated by the examples in (7).

(7) a. Sarah said **that the cat ate his breakfast**.
b. Oscar tried **to eat his breakfast**.

The function of complements of verbs that are full clauses, as in (7a), is COMP. The bold phrase in (7b) is slightly different. It is a clause, since it is built around a lexical verb, but it lacks a subject for *eat*. The meaning for the subject of *eat* will need to be "filled in" from the rest of the sentence (in Chapter 5 we will see how this is done). Such clausal complements are referred to as XCOMPs. So, an XCOMP is a COMP with "something missing" in the c-structure. There are good reasons to assume that even though this element is not there in the c-structure, it is present in f-structure, and it will in fact always be the subject. In (7b), the constituent filling the XCOMP function – *to eat his breakfast* – is built around the infinitival verb *to eat* (we will return to what c-structure to assign to such constituents in Section 2.3.2). However, other categories can also function as XCOMPs, and we will discuss such examples in Section 5.2.3.

We have so far focused on the selectional behaviour of verbs, but other categories may also select complements. Compare the examples in (8), where (8a) is a sentence and (8b) is a noun phrase.

(8) a. **Carl** studied ancient scripts.
b. **Carl**'s study of ancient scripts

The argument structure of nouns and the distribution of grammatical relations within noun phrases have not been quite as well explored in LFG as they have for verbs, and we will not go into a detailed account here. However, it is reasonable to assume that *study* in (8b) takes arguments much like *studied* does in (8a), and these arguments are expressed as grammatical functions. However, there are also differences. *Carl* is the SUBJ of *studied* in (8a), but there are reasons not to assign *Carl* the same function with respect to *study* in (8b). Consider the sentences in (9), all of which also have a possessive noun phrase preceding a noun.

(9) a. **Sarah**'s car has a dent.
b. **The car**'s exhaust is nearly falling off.
c. After **an hour**'s delay, Sarah gave up waiting.

In these examples, the possessive phrase is not closely related to a corresponding subject. In (9a) *Sarah* is the owner – the possessor – of the car, and we will use the grammatical relation POSS to refer to all possessive phrases. It is a well-known fact that the relationship between the head noun and the possessor noun phrase extends beyond canonical possession, so that the function POSS must not be taken too literally. We have already seen in (8) that some possessor phrases share properties with subjects, and in (9b) and (9c) *the car* and *an hour* do not "possess" – in any normal sense of the word – the *exhaust* and the *delay*, but we will still use POSS as the label for the grammatical relation. In Chapter 7 we will explore ways in which SUBJ and POSS behave in similar ways.

These are all the governable functions in LFG. Not everything present in a sentence is there because it is required by another element, however. Consider the bold phrases in (10).

(10) a. Oscar put the cat's breakfast on the floor **before he went to work**.
b. **Yesterday** Sarah said that the cat ate his breakfast.
c. Oscar tried to eat his breakfast **very slowly**.

The bold phrases in (10) are all optional as indicated by the grammaticality of (5b), (7a) and (7b). Such optional phrases that the speaker uses to add information, not because it is required by another element, are referred to as ADJ (for 'adjunct'). The examples in (10) illustrate the fact that ADJs can be of many different categories; *before he went to work* is a clause, *yesterday* is a noun phrase and *very slowly* is an adverb phrase (we will have more to say about categories and how they are organised in Section 2.3).

Since some such phrases may lack a subject, just like XCOMPs, there is also a function XADJ for adjuncts that lack a SUBJ. The bold phrases in (11) are examples of XADJs with the SUBJ absent in the c-structure.

(11) a. **Having put the cat's breakfast on the floor**, Oscar went to work.
b. **Encouraged by the cats' enthusiasm**, Oscar gave them some more food.

Whereas grammatical relations such as SUBJ and OBJ can occur only once in a clause, there can be more than one ADJ, as in (12a), where we have three ADJs: *quickly*, *in the kitchen* and *yesterday*. ADJs can also occur inside noun phrases, as in (12b), where again we have three ADJs: *big*, *ginger* and *behind the sofa*.

(12) a. The cat ate his breakfast **quickly in the kitchen yesterday**.
b. the **big ginger** cat **behind the sofa**

The fact that we can have more than one ADJ means that we must deal with them in a different way from SUBJ and OBJ. If we made *quickly*, *in the kitchen* and *yesterday* all be the value of one ADJ feature in f-structure, we would get the f-structure in (13), which violates the Uniqueness Condition since PRED does not have a unique value (the phrase *in the kitchen* should of course have a more complex analysis, but we hope this serves to illustrate the point). Instead, the value of ADJ is a **set** of f-structures, as indicated by the curly brackets in (14).

(13) $* \left[\text{ADJ} \left[\text{PRED} \quad \text{`QUICKLY' `IN THE KITCHEN' `YESTERDAY'} \right] \right]$

(14)

$$\left[\begin{array}{ll}\text{ADJ} & \left\{\begin{array}{l}\left[\text{PRED} \quad \text{`QUICKLY'}\right]\\ \left[\text{PRED} \quad \text{`IN THE KITCHEN'}\right]\\ \left[\text{PRED} \quad \text{`YESTERDAY'}\right]\end{array}\right\}\end{array}\right]$$

Now compare the sentences in (15b) and (15c) with that in (15a).

(15)
a. Oscar fed our dog.
b. **Which dog** did Oscar feed?
c. **Our dog**, Oscar refuses to feed (though he seems happy enough to feed the neighbour's cat).

In (15a), *fed* is immediately followed by its object. Since *fed* has the PRED value 'feed <SUBJ, OBJ>', and the object generally follows its verb, this is what we would expect. In (15b) and (15c), on the other hand, nothing follows *feed*, but the sentences are still grammatical. The reason is of course that the bold phrases in (15b) and (15c) fill the object function. They are, however, in an unusual position. The effect that is achieved by placing the element in a non-canonical position is related to information packaging, or discourse, and these types of function are then called DISCOURSE FUNCTIONS (or sometimes OVERLAY FUNCTIONS). We will recognise two discourse functions in f-structure: TOPIC – associated with old information, informally "that which we are talking about" – and FOCUS – referring to information that is new in the discourse or on which there is emphasis of some kind. In both (15b) and (15c), the bold phrase has two functions: its governable OBJ function and its discourse function FOCUS. This is a general property of elements that have a discourse function within a sentence; they must also be linked to some non-discourse function. We will return to how this is dealt with within LFG in Chapter 6.

In (15c), structural means, that is, position within the sentence, are used to indicate the information-structure status of *our dog*. However, the word order of English is quite rigidly determined by syntactic constraints, and there is generally little scope for using structure to indicate the information-structural status of a phrase in this way; instead prosody may be used – heavy stress may be put on an element to indicate FOCUS. When a language has a structural position reserved for particular discourse functions, we refer to these as GRAMMATICALISED DISCOURSE FUNCTIONS, and they form part of the f-structure. Hence we can refer to TOPIC and FOCUS as **GRAMMATICALISED** DISCOURSE FUNCTIONS in English. As mentioned briefly in Section 1.2, for the full complexity of information structure, there is a dimension in LFG that deals with information packaging, i-structure. We will not have much to say about this here, but suggestions for further reading can be found in Chapter 9.

SUBJ can also function as a discourse function, in that a speaker may organise the sentence in such a way that a topical constituent becomes the subject, for instance by using a passive construction. If the topic of our conversation is 'Oscar' and we want to add to the discourse the information that he has fed the cat, we are more likely to use (16a) than (16b), but if we are having a conversation about 'the cat' and we want to add the new information that Oscar has fed it, we may well use (16b) instead of (16a) (of course a pronoun is also often used to refer to an entity that has been mentioned before).

(16) a. Oscar has fed the cat.

b. The cat has been fed by Oscar.

SUBJ is then both a governable function and a grammaticalised discourse function. To some extent, the traditional terminology reflects this; in everyday language, *topic* and *subject* have quite similar meanings.

The functions we have introduced can be summed up as in Table 2.2. At this point, these concepts will sound pretty abstract, but the role of the different grammatical functions and the categorisation of them will become clearer as we work through examples in later chapters. We will use GF, for grammatical function, to refer to all functions which are not discourse functions, and for discourse functions we will use DF.

Earlier in this chapter, we introduced the Uniqueness Condition, which states that an attribute can have only one value in a given f-structure. This condition ensures that **this cats* is ungrammatical, because *this* and *cats* contribute incompatible values SG and PL to the NUM feature. There are two other well-formedness conditions: COMPLETENESS and COHERENCE.

Completeness: all governable functions which are part of the value of a PRED feature must be present in the local f-structure. All functions that have a θ-role must themselves have a PRED value.

Table 2.2 *Grammatical functions*

<table>
<tr><td colspan="2">NON-GOVERNABLE</td><td>TOPIC
FOCUS</td><td rowspan="2">DISCOURSE</td></tr>
<tr><td rowspan="7">GOVERNABLE</td><td rowspan="3">TERM</td><td>SUBJ</td></tr>
<tr><td>OBJ</td><td rowspan="8">NON-DISCOURSE</td></tr>
<tr><td>OBJθ</td></tr>
<tr><td rowspan="4">NON-TERM</td><td>OBLθ</td></tr>
<tr><td>POSS</td></tr>
<tr><td>COMP</td></tr>
<tr><td>XCOMP</td></tr>
<tr><td colspan="2" rowspan="2">NON-GOVERNABLE</td><td>ADJ</td></tr>
<tr><td>XADJ</td></tr>
</table>

Coherence: all governable functions present in an f-structure must occur in the value of a local PRED feature. All functions that have a PRED value must have a θ-role.

The first part of the Completeness Condition ensures that sentences such as those in (17) are ruled out and the Coherence Condition does the same for (18).

(17) a. *The cat devoured.
b. *The teacher put the book.

(18) a. *The cat devoured the dog the breakfast.
b. *The child smiled the dog.

The verb *devoured* has the PRED value 'devour <SUBJ, OBJ>', but in (17a), there is only a SUBJ. Similarly, *put* requires a SUBJ, an OBJ and an OBL_θ, but in (17b), there is no phrase that can function as OBL_θ. In (18a), there are three noun phrases that need grammatical relations – *the cat*, *the dog* and *the breakfast* – but *devour* only requires two: SUBJ and OBJ. Similarly in (18b), there is one noun phrase without a function since *smile* only requires a SUBJ. Hence the examples in (17) are incomplete and the ones in (18) are incoherent.

The second part of each condition refers to the need for a function that has a θ-role to have a value for PRED. There are elements that can function as subjects, but which do not have a PRED value because they have no semantics, examples from English are *there* and *it* as in (19). These elements are usually referred to as EXPLETIVES. We will see that expletives can be used in syntactic argumentation in Chapter 5.

(19) a. There is a man in the wardrobe.
b. It is snowing.

By Completeness and Coherence, these elements can then only be the subject of verbs that do not assign a θ-role to their subjects. In Section 4.2.4, we will see other effects of these two constraints.

2.3 C-structure

2.3.1 X-bar Syntax

Underlying LFG's c-structure is an approach to constituent structure referred to as X-bar theory. It is a bit misleading to refer to it as a 'theory', but that is the term usually used. It is a scheme for generalising across categories to capture similarities between them. The ideas behind X-bar theory are implemented in some form in a number of syntactic frameworks, but with some modifications. Here we will describe the general approach, but from the point of view of its implementation in LFG.

Two major kinds of categories can be distinguished: LEXICAL CATEGORIES and FUNCTIONAL CATEGORIES. The generalisations of X-bar theory are intended to hold for both, but we will see that the introduction of functional categories may lead to some changes in the analysis of lexical categories. Lexical categories consist of contentful words, like *cat*, *devour* and *breakfast*, though as we saw when discussing Latin in Chapter 1, S in the list below is different from other lexical categories in this sense. Words belonging to functional categories, on the other hand, have more abstract meanings like DEFINITE for *the* or PAST TENSE for *did*. The following categories are generally used in LFG, though a smaller or larger set of categories may be motivated for some languages.

- Lexical: **N**oun, **V**erb, **A**djective, **Adv**erb, **P**reposition, **S**entence
- Functional: **C**omplementiser, **I**nflection, **D**eterminer

In X-bar syntax, categories are said to PROJECT to phrases. This means that a phrase is assumed to be built up around a central item – the HEAD. For example, *hungry* could head a phrase *very hungry*, and since *hungry* is of the category A for adjective, we can refer to *very hungry* as an AP, an adjective phrase. It can be expanded further: *very hungry for ice cream* etc. Phrases that are headed in this sense are described as endocentric, a term we introduced in Section 1.2. In LFG, NON-PROJECTING categories are also assumed, most notably S, which is used for clauses where there is no argument in favour of assigning head status to any particular element. Such non-headed categories are referred to as exocentric. In Chapter 1 we argued that there are no obvious reasons for assuming that in Latin the verb and the object NP form a VP, and this is a degree of exocentricity, though we will see more extreme examples of exocentricity in Section 2.3.4. Unfortunately, the term LEXICAL tends to be used also to contrast with PHRASAL, so that N is lexical, and NP is phrasal; I is lexical in this sense – though it is functional in the sense used above – and contrasts with IP, which is phrasal. It is unlikely though that this ambiguity in the use of 'lexical' will cause confusion.

In the endocentric phrase *very hungry*, it is intuitively obvious why *hungry* rather than *very* is the head of the phrase, but we can't always rely on intuition to identify the head. Instead we will introduce some formal, morphosyntactic criteria for determining head status. As with many of the distinctions we make in linguistics, head status is not always absolutely clear-cut. Many elements that we analyse as the head of their phrase will not have all of the head properties; the main thing is that the head has more head properties than any other word in the phrase (otherwise that word would be the head). There are also cases where linguists disagree on what should be the head, and where the choice of head depends on more general theoretical assumptions. Still, here are some criteria we can use.

Certain elements can select another element. We saw in Section 2.2 that some verbs select for one phrase in addition to the subject, like *devour*, whereas others may select for two more, like *give*, or none, like *smile*. We also saw in examples (18) and (19) in Section 1.4 that even when two verbs combine with items that are semantically similar, they may require them to be of different categories; *enjoy* requires a noun phrase whereas *hope* requires a clause. This power to determine or constrain properties of the elements which they combine with is typical of heads, and the element that they select is sometimes referred to as the complement.

If a phrase has a particular feature, say NUM = PL or TENSE = PAST, and this feature is shown morphologically on one element, then that element is the MORPHOSYNTACTIC LOCUS and is assumed to be the head. The constituents in square brackets in (20) differ in tense: (20a) is PRESENT and (20b) is PAST. What is interpreted to be in the past is the whole phrase in brackets, but the marking is only on the verb *have* versus *had*. This is an argument for saying that *have/had* is the head of the phrase.

(20) a. The dogs [*have* chewed the furniture again].
b. The dogs [*had* chewed the furniture again].

In a similar vein, some items can put constraints on the shape of the elements that can co-occur with them. It is assumed that only heads can do this. This is illustrated in (21) and (22), where we see that *have* and *will* require their complements to have a particular feature. *Have* requires its complement to have the PAST PARTICIPLE form, whereas *will* requires the complement to be in the INFINITIVE. This is then evidence that *have/will* are the heads of *have chewed/will chew the furniture again*. Since it is the verb *chew/chewed* that carries that feature required by *have/will*, we can also conclude from this that *chew/chewed* is the head of the inner square bracket in (21a) and (22b) by the morphosyntactic locus criterion.

(21) a. The dogs [*have* [*chewed* the furniture again]].
b. *The dogs [*have* [*chew* the furniture again]].

(22) a. *The dogs [*will* [*chewed* the furniture again]].
b. The dogs [*will* [*chew* the furniture again]].

One further characteristic that heads are assumed to have is that they can represent the whole. Of course there are constituents where all parts are obligatory, and this criterion cannot be used for such constituents. However, if it is the case that one part can represent the whole, then that part is the head. Consider the sentences in (23).

(23) a. The dogs [have chewed the furniture again], but the cats *have not*.
b. The dogs [will chew the furniture again], but the cats *will not*.

What is understood to be negated by *not* here is not just *have* and *will*, respectively, but *have chewed the furniture again* and *will chew the furniture again*. The second part of both sentences is elliptic, so that *have* and *will* represent the whole constituent in brackets, and hence they are deemed to be the heads of their respective constituents by this criterion.

We will not have more to say about what criteria can be used to establish head status here, but we hope to have convinced you that *have* and *will* are the heads of their constituents and more generally of the head status of the AUXILIARY verb. In what follows we will use the criteria introduced to identify heads.

In the examples we have looked at here, all the evidence for head status rather neatly points in the same direction. However, this is not always the case. If you look at noun phrases in English, the situation is rather messier. Intuitively, you would think that in a noun phrase like *a hungry dog sitting by its food bowl*, the head would have to be *dog*; it is after all a "kind of" dog. However, if we forget lexical semantics and think of the functional side, it is not so clear. A crucial feature of a noun phrase like *the dog* is that it is definite, and this feature is marked only on the determiner in English. A feature like number is often marked on the noun, but in a noun phrase like *those sheep* it is marked only on the determiner. By the morphosyntactic locus criterion, the determiner could then be considered the head. In the sentence *Those dogs eat a lot*, either *those* or *dogs* could replace *those dogs* as a subject. For this reason there has been quite a debate about whether *a hungry dog sitting by its food bowl* should be considered an NP headed by *dog* or a DP (for Determiner Phrase) headed by the determiner *a*. Most linguists would now analyse it as a DP, and that is what we will assume for English. Of course *dog* is the head of the smaller NP constituent *hungry dog sitting by its food bowl*, which forms the complement of the D head of DP. In Section 2.3.3, when we have discussed the motivation for functional categories, we will come back to an argument in favour of assuming that the determiner is in fact the head and that hence English noun phrases are DPs. The arguments in favour of a DP do not apply to all languages, so we will assume that in some languages noun phrases are just NPs, and we will continue to use 'noun phrase' as a neutral term.

We have shown how a verbal head determines what complements (if any) it can co-occur with, but this selectional behaviour is not specific to verbs. Other categories can also take complements. If we return to the examples used in (8) in Section 2.2 (repeated here as (24)), we see that the lexical verb *studied* takes a DP (as we now call a noun phrase) complement in (24a) and that in a similar way the noun *study* takes a PP complement in (24b) and the preposition *of* takes a DP complement *ancient scripts*.

(24) a. **Carl** studied ancient scripts.
b. **Carl**'s study of ancient scripts

In (25), it is an adjective, *proud*, that takes a PP complement *of her dog*.

(25) Ingrid is **proud** *of her dog*.

This means that we can make a general statement that a head of any category can take a complement. The resulting category must be of the same kind as the head, of course, so nominal if the head is a noun, verbal if the head is a verb etc.

A lexical category and its complement do not necessarily form a full phrasal category; it is of an "in-between level". We will refer to this as an N′, pronounced 'N-bar', or V′ etc. depending on the category (we will come back to the use of N′ and V′ when we have introduced functional categories). Given that there are significant parallels between categories, we can use a variable and say that a head X can combine with a complement YP and form an X′. This can be stated in terms of a PHRASE STRUCTURE RULE using variables over categories. Such rules license small tree structures. In (26a), we have the COMPLEMENT RULE, which licenses the tree in (26b).

(26) a. $X' \rightarrow X\ YP$

b. X′

X YP

As we saw in Section 2.2, phrases that have the ADJ function behave differently from selected complements in that there can be more than one. The example in (24a) for instance can be expanded as in (27).

(27) a. Carl studied ancient scripts intensely.

b. Carl studied ancient scripts intensely every summer.

c. Carl studied ancient scripts intensely every summer because he loved it.

In principle, there are no formal limits to how many adjuncts can be added, though at a certain point, it becomes hard for the hearer to process. Since these phrases can be added freely, we need a new rule. The adjunct phrases are added to an X′, since they generally occur most naturally after a complement (the order in ?*Carl studied intensely ancient scripts* sounds odd) and the resulting phrase is also of category X′. We then get the ADJUNCT RULE in (28a), which permits the tree in (28b).

(28) a. $X' \rightarrow X'\ YP$

b. X′

X′ YP

A striking fact about the rule in (28a) is that X′ occurs on both sides of the arrow. This means that the rule can apply to its own output; it is RECURSIVE. If we take the V′ *studied ancient scripts*, created by the rule in (26a) and apply the rule in (28a) to add an adjunct *intensely* (which is of category AdvP), then the result is another V′. Since it is a V′, we can apply the rule in (28a) again and add another adjunct, this time the DP *every summer*. And so on. This would give the tree in (29), where the top two layers are licensed by the recursive application of rule (28a). Here and throughout this book we follow the convention of using triangles in trees to abstract away from detail we are not concerned with.

(29)

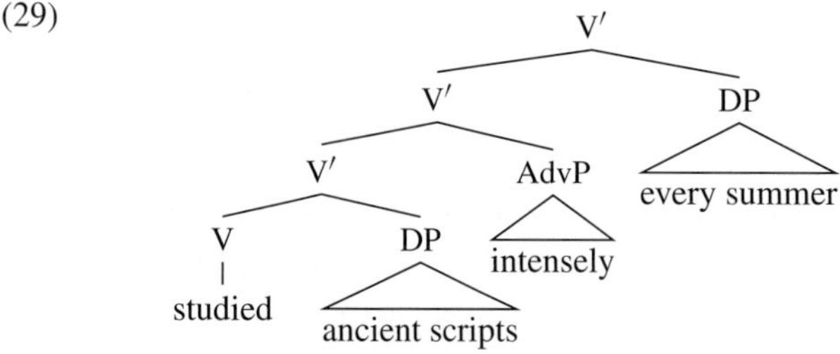

This recursiveness (or recursivity) is an important property of language.

A phrase like *studied ancient scripts* or indeed *studied ancient scripts intensely* is not complete. A subject needs to be added. This constituent is more like a complement than an adjunct in that it is required and it is unique. This means that we need a rule that is non-recursive. This gives the SPECIFIER RULE in (30a) which licenses the tree in (30b). The node that results from the application of the specifier rule is often referred to as X″, 'X double-bar', to link in with the intermediate X′. However, because there are only two bar levels, an X″ is always the same as an XP, and since we find XP clearer than X″, this is what we will use throughout this book. When we have discussed English clause structure and the use of functional categories in Section 2.3.2, we will see that in languages like English, where functional categories are motivated, there may have to be some modifications to our assumptions about lexical categories, but this serves to illustrate how X-bar syntax works.

(30) a. X″/XP → YP X′

b. X″/XP
   YP X′

We can then sum up the rules as in (31). Just to make clear that the complements, the adjuncts and the specifier can be of different categories, we have used a different variable for each. Notice the * in (31a). This is the so-called KLEENE STAR, and it is used to indicate 'zero or more', in this case because a head can have a number of complements, or no complements at all. We will find further use for the Kleene star throughout this book as we introduce further rules. In the specifier rule, we could have put the QP in brackets to indicate that it is also optional, but as we will see, there is a general convention in LFG that all phrase structure positions are optional.

(31) a. X′ ⟶ X YP* COMPLEMENT RULE

b. X′ ⟶ X′ ZP ADJUNCT RULE

c. XP ⟶ QP X′ SPECIFIER RULE

These are the standard general rules of X-bar theory, and they are particularly important in defining specifier and complement, terms that will be important throughout the book. With respect to adjuncts, it is generally recognised that they can also be attached at phrasal level, in which case they are said to ADJOIN to the phrase. This means we also need the rule in (32). Like the adjunct rule in (31), it has the property of being recursive, crucial to handling adjuncts. Which rule applies to an adjunct in a specific language is something that needs to be established empirically; the important thing here is to note that both positions are available within the LFG approach to X-bar syntax.

(32) XP ⟶ XP ZP PHRASAL ADJUNCT RULE

The standard X-bar syntax rules in (31) capture the parallels between different types of phrases nicely, but it is important to recognise that there are limits to the parallelisms; for instance, there may be limited scope for modifiers in a PP, and specifiers may not work quite this way in an AdvP. Like other frameworks that use X-bar syntax, LFG uses it with some modifications. For instance, we will need some additional rules to capture particles, like *on* in *catch on*, which are non-projecting. We will also argue that where functional categories are introduced above lexical categories, this can have consequences for the lexical categories, so that they do not project an intermediate X′ category in these circumstances. We will return to this in Section 2.3.2. In LFG, it is assumed that a language may not make use of a particular option, say, by not having a specifier for a specific category. It is also central to LFG's approach to structure that not all phrases need to be endocentric as assumed in standard X-bar theory; exocentric phrases are also permitted. We will return to this in Section 2.3.4.

An important principle that applies to c-structure is that of Lexical Integrity:

Lexical Integrity Principle: Morphologically complete words are leaves of the c-structure tree and each leaf corresponds to one and only one c-structure node.

This is in line with the general LFG assumption that there are separate dimensions of linguistic information with different processes operating within them. Words are assumed to be constructed in the morphology before they are inserted into the syntax. We will not be concerned here with the details of how this is done. Not only does morphology operate differently from syntax, but there is also evidence that syntax has no access to the morphological structure of the word. So, for instance, as far as syntax goes, there is no real difference between *test* and *pressed*, apart from the fact that the former has the feature TENSE = PRESENT and the latter TENSE = PAST. Morphologically, *test* consists of one morpheme only, whereas *press-ed* consists of two; however, to the syntax they are just two words of the category V, which can be inserted under a V node in a suitable tree.

Identifying when you have a V and a VP or an A and an AP is not that difficult in English (though there are languages where it may be), but knowing when you have a functional category may be less straightforward. In LFG, there is a relatively restrictive approach to functional categories. In general, they are only motivated when a particular functional feature is associated with a structural position. To illustrate the use of functional categories, we will now examine clause structure in a highly configurational language like English in some detail. In Section 2.3.4 we will compare it with languages with some degree of non-configurationality.

2.3.2 The C-structure of English Clauses

We established in Section 2.3.1 that *have* is the head of *The dogs have chewed the furniture again*, so that a clause in English is endocentric. The question now is what the category of this constituent is. In our first discussion of this we assumed that *have* is just a V, so that the whole sentence is a VP. However, we will now have reason to revise this. Auxiliary verbs such as *have* have special properties in English, but only when they are FINITE, that is, marked as present or past.

We will pick out three of the special properties: finite auxiliaries can carry negation (33a), they can invert with the subject to form a question (33b) and they can be used in an elliptic construction to replace the whole constituent (33c) (see also (23)).

(33)
a. The cat **has not / hasn't** scratched the furniture.
b. **Has the cat** scratched the furniture?
c. The cat has scratched the furniture, but the dog **has** not.

It is not the auxiliary as such that has these special properties, it is only when it has the feature value FINITE = +. In (34), HAVE occurs in its non-finite (FINITE = −) form *have* because it is preceded by another auxiliary, and we see that it does not have the special properties shown in (33). It should be pointed out that for (34a), the version with *have not* is possible, but this is a different use of the negation as the impossibility of using *haven't* shows.

(34)
a. *The cat will **have not / haven't** scratched the furniture.
b. ***Have the cat** will scratched the furniture?
c. *The cat will have scratched the furniture, but the dog will **have** not/**haven't**.

It is the feature FINITE = + that gives finite auxiliaries their special status, and it is exactly when functional features have special structural properties that we assume functional categories. We will analyse finite auxiliaries in English as belonging to the category I (for Inflection), and since they are the head, the phrase as a whole will be an IP. This gives us the tree in (35).

(35)

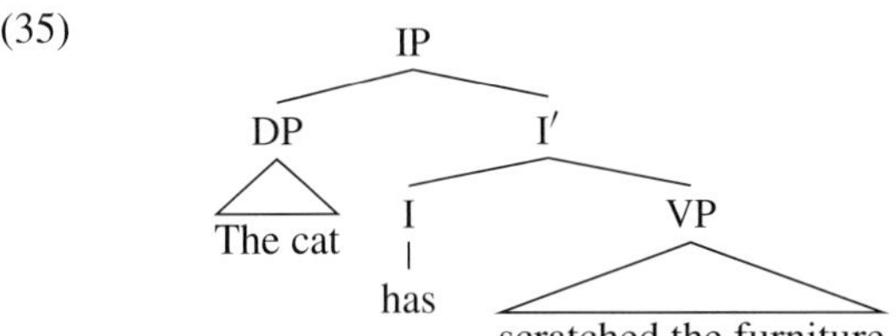

In (35), the subject DP *the cat* is found in the specifier of IP slot. In fact, we will **define** SUBJ in English as the DP that is in specifier of IP. It turns out that there is cross-linguistic evidence that the specifier positions of functional categories have special status; they tend to be the grammaticalised discourse functions. As you may remember from Table 2.2 in Section 2.2, this includes SUBJ, TOPIC and FOCUS. Non-discourse functions, on the other hand, are complements of lexical categories, so an OBJ, for instance, would be the complement of a verb. We will look at the mapping between c-structure and f-structure in Chapter 3, and in Chapter 6, we will see another example of a specifier of a functional category having a discourse function.

In English, lexical verbs, unlike auxiliaries, do not allow negation, questions and ellipsis even when finite, as the ungrammaticality of (36) shows.

(36)
a. *The cat **scratched not / scratchedn't** the furniture.
b. ***Scratched the cat** the furniture?
c. *The cat scratched the furniture, but the dog **scratched** not.

This means that we do not have any arguments for assuming that lexical verbs are found under an I node even when they are finite. In some approaches to grammar, this would mean that a zero element, an invisible and inaudible element, would be assumed to occupy the I position. However, since in LFG c-structure is assumed to be what you see (or hear), empty elements are generally not used: pre-terminal nodes (such as I, V, N) must dominate some terminal material (a word). However, in LFG, there is a convention that all phrase structure nodes are optional, including the pre-terminal or head positions. This means that all elements on the right side in a phrase structure rule are optional. This makes the LFG implementation of X-bar theory radically different from other uses of it.

For a sentence like *The cat scratched the furniture* we get the tree in (37) (remember that we use the triangle as a shorthand, indicating where we have omitted the details of internal structure).

(37)

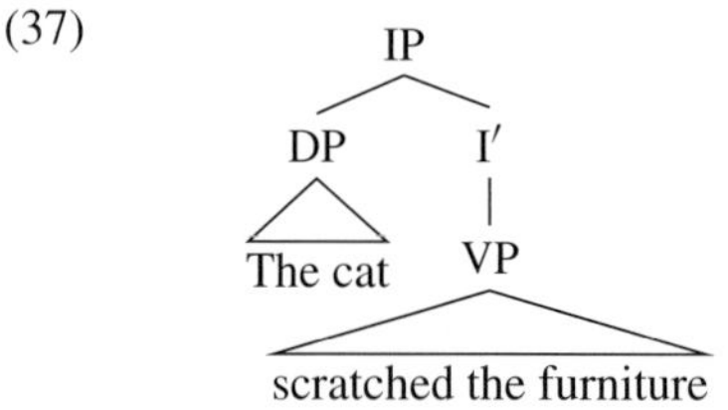

Here the I is not present since there is no element to fill it; however, the IP is still there, and there are a number of reasons for this. Since *scratched* is of the category V, if there was no I projection at all, this would make the whole sentence a VP rather than an IP. This would mean that *The cat scratched the furniture* would be of a different category from *The cat has scratched the furniture*, which would not be appropriate since they have the same distribution. Second, as we have already said and as we will see in Section 3.2, in English we actually define SUBJ in terms of its position as specifier of IP. This means that if the rule introducing IP and its DP and I′ daughters had not applied, there would be no position for the SUBJ. This is then one of the ways in which LFG departs from the strict X-bar approach.

We will assume that, at least in English, a lexical category that is embedded under a functional category is reduced in structure. Hence we will not use the V′ level in English VPs throughout this book. If there are good arguments for a more articulated structure, of course, there is nothing that prevents the use of V′, but it seems reasonable that the positioning of related functional material outside the VP may reduce VP-internal structure.

A non-finite auxiliary verb will also occur in V, since it is the feature value FINITE = + in combination with auxiliary status that is the motivation for the I node. *The cat will have scratched the furniture* then has the structure in (38).

(38)

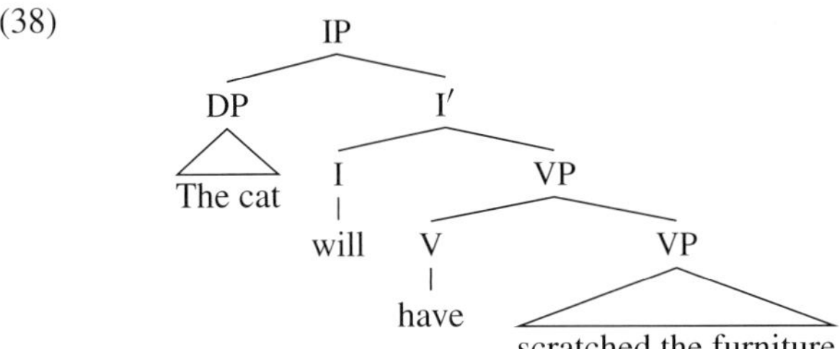

We will discuss constructions like that in (39) in Chapter 5, but let's just look briefly at the clause in bold here.

(39) Oscar would want **to feed the cat**.

We have said that one characteristic of heads in general and hence also of I is that they can take the place of the whole constituent in ellipsis. (40a) shows that *would* can do this and (40b) that *want* cannot. The example in (40c) shows interesting behaviour by the infinitival marker *to* in this respect.

(40) a. Oscar would want to feed the cat, but Ingrid *would* not.
b. *Oscar would want to feed the cat, but Ingrid would not *want*.
c. Oscar would want to feed the cat, but Ingrid would not want *to*.

In (40c), *to* represents the whole constituent *to feed the cat*, just like *would* represents *would want to feed the cat* in (40a). For this reason, we assume that the infinitival marker *to* is also an I element, so that we get the tree in (41) for the bold clause in (39). We'll return to the issue of how these trees fit into the tree for the sentence as a whole in Chapter 5.

(41)

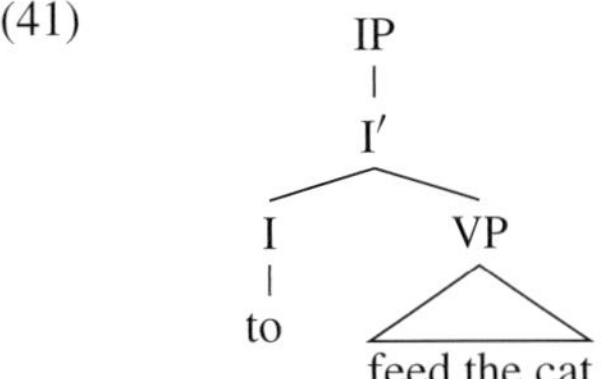

In English, finite subordinate clauses look much like main clauses. In fact, we can turn the main clause in (42a) into a subordinate clause as in (42b).

(42) a. The cats have scratched the furniture again.
b. Fred says **the cats have scratched the furniture again**.

However, there is another version of (42b) which looks slightly different in structure, namely (43).

(43) Fred says **that the cats have scratched the furniture again**.

There are also other elements which occur in subordinate clauses in this way, like *whether* and *if* in (44).

(44) a. Fred wonders **whether the cats have scratched the furniture again**.

b. **If the cats have scratched the furniture again**, Ingrid will be disgruntled.

These words actually have head properties, for instance in that verbs may select their complements with respect to that word. As the examples in (45a) and (45b) show, a verb like *hope* can combine with a subordinate clause introduced by *that*, but not *whether*. *Wonder*, which combined happily with a *whether* clause in (44a), shows the opposite behaviour as the ungrammaticality of (45c) shows.

(45) a. Fred hopes **that the cats have not scratched the furniture again**.

b. *Fred hopes **whether the cats have not scratched the furniture again**.

c. *Fred wonders **that the cats have scratched the furniture again**.

Heads like *that* and *whether* belong to a functional category; they contribute functional features, but no lexical meaning. The term COMPLEMENTISER is standardly used to refer to such elements, so it is assigned to category C, which forms a CP. C takes an IP as its complement, so that we get the tree in (46) for the sentence in (43). You see that the subordinate clause is the complement of the higher verb *says*.

(46)

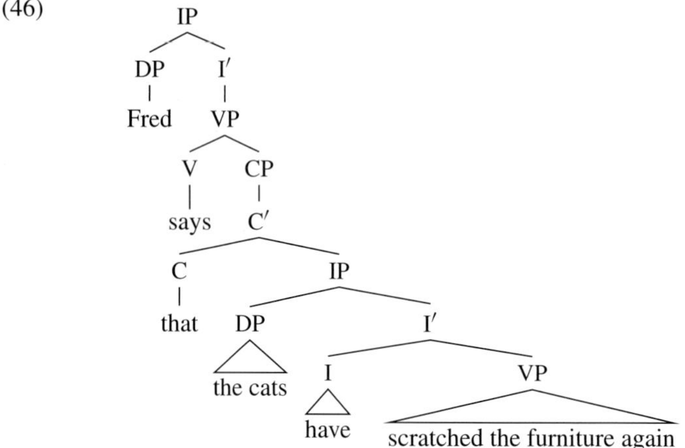

One of the characteristics of a head is that it contributes its features to the phrase as a whole. The subordinate clause CP in (46) is present tense because the head *has* has the feature value TENSE = PRES. The C element *that* also contributes features to the clause; it does for instance mark it as declarative, finite and subordinate, but of course the f-structure for the subordinate clause as a whole also has to include the PRED feature 'scratch <SUBJ, OBJ>', which is associated with the verb inside the VP in (46). In LFG, this is ensured by functional categories being CO-HEADS with the category below them; in (46), C, I and V are all co-heads, which means that the features of the mother's f-structure can come from any one of the co-heads, which in turn means that there must be no clashing feature values or Uniqueness would be violated (see Section 2.2). This also means that a functional category cannot have a PRED feature since this would always clash with the PRED feature of the lexical head. We can refer to this as PRED UNIQUENESS, since it is a violation of Uniqueness. We will see in Section 3.2 how this works formally.

To sum up, the phrase structure rules we have used to generate the English clauses we have considered so far are those in (47). We will of course have to expand this set of rules in order to be able to analyse other categories, like DPs, which we will consider in Section 2.3.3. In Section 2.3.4, we will show that some languages require a different set of rules for clauses.

(47)
a. CP ⟶ XP C′
b. C′ ⟶ C IP
c. IP ⟶ DP I′
d. I′ ⟶ I VP
e. VP ⟶ V DP DP PP CP ...
f. VP ⟶ VP XP

The rule in (47e) may look confusing: surely no verb in English would take four complements, two DPs, one PP and a CP? Recall, however, that all categories on the right-hand side of a phrase structure rule are interpreted as optional by convention. This means that a tree generated by the rule in (47e) would only include those complements required by the verb's PRED feature. This is ensured by the Coherence Condition. For *smile* there would only be a verb, since its PRED feature value would only include a SUBJ and no complements, for *give* there would be two DPs and for *put* there would be a DP and a PP. In fact, the rule in (47e) is not complete as it stands since verbs can also take clauses as complements. In Chapter 6, we will return to look at the CP and the XP that we have included in (47a).

As already indicated above, we assume a VP rule for English in (47e) which directly introduces the lexical head V (so that there is no V′). This is because it is not entirely clear that VPs in English make use of the specifier position for this category (as we will see in Section 2.3.3, the same argument may be made for the NP inside the DP in English), and this may then be an example of how the X-bar notation makes positions available that a language may opt not to make use of. Our intention here is not to provide a complete analysis of English clause structure, but rather to illustrate how X-bar syntax is implemented in LFG. If there is evidence in favour of elements occurring in the specifier position of VP in English, then a rule needs to be added to this set.

We have assumed in (47f) that adjuncts are added to the VP in English, but it is possible that arguments can be found in favour of different positions for modifiers, and then there may be a need for both V′ and VP modification.

We have referred to a number of general principles that hold for the correspondence between structure and function in a language like English, whose structure is endocentric and includes functional categories. We can sum them up here as general PRINCIPLES OF STRUCTURE–FUNCTION ASSOCIATION, applying to configurational languages such as English.

- A c-structure head and all its projections are mapped onto one f-structure.
- Functional categories and their complements are co-heads.
- Specifiers of functional categories are grammaticalised discourse functions.
- Complements of lexical categories are non-discourse functions.
- Constituents adjoined to a category by recursive rules are generally adjuncts.

2.3.3 The C-structure of Other Categories

Having introduced functional categories by looking at clause structure in English, we now briefly return to English noun phrases before moving on to consider mapping to f-structure. We said in Section 2.3.1 that the headedness criteria do not provide unambiguous evidence for the head status of either D or N in English noun phrases, but there is certainly an argument in favour of assuming that the D is a morphosyntactic locus. Now we have introduced the idea that a functional category is motivated when a functional feature is associated with a particular position. Applying this to noun phrases, we can argue that the feature DEF = ± is associated with the left edge of the noun phrase (ignoring the so-called predeterminers like *all* or *both*) and that this is an argument for a DP. As we said in Section 2.3.1 this is generally how English noun phrases are analysed in the current literature, and hence it is the assumption we will make here. The rules we will assume for noun phrases in English are provided in (48). As with VP in English clauses, we have skipped the single-bar stage for NP, and as we did for the complement rule for V, we include all potential complements in one rule, with … indicating that there may be more than the ones provided here. We assume that modifiers adjoin to NP, that is attach to an NP to form a new NP, as indicated in (48d). It is not just APs that can modify a noun, and in (48e), we include a recursive rule for PP modifiers. These are not the only categories that can modify nouns, but we are not aiming to be exhaustive here, just to illustrate the workings of c-structure. There may be arguments in favour of having more than one position for nominal modifiers, but that is a level of language-specific detail we will not get into here. For illustration, we provide examples of noun phrases with a PP complement and a CP complement, respectively, in (49) and a tree for the noun phrase in (12b) in (50). In order to be able to analyse the noun phrases fully, we also add a simple rule for PPs in (48f). We will return to PPs in Section 3.3. In (50) we have put the APs lower than the PP, but since the NP is recursive, the rules allow for both possibilities. We will not go into the empirical arguments for the different options here.

(48)
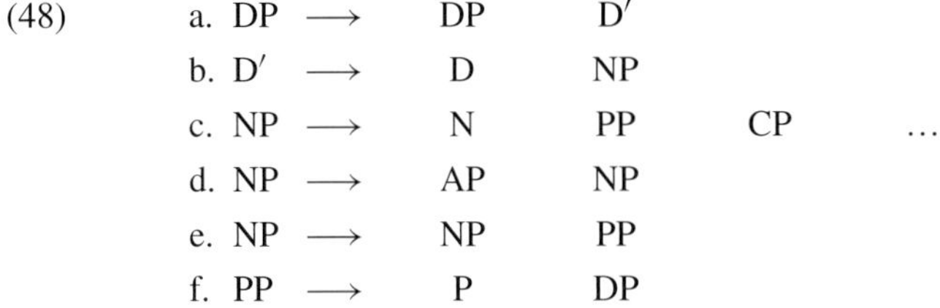

a. DP ⟶ DP D′
b. D′ ⟶ D NP
c. NP ⟶ N PP CP …
d. NP ⟶ AP NP
e. NP ⟶ NP PP
f. PP ⟶ P DP

(49)
a. a **lover** *of cats*
b. the **fact** *that they love cats*

(50)
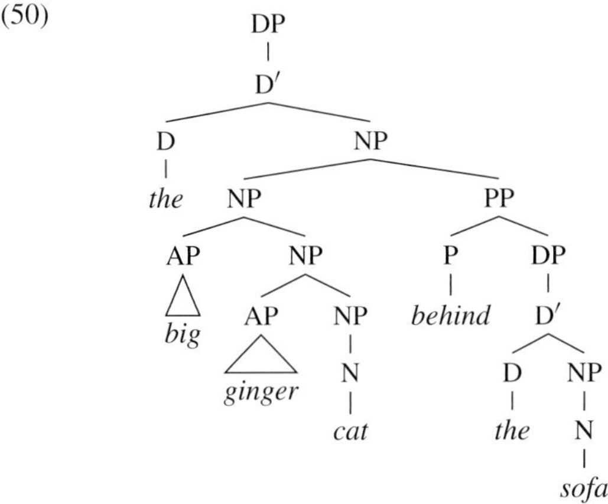

The rules in (47) and (48) can account for many structures of English, but they cannot generate examples such as those in (51).

(51)
a. Carl studied ancient scripts and Eve studied astrophysics.
b. Carl studied ancient scripts and classical languages.
c. Carl studied ancient and modern languages.

In (51a), two full clauses are coordinated, in (51b) two noun phrases are coordinated and in (51c) two adjective phrases. Coordination can combine any constituents as long as they are all of the same category and bar level; the result is a constituent that is also of that category and bar level. More than two items can be coordinated, but then it is generally just the last one that has an explicit coordinator.

(52)
a. Carl studied ancient scripts, Eve studied astrophysics and Ingrid studied philosophy.
b. Carl studied ancient scripts and classical languages, but not history.
c. Carl studied ancient, modern and artificial languages.

To capture these coordination structures, we can postulate the c-structure rule in (53). Here we have used α to generalise over any category at X, X′ or XP level. We introduced the Kleene star in the rules in (31), and here we introduce the KLEENE PLUS in the form of the superscripted $^+$, which means 'one or more', so that the rule allows for one or more categories before the overt conjunction

Conj. We have assumed here that there is an overt conjunction only for the final conjunct, but this will vary between languages and constructions.

(53) $\alpha \longrightarrow \alpha^{+} \quad \text{Conj} \quad \alpha$

2.3.4 Variation in C-structure

In Section 1.2 we saw that constituent order was less constrained by syntactic rules in Latin than in English. In particular, we saw no argument for a VP in Latin, and though one word order is more common, it varies depending on the information-structural properties of the constituents. This means that we cannot establish a syntactically determined position for the V, and hence the structure we assume for Latin is (54), where the order of the daughters is not specified. Latin is non-configurational in the sense that it can be argued not to have VPs.

(54)

```
       S
   ____|____
  NP   NP   V
```

The clause structures of languages across the world show more variation than that which we see when we compare English and Latin, however. There are for instance languages which are more radically non-configurational than Latin. Consider the data from Wambaya in (55) (from Nordlinger, 1998, 27–8). Wambaya is an indigenous language originally spoken in the Northern Territory, Australia, which now has few fluent speakers left.

(55)
a. Dawu gin-a alaji janyi-ni.
bite 3SG.M.SUBJ-PST boy.I(ACC) dog.I-ERG

b. Alaji gin-a dawu janyi-ni.
boy.I(ACC) 3SG.M.SUBJ-PST bite dog.I-ERG

c. Alaji gin-a janyi-ni dawu.
boy.I(ACC) 3SG.M.SUBJ-PST dog.I-ERG bite

d. Dawu gin-a janyi-ni alaji.
bite 3SG.M.SUBJ-PST dog.I-ERG boy.I(ACC)

e. Janyi-ni gin-a alaji dawu.
dog.I-ERG 3SG.M.SUBJ-PST boy.I(ACC) bite

f. Janyi-ni gin-a dawu alaji.
dog.I-ERG 3SG.M.SUBJ-PST bite boy.I(ACC)
'The dog bit the boy.'

Some explanation of the glossing is in order here. The I indicates the class of the noun (similar to gender in French or German), and ERGative and ACCusative are case markers. Wambaya has a different organisation of grammatical relations from English; it is a (partially) ERGATIVE language, which means that it marks the subject of a transitive verb like 'bite' with ERGative case. Subjects of intransitive verbs and objects of transitive verbs are marked with the same case. This means that in (55), 'dog' is the subject. The element *gina* can be compared to auxiliaries like *did* in English; it consists of an agreement marker and a past tense marker. The most striking property of these Wambaya sentences is that as long as *gina* occurs in the second position, all the orders between the words are acceptable sentences and have the same basic meaning. Which one is used depends mainly on how the speaker wants to present the information. The association between a functional feature, TENSE, and a structural position, second position, is an argument for the positing of a functional category, in this case I. We can then assume that like in English, Wambaya clauses are of category IP, and that the specifier of the IP involves a grammaticalised discourse function. However, beyond this there are few structural similarities with English at clausal level. Given the data in (55), it would be difficult to argue for there being a VP; the verb and the NP *alaji* 'boy' (note that there is no equivalent of *the* and no argument in favour of assuming a DP) do not have to occur next to each other and can occur in either order. In this sense, the Wambaya structure has more in common with Latin than with English, and we will assume that its structure also involves an exocentric category S. The resulting tree for Wambaya is provided in (56); it has both an IP and an S. Here we have assumed the order in (55b), but the order within the S is free, and any one of those elements could have occurred in the specifier of IP position under the right information-structural circumstances.

(56)

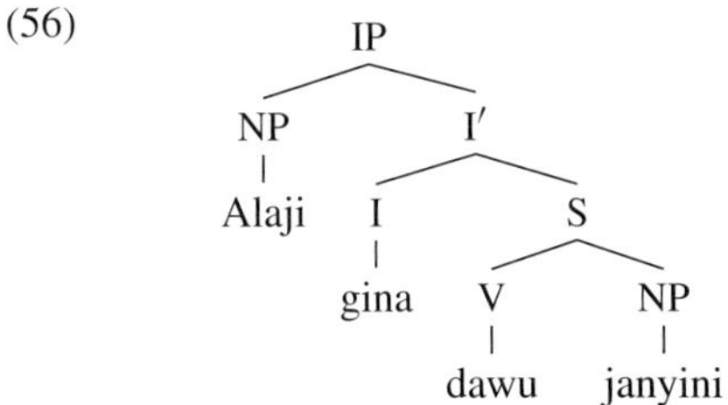

This very brief look at clause structure in three languages reveals just how much languages can vary in their syntactic structure, and it is important that our representation of c-structure can capture this variation. It is not just for clauses that we find great variation in structure between languages. Consider the noun phrases from Macedonian, a South Slavic language, in (57), for instance.

(57)

a. čovek=ot
man=DEF
'the man'

b. dobr=iot čovek
good=DEF man
'the good man'

c. dobr=iot mal čovek
good=DEF little man
'the good little man'

d. moj=ot casovnik
my=DEF watch
'my watch'

e. cetiri=te stotini lug'e
four=DEF hundred people
'the four hundred people'

Here you see that the equivalent of the English *the* occurs in the second position, much like the finite element did in Wambaya. It is what is called a CLITIC, that is, a bound element – in the sense that it attaches to another word – but one that differs from an affix in that it is positioned by syntactic rather than morphological rules (this is why it is linked with = rather than -). The key property for us is that it always occurs in second position and can attach to different categories; in (57a) it attaches to a noun, to an adjective in (57b) and (57c), to a possessive pronoun in (57d) and to the first part of a complex numeral in (57e). On the assumption that a functional feature associated with a specific structural position indicates the presence of a projecting functional category, we can take the distribution of DEF in (57) as evidence for a DP. There is no evidence here for the nominal equivalent of S, that is, a nominal exocentric phrase, however, since we do not see the freedom of word order in these noun phrases that we saw in Latin or Wambaya clauses, but we would assume that the complement of D is an NP.

We provided the set of phrase structure rules required for English clauses in (47), but we need to expand this set somewhat if the rules are to be general enough to account for the Latin and Wambaya data. Though we have not provided any data for noun phrases in the two languages, there is in fact no evidence for a DP in either, so that in addition to the phrase structure rule in (47c), we need to have (58a), and (58b) is an alternative to (47d). Finally, we need a rule to expand S, and this is found in (58c). Here we use commas to indicate that the order of the daughters of S is not specified.

(58)
a. IP $\longrightarrow$ NP I′
b. I′ $\longrightarrow$ I S
c. S $\longrightarrow$ V, NP, NP ...

It turns out that there are languages that show a higher degree of non-configurationality than that indicated by the rule in (58c). An example from Jiwarli, an indigenous language which was spoken in Western Australia, but that now has no fluent speakers left, is provided in (59) (Austin, 2001, 311).

(59) Yinha nhurra parlura-rni-nma payipa nganaju
this.ACC 2SG.ERG full-CAUS-IMP pipe.ACC 1SG.DAT.ACC
'You fill up this pipe of mine!'

This example may require a bit more explanation. The glossing shows that the verb *parlura-rni-nma* literally means 'cause to become full!', but it is idiomatically translated as 'fill!'. As in Wambaya, the phrase-marked ergative, *nhurra*, is the subject of the transitive verb. The three elements marked with accusative case together mean 'this my pipe', or as in the idiomatic translation; 'this pipe of mine'. The remarkable thing here is that the demonstrative *yinha* is separated from the rest of the noun phrase *payipa* and *nganaju*. Arguing the same way we did when it came to the absence of a VP in Latin, this means that there is no NP in Jiwarli, and the tree for (59) will be something like (60). Note that as far as we can tell from this limited data, Jiwarli clause structure does not involve an IP.

(60)

```
              S
  ___________/|\___________
 /      /     |     \      \
Dem    N      V      N    Poss
```

In principle, we would then need an alternative to the rule in (58c), as in (61).

(61) S $\longrightarrow$ Dem, N, V ...

However, it would be preferable to be able to generalise over the two types of languages that have the category S and formulate a general rule for S in non-configurational languages. This is done in LFG by the rule in (62).

(62) S $\longrightarrow$ V, X*

The Kleene star used in (62) was introduced in the rules in (31). The reason we need 'zero or more' here is that some languages may not need separate arguments; think of Latin *veni, vidi, vici*, which means 'I came, I saw, I conquered', without the need for a pronoun in c-structure (we will see how these are analysed in LFG in Section 4.2.3). Since X stands for any category, the rule in (62) states that a mother node S can have a V daughter and zero or more daughters of any category. This rule replaces (58c) and (61). Since the non-configurational languages we have looked at differ in their degree of non-configurationality, we need to specify what the variable X in (62) can be, and this is done as in (63), where $\in$ is the logical symbol meaning 'belongs to' and the curly brackets indicate a set of elements. We are not intending to provide an exhaustive or in-depth analysis of the two languages here, but rather to illustrate how the LFG tools can be used to analyse non-configurational clause organisation.

(63)
a. Latin: X $\in$ {NP, PP, CP}
b. Wambaya: X $\in$ {NP, ...}
c. Jiwarli: X $\in$ {N, A, D, ...}

If we replace the rules in (58c) and (61) with (62) and include those in (47) and (58b), we have the set of rules involved in licensing clause-level constituents which is provided in (64). We have not included any of the rules for adjuncts here; they would involve recursive rules expanding VP or V′.

(64)
a. CP $\longrightarrow$ XP C′
b. C′ $\longrightarrow$ C IP
c. IP $\longrightarrow$ DP I′
d. I′ $\longrightarrow$ I VP
e. I′ $\longrightarrow$ I S

f. VP ⟶ V DP DP PP CP ...

g. S ⟶ V X*

These may not be exhaustive, but the assumption is that there is a limited set of c-structure rules, and that a language employs a subset of these rules. A rule defines a subtree, and any tree must have each part of it licensed by some set of rules relevant to the language in question. As we have said, in LFG, all categories on the right-hand side of a c-structure rule are optional and hence need not be there in the tree. This was exemplified in the tree in (37), where there is no I, so that I′ only has one daughter, VP. However, a subtree where one daughter is "missing" must still have been licensed by one of the applicable rules.

In this chapter, we have introduced the elements of a-structure, f-structure and c-structure. We have shown how c-structure can vary quite radically between languages. In Chapter 3 we will turn to the mapping between these dimensions, and we will see how the differences in c-structure organisation lead to differences in the mapping between c-structure and f-structure. In Chapter 3, we consider the mapping for a language like English, which relies heavily on structure for the identification of grammatical functions. This is contrasted in Chapter 4 with languages where morphology plays a crucial role in mapping between c-structure and f-structure. In Chapter 8 we return to the mapping between a-structure and f-structure.

Reading

In this chapter, we assumed nine θ-roles, and this is what we will be working with when we come to consider the mapping between a-structure and f-structure in more detail in Chapter 8. If you are interested in an approach that generalises more about different θ-roles, then look at Dowty (1991), who works with two overarching roles: Proto-Agent and Proto-Patient. A different approach to θ-roles that has influenced work within LFG can be found in Jackendoff (1990).

We presented the standard approach to grammatical relations in LFG in Section 2.2, and there is broad agreement on the inventory of functions we have assumed here. However, as in any healthy grammatical framework, there is still debate on some issues. Kroeger (1993) provides a discussion of grammatical functions, and of SUBJ particularly, in light of data from Tagalog. The distinction between OBJ and COMP is made partly in terms of category; an OBJ is a DP (or NP) and a COMP is a CP (or maybe IP or S). Given the emphasis in LFG on a separation between c-structure and f-structure, it may seem odd to define a function in terms of a c-structure category, and Alsina et al. (2005) sparked some debate on the issue, which is also picked up by Dalrymple and Lødrup (2000), who argue that finite clausal complements can be either COMP or OBJ. Similarly the issue of the possible c-structure categories that can fill the SUBJ function is a matter for debate. Bresnan (1994) argues that at least in some constructions, PPs can fill the SUBJ function. She illustrates this with examples from English and Chicheŵa. However, it is generally assumed that constituents that may appear to be clausal subjects do not in fact appear in the canonical SUBJ position, but in a TOPIC position from where they are linked to the SUBJ function. The distinction between OBJ and OBJ_θ is discussed in Börjars and Vincent (2008). Further discussion of Recipient or Goal OBJ_θ can be found in Kibort (2008) and Sadler and Camilleri (2013).

Though we have presented a number of criteria for head status here, it was obvious that it is not always easy to establish an unambiguous head, particularly not within noun phrases. The idea of a DP, rather than an NP, was first proposed by Abney (1987) based on different assumptions from those that underpin LFG. An interesting exchange on the notion of headedness is that between Zwicky (1985) and Hudson (1987).

Arguments for the rather strict approach to functional categories proposed here can be found in Kroeger (1993) and Börjars et al. (1999). Lexical Integrity standardly applies to words only, but Asudeh et al. (2013) have suggested that there may be some multi-word expressions that show similar properties. The fact that all categories on the right-hand side of c-structure rules are optional is captured in Bresnan et al. (2016, 90) as the Principle of Economy of Expression. Dalrymple et al. (2015) provide a critical discussion of this principle.

In this chapter, we exemplified CP clauses where the sister of C is either an IP or an S. There are also analyses within LFG where there is a rule that expands C′ as a C and a VP daughter, but not IP or S. One example is the analysis of Dutch and German by Kaplan and Zaenen (2003). This is relevant to Question 2.6 in the exercises about Swedish clauses.

For more on the role of grammaticalised discourse functions and their connection with the projection of functional categories, see for instance Bresnan and Mchombo (1987) or King (1995).

Our analysis of POSS as a grammatical relation within the noun phrase implies that a noun (optionally) takes a POSS as an argument. An approach along these lines has been independently argued for by Payne et al. (2013).

In Section 2.3.1 we made reference to particles like *on* in *catch on* and said that they may be considered non-projecting, something that has not been accounted for in this chapter. You can find out more about how to analyse non-projecting categories in Toivonen (2003).

Exercises

2.1 Consider the pairs of sentences in (65) to (67) from the point of view of a-structure and f-structure. Consider questions such as: how many arguments does the verb in each sentence have? Are the arguments always obligatory? Are the θ-roles involved the same? Are the same grammatical functions (SUBJ, OBJ etc.) involved?

(65) a. Oscar slept the whole night.
b. Oscar ate the whole biscuit.

(66) a. Elizabeth likes Darcy.
b. Darcy hits Wickham.

(67) a. Fred boiled the kettle.
b. The kettle boiled.

2.2 What phrases in English do the following f-structures represent?

(68)

$$\begin{bmatrix} \text{PRED} & \text{`RAT'} \\ \text{NUM} & \text{SG} \\ \text{DEF} & - \end{bmatrix}$$

(69)

$$\begin{bmatrix} \text{PRED} & \text{`LIKE <SUBJ, OBJ>'} \\ \text{TENSE} & \text{PAST} \\ \text{SUBJ} & \begin{bmatrix} \text{PRED} & \text{`CHILD'} \\ \text{NUM} & \text{SG} \\ \text{DEF} & + \end{bmatrix} \\ \text{OBJ} & \begin{bmatrix} \text{PRED} & \text{`BISCUIT'} \\ \text{NUM} & \text{PL} \\ \text{DEF} & + \end{bmatrix} \end{bmatrix}$$

(70)

$$\begin{bmatrix} \text{PRED} & \text{`THINK <SUBJ, COMP>'} \\ \text{TENSE} & \text{PRES} \\ \text{SUBJ} & \begin{bmatrix} \text{PRED} & \text{`NEIGHBOUR'} \\ \text{NUM} & \text{PL} \\ \text{DEF} & + \end{bmatrix} \\ \text{COMP} & \begin{bmatrix} \text{PRED} & \text{`SMELL<SUBJ>'} \\ \text{TENSE} & \text{PRES} \\ \text{SUBJ} & \begin{bmatrix} \text{PRED} & \text{`DOG'} \\ \text{NUM} & \text{PL} \\ \text{DEF} & + \end{bmatrix} \end{bmatrix} \end{bmatrix}$$

(71)

$$\begin{bmatrix} \text{PRED} & \text{`BARK <SUBJ>'} \\ \text{TENSE} & \text{PAST} \\ \text{SUBJ} & \begin{bmatrix} \text{PRED} & \text{`DOG <(POSS)>'} \\ \text{NUM} & \text{PL} \\ \text{POSS} & \begin{bmatrix} \text{PRED} & \text{`OSCAR'} \end{bmatrix} \end{bmatrix} \end{bmatrix}$$

2.3 What is wrong with each of the following f-structures? Make the necessary corrections and state what phrase it represents when corrected.

(72)

$$\begin{bmatrix} \text{PRED} & \text{`KICKED<SUBJ, OBJ>'} \\ \text{TENSE} & \text{PAST} \\ \text{SUBJ} & \begin{bmatrix} \text{PRED} & \text{`OSCAR'} \\ \text{GEND} & \text{MASC} \end{bmatrix} \\ \text{OBJ} & \begin{bmatrix} \text{PRED} & \text{`BALL'} \\ \text{NUM} & \text{SG} \\ \text{DEF} & + \end{bmatrix} \end{bmatrix}$$

(73)

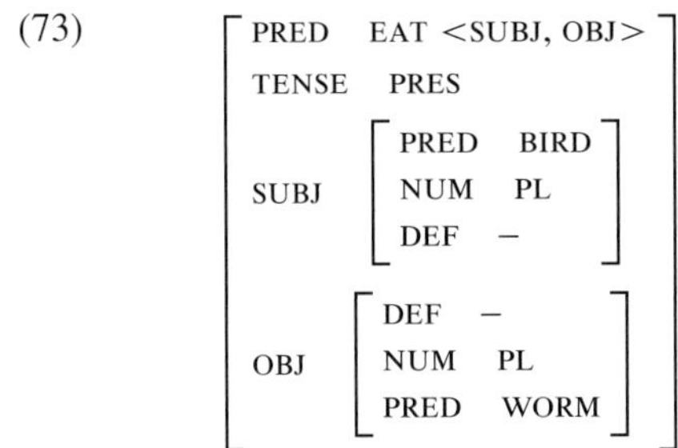

(74)

PRED 'SNOOZE'
TENSE PAST
PRED 'KITTEN'
NUM SG
DEF +

2.4 Which constraints do the ungrammatical sentences in (75) violate?

(75)
a. *That dogs chased ducks.
b. *The little lady tickled.
c. *A small kitten eat very little.
d. *Oscar wants.
e. *Sarah headed the ball the goal.

2.5 In Section 2.2, we said that regular noun phrases are third person. Discuss this in the light of the features of the components of the bold noun phrases in (76).

(76)
a. **Those dogs** hurt themselves.
b. **The girl** washed herself.
c. **We pensioners** look after ourselves.
d. **You students** only think about yourselves.

2.6 The sentences in (77) are typical of Swedish clausal word order. Given LFG assumptions, what can we assume about the position of the finite verb? How about the position of the initial element? If we assume that Swedish clause structure after the finite verb consists of just a VP (no IP), as suggested by Kaplan and Zaenen (2003), can you provide the c-structure for the whole sentence for each example in (77)?

(77)
a. Nils åt fyra pannkakor igår.
Nils eat.PST four pancake.PL yesterday
'Nils ate four pancakes yesterday.'

b. I förrgår åt han köttbullar
the day before yesterday.DEF eat.PST he meatball.PL
istället.
instead
'The day before yesterday he ate meatballs instead.'

c. Ägg gillar han inte.
egg like.PRS he not
'Eggs he doesn't like.'

d. Honom ger hon gärna alla sina pannkakor.
him give.PRS she gladly all her pancake.PL
'She happily gives **him** all her pancakes.'

3 Mapping between C-structure and F-structure

3.1 Sources of F-structure Information

In Section 1.3, we saw that different correspondences between c-structure and f-structure hold for English and Latin, reflecting the fact that f-structures are largely invariant cross-linguistically but c-structures differ considerably, as shown in (15) of Chapter 1. We will now go through the mapping for English in some detail, and we will return to the type of mapping that is required for Latin in Chapter 4.

With each node in the c-structure, there will be an associated f-structure, that is to say that there will be an f-structure associated with each constituent. This is what we indicated in Section 1.3 by drawing lines between nodes in trees and parts of f-structures. The f-structure for any constituent larger than a word is built up from the f-structures of the constituents which form part of it. The content of the f-structure of a constituent comes from two sources:

- the f-structure information associated with the lexical entry for each word in the string
- c-structure rules which are annotated with functional information

In the lexicon, words are associated with EQUATIONS specifying f-structure information. A basic type of equation is illustrated in (1), where *f* is the name of an f-structure.

(1) (*f* FEATURE) = VALUE

To take a more concrete example, a word like *dogs* would have the equations in (2) associated with it in the lexicon.

(2) *dogs* N (*f* PRED) = 'DOG'
(*f* NUM) = PL

A collection of equations like this is referred to as an F-DESCRIPTION. We will see more impressive f-descriptions when we consider whole sentences below. The collection of equations in (2) can be read as 'there is an f-structure *f* which contains a feature PRED and a feature NUM with the value 'DOG' and PL, respectively'. Any constituent of which *dogs* forms a part will have associated with it an f-structure which contains PRED = 'DOG' and NUM = PL. More formally, these equations express CONSTRAINTS on the f-structure associated with the word *dog*. This may be a little abstract at the moment, but it will become clearer as we work our way through an example. In Section 3.2, when we start putting lexical entries into trees, we will replace the *f* in the lexical entries with a different notation for referring to f-structures that links in with the trees we draw for c-structure.

The other source of information about f-structures is the c-structure rules. The more configurational a language is, the bigger the contribution that the c-structure, rather than the lexical entries, makes to f-structure. We have said that in English the subject is found in the specifier of IP position. This information then has to be included in the phrase structure rule we introduced in (47c) in Section 2.3.2. This is done by ANNOTATING the phrase structure rules; the annotated version of (47c) is provided in (3). The equation underneath the category node is often referred to as a SCHEMA (the plural form used is *schemata*).

(3) $$\text{IP} \longrightarrow \underset{(\uparrow \text{SUBJ}) = \downarrow}{\text{DP}} \qquad \underset{\uparrow = \downarrow}{\text{I}'}$$

The new symbols require some explanation. First, remember that every phrase structure node is associated with an f-structure. We have used shorthand terminology to link c-structure and f-structure so far. We have said 'the DP daughter of IP is the subject', whereas this should really be 'the f-structure associated with the IP node will contain a feature SUBJ and the value of that feature will be the f-structure associated with the DP node in the specifier position in this particular tree'. The equation under the DP in (3) says exactly this. To make it visually easy, the symbol ↑ is used to mean 'the f-structure associated with the node above this one', and ↓ is used for 'the f-structure associated with this node'. Because the schema tends to be written below the category label, it is sometimes tempting to read the ↓ as 'the node below this one', but remember that ↓ refers to the f-structure of the node itself, not the one below. So in the equation under the DP in (3), ↓ refers to the f-structure associated with the DP itself. With this interpretation of the up and down arrows, we can read the equation under the DP as 'the f-structure associated with my mother node contains a feature SUBJ and the value of that feature is the f-structure associated with this node'.

Formally, every node in a c-structure is related to a piece of f-structure by a MAPPING FUNCTION, which we call ϕ. The symbol ↓ is itself shorthand for 'the function ϕ applied to the current node', or $\phi(*)$ where $*$ is a VARIABLE which stands for the current node, and ↑ is shorthand for 'the function ϕ applied to the mother of this node', or $\phi(M(*))$ where $M(*)$ is the node immediately dominating the current node. Because $*$ is itself a variable over c-structure nodes, formally the f-structure variables ↑ and ↓ are actually METAVARIABLES (that is, variables over variables). If you found this explanation of the formal side of things hard to digest, don't worry; throughout the book we just refer to them as the f-structure variables ↑ and ↓ and when we explain how the mapping works we will stick to more informal language.

The equation under I′ in (3) states that its f-structure is shared with its mother: 'the f-structure associated with the mother node is the same as the f-structure associated with this node'. This is exactly what we should get on the head in a subtree. All f-structure information associated with a head is also associated with its mother, and the other way around.

In order to make it easier to refer to the f-structures associated with the different nodes as we explain the mapping function, we will name them. We will use the variables f_1, f_2, f_3 etc. to name the f-structures associated with nodes. Note that the names, f_1 etc. are not significant in themselves; they just give a unique way of referring to the f-structure associated with each node in the tree (rather than saying 'the f-structure associated with the DP daughter of IP', which is rather cumbersome). We'll start with the tree corresponding to the rule in (3), shown in (4).

(4)

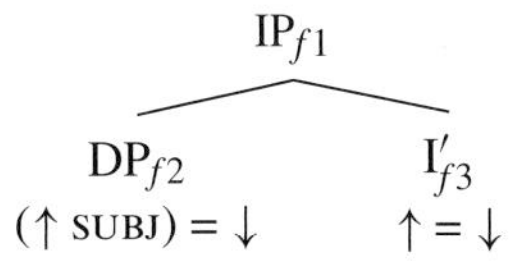

$$\begin{array}{ccc} & \text{IP}_{f1} & \\ \text{DP}_{f2} & & \text{I}'_{f3} \\ (\uparrow \text{SUBJ}) = \downarrow & & \uparrow = \downarrow \end{array}$$

We can now instantiate the f-structure variables ↑ and ↓ to the f-structures which they actually stand for in the context of this tree. Remember that ↓ means 'the f-structure associated with **this** node' (or, more formally, 'the result of applying the mapping function ϕ to this node') and ↑ means 'the f-structure associated with the **mother** of this node' (or more formally, 'the result of applying the mapping function ϕ to the mother of this node'), so ↓ actually names the f-structure of the (current) node and ↑ names the f-structure of the mother node. Looking at the DP, ↑ refers to the f-structure of the node above, which we have named f_1. ↓ refers to the f-structure of the DP node itself, which is f_2. Hence we get the equation in (5a). In a similar way, ↑ = ↓ under I′ gives us the equation in (5b).

(5)
a. $(f_1 \text{ SUBJ}) = f_2$
b. $f_1 = f_3$

The equation in (5b) tells us that the f-structure associated with the I′ is identical to that of the mother node; all f-structure information associated with IP is also associated with I′. This means that if the f-structure associated with the DP is the SUBJ of IP, as the equation in (5a) states, then it is also the SUBJ of I′. When we get further down into the tree, we will see that the headedness trail through the tree will make this the SUBJ of the verb.

We can now annotate the other rules required for English that were provided in (47) and (48) of Chapter 2, which are the ones we need to generate a basic clause. The notion of co-head was introduced in relation to (46) in Section 2.3.2. In (6a) and (6d), the two daughters of I' and D', respectively, are co-heads as indicated by ↑ = ↓ on both constituents on the right-hand side. The f-structures associated with both constituents will contribute equally to the f-structure of the mother.

We will see how this works formally in Section 3.2. In order to keep things simple, in the rule for VP in (6b), we have not included all the potential complements we included in (47e) in Section 2.3.2, and we have not given an exhaustive set of rules here. We will return to the CP structure in Chapter 6.

(6)

a. I′	$\longrightarrow$	I	VP		
		$\uparrow = \downarrow$	$\uparrow = \downarrow$		
b. VP	$\longrightarrow$	V	DP	DP	...
		$\uparrow = \downarrow$	$(\uparrow \text{OBJ}) = \downarrow$	$(\uparrow \text{OBJ}_\theta) = \downarrow$	
c. DP	$\longrightarrow$	DP	D′		
		$(\uparrow \text{POSS}) = \downarrow$	$\uparrow = \downarrow$		
d. D′	$\longrightarrow$	D	NP		
		$\uparrow = \downarrow$	$\uparrow = \downarrow$		
e. NP	$\longrightarrow$	AP	NP		
		$\downarrow \in (\uparrow \text{ADJ})$	$\uparrow = \downarrow$		
f. NP	$\longrightarrow$	N	PP	CP	...
		$\uparrow = \downarrow$	$(\uparrow \text{OBL}_\theta) = \downarrow$	$(\uparrow \text{COMP}) = \downarrow$	
g. PP	$\longrightarrow$	P	DP		
		$\uparrow = \downarrow$	$(\uparrow \text{OBJ}) = \downarrow$		

We showed in Section 2.2 that ADJ needs to have a set of f-structures as its value since adjuncts can occur recursively. This is indicated by the annotation $\downarrow \in (\uparrow \text{ADJ})$ in (6e), which we can read as 'the f-structure associated with this node is a member of the set of f-structures that forms the value of ADJ'. Note that it is not necessary to use { } here to indicate that the value is a set. We will have reason to return to the annotation of prepositions once we have worked through structure–function mapping in Section 3.2.

The coordination rule we introduced in (53) in Section 2.3.3 also involves a set. The annotated version of the rule is provided in (7).

(7)

α	$\longrightarrow$	α^+	Conj	α
		$\downarrow \in \uparrow$		$\downarrow \in \uparrow$

This rule makes sure that the f-structure associated with each of the conjuncts becomes a member of the set that forms the f-structure of the mother. The f-structure of the whole coordinated phrase is the set of the f-structures of all the conjuncts.

3.2 Mapping C-structure to F-structure

We will work through the simple example in (8), and we will do so very gradually because it is important that the technicalities of the mapping are clear before we move on to more interesting data.

(8) The dog eats sausages.

The four lexical items we need are (9) to (12), each item with the associated functional information in the form of functional equations forming an f-description. More information could be added, but these partial lexical entries will serve to illustrate the point.

(9) *the* D (↑ DEF) = +

(10) *dog* N (↑ PRED) = 'DOG'
(↑ NUM) = SG

(11) *eats* V (↑ PRED) = 'EAT<SUBJ, OBJ>'
(↑ TENSE) = PRES

(12) *sausages* N (↑ PRED) = 'SAUSAGE'
(↑ NUM) = PL

The tree generated for the sentence in (8) by the annotated rules in (6a) to (6d) and the lexical entries above is provided in (13). We know that the mapping function relates every c-structure node to some f-structure, and so we have provided labels for those f-structures in the tree, where f_1 is the name of the f-structure associated with the IP node and so on. Note that since there is no finite auxiliary, there is no I node.

(13)

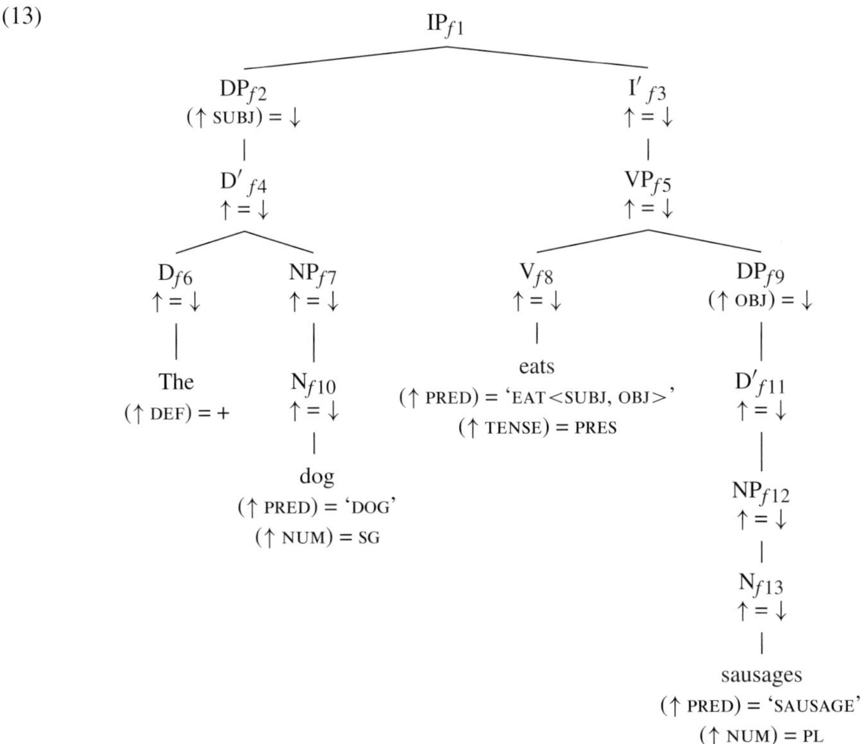

We will now instantiate the f-structure variables ↑ and ↓ in the equations annotated to the nodes. Informally, this means replacing them with the name we have given to the f-structure the arrow refers to. We will start from the IP at the top, although of course we could have started from any node in the tree. Looking at the DP above *the dog*, the f-structure associated with the mother node is f_1 and the node itself is associated with an f-structure referred to as f_2. This gives us the equation in (14a). The mother node of I′ has the f-structure f_1 associated with it, and the node itself is associated with f_3. This gives us the equation in (14b). This is what we established when we looked at the top part of the tree in (4).

(14)
a. $(f_1 \text{ SUBJ}) = f_2$
b. $f_1 = f_3$

If we carry on down from this DP node, we get the equations in (15a)–(15d) since D′, D, NP and the N nodes are all associated with $\uparrow = \downarrow$ so that the f-structure information is identical for the different nodes. This means that D and N are co-heads. This can of course also be written as (15e).

(15)
a. $f_2 = f_4$
b. $f_4 = f_6$
c. $f_4 = f_7$
d. $f_7 = f_{10}$
e. $f_2 = f_4 = f_6 = f_7 = f_{10}$

Turning to the I′ node and below, we can state the equations in (16).

(16)
a. $f_3 = f_5$
b. $(f_5 \text{ OBJ}) = f_9$
c. $f_5 = f_8$
d. $f_9 = f_{11}$
e. $f_{11} = f_{12}$
f. $f_{12} = f_{13}$

We have now stated all the equations resulting from the annotated phrase structure rules and turn to the information from the lexical entries for the words. We get the equations in (17).

(17)
a. $(f_6 \text{ DEF}) = +$
b. $(f_{10} \text{ NUM}) = \text{SG}$
c. $(f_{10} \text{ PRED}) = \text{'DOG'}$
d. $(f_8 \text{ PRED}) = \text{'EAT <SUBJ, OBJ>'}$
e. $(f_8 \text{ TENSE}) = \text{PRES}$
f. $(f_{13} \text{ PRED}) = \text{'SAUSAGE'}$
g. $(f_{13} \text{ NUM}) = \text{PL}$

Let's now build the f-structure defined by this f-description. This is done by SOLVING the set of equations that form the f-description. The equation in (14a) states that there is an f-structure referred to as f_1 that contains a feature SUBJ and that the value of that feature is another f-structure referred to as f_2. (14b) tells us that there is an f-structure f_3 which is identical to f_1. These equations specify the f-structure in (18). F-structures are sets of feature–value pairs, and we use square brackets to keep sets of feature–value pairs together. As we saw in Section 2.2, the term attribute is sometimes used instead of feature, and a set of attribute–value pairs is referred to as an attribute–value matrix, or AVM.

(18)

$$f1,f3\begin{bmatrix}\text{SUBJ} & f2\begin{bmatrix}\ \end{bmatrix}\end{bmatrix}$$

The equations in (15) add the information that the f-structure f_2 is identical to f_4 and that f_4 in turn is identical to f_6, which is the same as f_7 and f_{10}. This means that any information that is contributed by f_2, f_4, f_6, f_7 or f_{10} becomes part of the same f-structure. The many different names for one f-structure are the result of the $\uparrow = \downarrow$ equations, which are characteristic of heads. We can expand the f-structure in (18) to that in (19), which is the smallest f-structure which satisfies the constraints we have considered so far.

(19)

$$f1,f3\begin{bmatrix}\text{SUBJ} & f2,f4,f6,f7,f10\begin{bmatrix}\ \end{bmatrix}\end{bmatrix}$$

Turning now to the equations in (16), they define identity between f_3, f_5 and f_8, and we know from (14b) that this is equal to f_1, so we can add these to the f-structure as in (20). (16b) states that f_5, one of the many ways of referring to the main f-structure, contains the feature OBJ and that this feature has as its value an f-structure known as f_9. (16d) to (16f) then state that this f_9 is identical to another f-structure f_{11}, which in turn is identical to f_{12} and f_{13}. This means we can expand our f-structure as in (20), which is the smallest f-structure which satisfies all the constraints we have now taken into account.

(20)

$$f1,f3,f5,f8\begin{bmatrix}\text{SUBJ} & f2,f4,f6,f7,f10\begin{bmatrix}\ \end{bmatrix}\\ \text{OBJ} & f9,f11,f12,f13\begin{bmatrix}\ \end{bmatrix}\end{bmatrix}$$

The equations in (17), finally, add the information from the lexical entries. They add information to f_6 and f_{10}, which together contribute to the f-structure that forms the value of the SUBJ feature. The equations also provide information about the features of f_8, which is the main f-structure. In the final two equations in (17) information is added about f_{13}, which is the f-structure which forms the value of the OBJ feature. This gives us the f-structure in (21).

(21)

$$f1,f3,f5,f8\left[\begin{array}{ll}\text{PRED} & \text{'EAT<SUBJ, OBJ>'}\\ \text{TENSE} & \text{PRES}\\ \text{SUBJ} & f2,f4,f6,f7,f10\left[\begin{array}{ll}\text{DEF} & +\\ \text{NUM} & \text{SG}\\ \text{PRED} & \text{'DOG'}\end{array}\right]\\ \text{OBJ} & f9,f11,f12,f13\left[\begin{array}{ll}\text{PRED} & \text{'SAUSAGE'}\\ \text{NUM} & \text{PL}\end{array}\right]\end{array}\right]$$

And there we are: we have used the annotated phrase structure rules and the lexical entries to construct the tree, named the f-structures associated with every constituent, used those to replace the f-structure variables in the equations and then we have solved the equations to build the f-structure which satisfies **all and only** the constraints stated in the equations: this f-structure is often called the MINIMAL SOLUTION in LFG. The f-structure in (21) is Complete; the argument functions which are part of the PRED value for *eats* are present in the f-structure and they have their own PRED values. It is also Coherent; there are no extra argument functions that are not required by a predicate. The process added information at every stage; at no point was information lost or overwritten. This is the property of monotonicity, which we introduced in Section 2.2. We have seen that the relationship between c-structure and f-structure is stated in terms of a simple mapping function putting nodes of the c-structure and pieces of f-structure in correspondence. This formal robustness and explicitness makes LFG testable and eminently suitable for computational work.

We emphasised above that the f-structure we are interested in is always the **smallest** f-structure (or the minimal solution) which satisfies the constraints expressed in the equations in the f-description that we have. This is important. Consider again the set of equations in (14), repeated here as (22). In principle, the constraints put on an f-structure by these equations are satisfied also by the f-structure in (23); there is an f-structure f_1 which has a SUBJ feature, and the value of that is an f-structure referred to as f_2, and the f-structure f_1 is identical to f_3. Still, we would not want (23) to be the f-structure satisfying the f-description in (22), because it contains additional information. This is why we insist on the solution being the smallest f-structure which satisfies the constraints expressed by the equations. Of course, if we had an f-description containing further information about an anteater that sneezed in addition to (22), then (23) may be the smallest f-structure satisfying that f-description, but it is not the smallest one satisfying (22).

(22)

a. $(f_1\ \text{SUBJ}) = f_2$

b. $f_1 = f_3$

(23)

$$f1,f3\left[\begin{array}{ll}\text{PRED} & \text{'SNEEZE<SUBJ>'}\\ \text{TENSE} & \text{PAST}\\ \text{SUBJ} & f2\left[\begin{array}{ll}\text{PRED} & \text{ANTEATER}\\ \text{NUM} & \text{SG}\end{array}\right]\end{array}\right]$$

Let's look again at the (partial) lexical entry for *eats* in (11), repeated here as (24).

(24) *eats* V (↑ PRED) = 'EAT<SUBJ, OBJ>'
(↑ TENSE) = PRES

There is some crucial information missing here, in particular the information which ensures that (25) is correctly ruled out by the grammar.

(25) *The cats eats tuna.

We know that this is ungrammatical because *eats* requires a third person singular subject and *the cats* is plural. The information that the verb requires a third person singular subject needs to be included in the lexical entry. This is done by expanding the lexical entry as in (26), where the NUM value of the SUBJ f-structure is specified as having the value SG and SUBJ PERS is also given a value. These equations use a string of attributes to specify a PATH through an f-structure, and we will see more of these in later chapters.

(26) *eats* V (↑ PRED) = 'EAT<SUBJ, OBJ>'
(↑ TENSE) = PRES
(↑ SUBJ NUM) = SG
(↑ SUBJ PERS) = 3

The equations associated with lexical entries that we have looked at so far **build** or **define** f-structure in the sense that they contribute features and values to an f-structure. We refer to this type of equation as DEFINING EQUATIONS. The equations in (26), along with that for *tuna*, build or define the f-structure in (27).

(27)

$$\left[\begin{array}{ll} \text{PRED} & \text{`EAT<SUBJ, OBJ>'} \\ \text{TENSE} & \text{PRES} \\ \text{SUBJ} & \left[\begin{array}{ll} \text{NUM} & \text{SG} \\ \text{PERS} & 3 \end{array}\right] \\ \text{OBJ} & \left[\begin{array}{ll} \text{PRED} & \text{`TUNA'} \end{array}\right] \end{array}\right]$$

Here we see how the verb has added information about the subject. However, we do not have a complete sentence. This is where the second part of the Completeness Condition introduced in Section 2.2 comes in. The f-structure in (27) violates the Completeness Condition since the SUBJ lacks a PRED feature. The values for SUBJ NUM and SUBJ PERS do, however, ensure that if we try to combine *eats tuna* with a subject that has any other value for NUM or PERS, like *the cats* (NUM = PL, PERS = 3), the resulting structure would be ruled out. In this case, the verb *eats* would assign the value NUM = SG to the SUBJ, and the subject *the cats* would itself give the same SUBJ the value NUM = PL. This would mean that NUM would have two incompatible values and hence would violate Uniqueness. The sentence **The cats eats the tuna* would correctly be ruled out as ungrammatical by our grammar.

Alongside defining equations, there is another type of equation that does not itself contribute or define f-structure information, but rather checks that the information it specifies is present in the minimal f-structure. These are called CONSTRAINING EQUATIONS. Say we had a language with a verb with the equations in (28) as part of its lexical entry. In these equations, $=_c$ indicates that it is constraining, not defining.

(28) (↑ SUBJ NUM) $=_c$ SG
(↑ SUBJ PERS) $=_c$ 3

In this case, the verbal lexical entry does not **itself** contribute information to the f-structure of the SUBJ, but rather the equations in (28) require that the SUBJ in the minimal solution already **contains** the value SG for the NUM feature and 3 for the PERS feature. These constraints are only satisfied if those values are defined elsewhere, for example, contributed by the subject noun itself. Can we be sure that English verbs do not have constraining equations for PERS and NUM? If we take a subject that is not itself marked for number, and hence can be assumed not to have values for PERS and NUM, like *sheep*, then both examples in (29) would correctly be predicted to be grammatical only if the equations were defining rather than constraining. The constraining equations in (28) would require the noun to have those features.

(29) a. The sheep lives in the field.
b. The sheep live in the field.

There is a further reason to assume that the values for SUBJ NUM and SUBJ PERS associated with the verb are defining. Defining equations would actually make sure that the noun was specified for NUM and PERS in (29) and this is correct since once you combine *the sheep* with *lives*, *the sheep* is treated as singular. This is clear from pronoun use for instance. So if we continue to talk about *the sheep*, we get the pronoun use in (30).

(30) a. The sheep lives in the field. It is / *They are quite happy there.
b. The sheep live in the field. *It is / They are quite happy there.

If the equations are defining, then the subject of (29a) receives the features NUM = SG and PERS = 3 from the verb, and the grammaticality pattern in (30a) would be predicted. Similarly for the plural interpretation in (30b).

3.3 Mapping for Prepositional Phrases

In (6g) in Section 3.1, we provided an annotated c-structure rule for PPs, repeated here in (31).

(31) PP ⟶ P DP
↑ = ↓ (↑ OBJ) = ↓

We need to say a little more about how prepositions are dealt with here. We can distinguish two types of prepositions in English: those like *behind* in (32a) that make a full semantic contribution in that they describe a specific relationship between two entities, and others like *to* in (32b) that simply indicate a grammatical relation.

(32) a. Oscar ate the sweets behind the bike shed.
b. Oscar donated clothes to the charity shop.

The difference between the two types of preposition is illustrated in (33), where we see that the semantic preposition can be replaced by other semantic prepositions with different meanings, whereas the grammatical preposition is determined by the syntactic context and cannot be replaced without changing the structure of the sentence.

(33) a. Oscar ate the sweets above/on/under the bike shed.
b. Oscar donated clothes *of/*on the charity shop.

Of course prepositions can have other functions too, for instance in prepositional verbs like *deal with* or *rely on*, but here we are interested in the major distinction between semantic and grammatical prepositions. We should point out here that *to* in English also has a semantic use indicating direction, as in (34), where it does alternate with other semantic prepositions, but we will focus on the grammatical use, so when we refer to *to* here, we refer to the grammatical use in (32b).

(34) Oscar drove the car as fast as he could to/from the station.

The difference between elements that have meaning and those that do not lies in the PRED feature in LFG; *behind* will have a PRED feature in (32a), whereas *to* in (32b) will not. The rule in (31) will then only be relevant for prepositions like *behind* that have a PRED feature and require an OBJ; without a PRED feature, *to* cannot select an OBJ. Prepositions that mark a grammatical relation, on the other hand, share properties with functional categories like C, I and D in that they are functional co-heads with their noun phrase complement. This gives the rule in (35), to be contrasted with (31).

(35) PP $\longrightarrow$ P DP
$\uparrow = \downarrow$ $\uparrow = \downarrow$

The lexical entries for the two prepositions will also need to be different. *Behind* will have a PRED feature as illustrated in (36a) (though we will see in Section 5.2.3 that there will be more to say about prepositions). The lexical entry for *to*, on the other hand, lacks a PRED feature and only has information about what grammatical relation it marks, in this case $\text{OBL}_{Rec(ipient)}$. This is done through a feature PCASE, which takes the name of a grammatical relation as its value, making OBL_{Rec} both the value of a feature PCASE and a grammatical relation in its own right.

(36) a. *behind* P ($\uparrow$ PRED) = 'BEHIND<OBJ>'
b. *to* P ($\uparrow$ PCASE) = OBL_{Rec}

The fact that the name of a grammatical relation is also a value of the feature PCASE may seem counterintuitive, but it means that the preposition licenses a noun phrase to have this function; it links a noun phrase with the OBL_{Rec} function. Functionally, this makes it resemble a case marker like the Finnish ILLative case marker *-an* in (37a) which allows the noun *hyväntekeväisyyskauppa* to function as the OBL_{Rec}. This can be contrasted with *takana* in (37b), a semantic postposition which corresponds to the preposition *behind* in English, though differing from it in that it follows rather than precedes the noun phrase with which it combines. The gloss PTV stands for PARTITIVE case, which is one of the cases that an object can take in Finnish.

(37) a. Oskar lahjoitti vaatteita hyväntekeväisyyskauppaan.
Oscar donate.PST piece of clothing.PL.PTV charity shop.ILL
'Oscar donated clothes to the charity shop.'

b. Oskar söi makeisia polkupyörävajan takana.
Oscar eat.PST sweet.PL.PTV bike shed.GEN behind
'Oscar ate the sweets behind the bike shed.'

The verb *donated* in (32b) will have the PRED feature in (38a). The rule in (38b) applies; this is a special case of the VP rule in (64f) in Section 2.3.4 (and a version of (6b)). Unlike (64f), it is now annotated.

(38) a. *donate* V $(\uparrow \text{PRED}) = \text{'DONATE <SUBJ, OBJ, OBL}_{Rec}\text{>'}$

b. VP $\longrightarrow$ V DP PP
$\uparrow = \downarrow$ $(\uparrow \text{OBJ}) = \downarrow$ $(\uparrow (\downarrow \text{PCASE})) = \downarrow$

To show how this works, we will work through the mapping for *donated clothes to charity*, where we have simplified the final noun phrase in order to concentrate on the issue of how PCASE works. The c-structure is provided in (39).

(39)

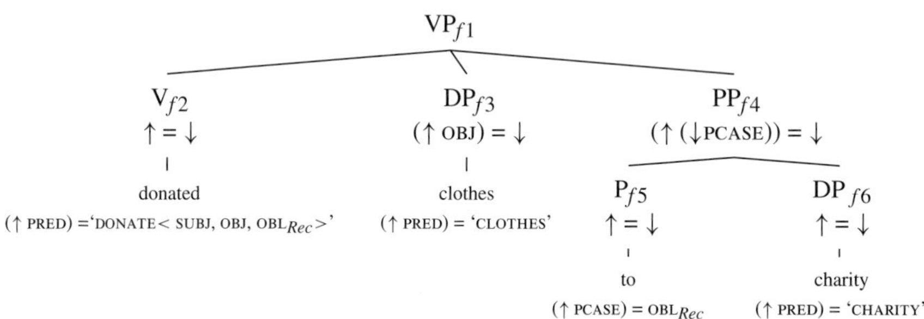

From this tree, we can derive the f-description in (40).

(40) a. $f_1 = f_2$

b. $(f_1 \text{ OBJ}) = f_3$

c. $(f_1 \ (f_4 \text{PCASE})) = f_4$

d. $f_4 = f_5$

e. $f_4 = f_6$

f. (f_2 PRED) = 'DONATE <SUBJ, OBJ, OBL_{Rec}>'

g. (f_3 PRED) = 'CLOTHES'

h. (f_5 PCASE) = OBL_{Rec}

i. (f_6 PRED) = 'CHARITY'

Now we come to the crucial part of the analysis involving PCASE. The equation in (40d) states that the two f-structures f_4 and f_5 are identical. This means that (40h) can be restated as (f_4 PCASE) = OBL_{Rec}. This in turn means that we can replace (f_4 PCASE) in (40c) by the value OBL_{Rec} to get the equation in (41).

(41) (f_1 OBL_{Rec}) = f_4

This f-description gives the f-structure in (42).

(42)

$$
f1,f2 \begin{bmatrix} \text{PRED} & \text{`DONATE <SUBJ, OBJ, OBL}_{Rec}\text{>'} \\ \text{OBJ} & f3 \begin{bmatrix} \text{PRED} & \text{`CLOTHES'} \end{bmatrix} \\ \text{OBL}_{Rec} & f4,f5,f6 \begin{bmatrix} \text{PRED} & \text{`CHARITY'} \\ \text{PCASE} & \text{OBL}_{Rec} \end{bmatrix} \end{bmatrix}
$$

In this section we have seen that the attribute name of an oblique function is provided by 'picking up' the value of the PCASE attribute associated with the preposition itself. In the case we discussed, the grammatical (PRED-less) use of *to* is associated with the PCASE value of OBL_{Rec}.

Turning now to a contentful preposition in an OBL_θ function, we see that things work in the same way. The PP *on the table* in (43a) is an argument of the verb, which has the PRED feature in (43b). The preposition *on* here is clearly a semantic preposition because it can be replaced by other locational prepositions, such as *under* or *behind*. The c-structure rule in (38b) applies, and we repeat it as (44a), alongside (31), repeated here as (44b).

(43)

a. Robin put food on the table.

b. *put* V (↑ PRED) = 'PUT <SUBJ, OBJ, OBL_{Loc}>'

c. *on* P (↑ PRED) = 'ON <OBJ>'
(↑ PCASE) = OBL_{Loc}

(44)

a. VP ⟶ V DP PP
↑ = ↓ ↑ OBJ = ↓ (↑ (↓PCASE)) = ↓

b. PP ⟶ P DP
↑ = ↓ (↑ OBJ) = ↓

As we see in (43c), the preposition *on* has a PCASE value of OBL_{Loc}, which will mean that the f-structure for the sentence in (43a) will be as shown in (45) (we leave it to the reader to work through the details of this example!).

(45)

$$\left[\begin{array}{ll} \text{SUBJ} & \left[\begin{array}{ll}\text{PRED} & \text{`ROBIN'}\end{array}\right] \\ \text{OBJ} & \left[\begin{array}{ll}\text{PRED} & \text{`FOOD'}\end{array}\right] \\ \text{OBL}_{Loc} & \left[\begin{array}{ll} \text{PCASE} & \text{OBL}_{Loc} \\ \text{PRED} & \text{`ON<OBJ>'} \\ \text{OBJ} & \left[\begin{array}{ll}\text{PRED} & \text{`TABLE'} \\ \text{DEF} & + \end{array}\right] \end{array}\right] \\ \text{PRED} & \text{`PUT <SUBJ, OBJ, OBL}_{Loc}\text{>'} \end{array}\right]$$

There is more to say about the use of prepositional phrases in other contexts, and we suggest further reading for this at the end of the chapter.

Reading

The approach to mapping between c- and f-structure described here is standard for LFG; the only variation is in the analysis of prepositions, where an alternative analysis can be found in Butt et al. (1999, 125–9).

Exercises

3.1 For each of the set of f-descriptions in (46) to (48), provide the resulting f-structure. For each of the resulting f-structures, determine whether it violates any of the Uniqueness, Completeness or Coherence Conditions.

(46)
a. $f_1 = f_3$
b. $f_6 = f_7$
c. $f_2 = f_4$
d. (f_1 SUBJ) = f_2
e. (f_1 PRED) = 'ANNOY <SUBJ, OBJ>'
f. (f_1 TENSE) = PAST
g. (f_3 OBJ) = f_6
h. (f_6 PRED) = 'PENSIONER'
i. (f_7 DEF) = +
j. (f_7 NUM) = PL
k. (f_4 POSS) = f_5
l. (f_5 PRED) = 'INGRID'
m. (f_2 PRED) = 'DOG <(POSS)>'

(47)
a. (f_1 PRED) = 'TYPE <SUBJ, OBJ>'
b. (f_1 TENSE) = PRES
c. (f_1 SUBJ NUM) = SG
d. (f_1 SUBJ PERS) = 3
e. $f_2 = f_4$
f. (f_1 OBJ) = f_2

g. $(f_2$ PRED) = 'LETTER'
h. $(f_4$ DEF) = –
i. $(f_4$ NUM) = PL

(48) a. $(f_1$ PRED) = 'CHEW <SUBJ, OBJ>'
b. $(f_1$ TENSE) = PRES
c. $(f_1$ SUBJ NUM) = SG
d. $(f_1$ SUBJ PERS) = 3
e. $(f_1$ SUBJ) = f_8
f. $(f_8$ PRED = 'DOG'
g. $(f_8$ NUM) = PL
h. $(f_1$ OBJ) = f_2
i. $(f_2$ PRED) = 'SHOE'
j. $(f_2$ DEF) = –
k. $(f_2$ NUM) = PL

3.2 Use the rules provided in (3), (6) and (7) and appropriate lexical entries to draw the annotated c-structure tree for the sentences in (49).

(49) a. The cat likes milk.
b. The teacher gave the children a good book.
c. The dog's basket smells.
d. The cats and the dogs chased a mouse.

3.3 In exercise 2.5, we asked you to consider the noun phrases in bold in (50) in the light of the feature PERS and the claim in Section 2.2 that regular noun phrases are third person. Now you should be able to provide the lexical entries for the elements in bold, use the annotated phrase structure rules given for noun phrases in Section 2.3.3 to draw the appropriate tree, provide the f-description and solve the equations to give you the f-structure for each noun phrase.

(50) a. **Those dogs** hurt themselves.
b. **The girl** washed herself.
c. **We pensioners** look after ourselves.
d. **You students** only think about yourselves.

4 Morphology and F-structure

4.1 Introduction

In Chapter 2 we introduced the Principle of Lexical Integrity, which requires that the terminal nodes of c-structure trees are morphologically complete words and that each word can correspond to only one c-structure node. This ensures a clear separation between the morphology and the syntax, such that syntactic processes have access only to morphologically complete words, and cannot therefore apply to the internal properties of words. However, this does not mean that words cannot contribute information that is relevant to the syntax since, due to LFG's parallel architecture, information that is associated with the inflected forms of words can be contributed directly to the f-structure without violating Lexical Integrity. This allows for an account of the many different ways in which morphology and syntax interact in the world's languages. In this chapter we begin by discussing languages which use morphology to encode information about grammatical relations such as subject and object. We then discuss some of the more complex phenomena involving morphology–syntax interaction, such as concord within the noun phrase, tense marking in noun phrases and agreement in coordination.

4.2 Morphological Marking of Grammatical Relations

English is a language that relies heavily on syntactic structure for identifying grammatical relations. In Chapter 3, we saw how this can be accounted for by assuming that phrase structure rules are annotated with functional equations which associate nodes in the c-structure with grammatical functions in the f-structure. We also saw, however, that languages vary in their c-structures and that many of the world's languages, including Latin and Wambaya, identify their grammatical relations by morphological means. Some languages have marking on the verb, known as VERBAL AGREEMENT. Since the verb is the lexical head of the clause, this is also referred to as HEAD MARKING. Others have the marking on the argument noun phrases themselves, using case morphology; this is referred to as DEPENDENT MARKING since the marking is not on the head (the verb) but on the dependents of the head (the arguments). Many languages use a mixture of head marking and dependent marking, as well as a mixture of morphological and syntactic means for identifying grammatical relations, such as Latin for example. As we will see, in LFG this is captured by the information from different sources – be that the head, the dependent or c-structure annotations – all contributing to one f-structure.

In Chapter 1 we introduced the term non-configurational to describe languages like Latin, Wambaya and Jiwarli, for which there is no evidence for a VP. The absence of a VP means that core grammatical functions such as subject and object cannot clearly be defined in structural terms as they can in languages like English; these languages identify their grammatical relations by morphological means instead. Thus, in non-configurational languages we don't find a fixed association between grammatical functions and positions in the phrase structure, which means that annotating phrase structure rules with functional equations will not be a useful way to identify grammatical functions. Instead we need to be able to identify grammatical functions via the morphology. In this chapter we will see how this can be done for both dependent marking (Section 4.2.1) and head marking (Section 4.2.2) morphology.

4.2.1 Dependent Marking

Remember the Latin data from Chapter 1, repeated in (1).

(1)

a. Caesar suas copias in
Caesar.NOM REFL.ACC.F.PL troop.ACC.F.PL in
proximum collem subducit
nearest.ACC.M.SG hill.ACC.M.SG withdraw.PRS.3SG
'Caesar withdraws his (own) forces to the nearest hill.'
[*De bello Gallico* 1.22]

b. copias suas Caesar in
troop.ACC.F.PL REFL.ACC.F.PL Caesar.NOM in
proximum collem subducit
nearest.ACC.M.SG hill.ACC.M.SG withdraw.PRS.3SG
[*De bello Gallico* 1.24]

c. copias suas in proximum
troop.ACC.F.PL REFL.ACC.F.PL in nearest.ACC.M.SG
collem subducit Caesar
hill.ACC.M.SG withdraw.PRS.3SG Caesar.NOM
[constructed]

d. non respuit condicionem Caesar
NEG reject.PRS.3SG proposal.ACC.SG Caesar.NOM
'Caesar did not reject the proposal.' [*De bello Gallico* 1.42]

As we saw in Chapter 1 all orderings of the major constituents in (1) are grammatical in Latin. Since the verb is not necessarily structurally close to the object noun phrase, there is no evidence that would lead us to assume that there is a VP. There is also no evidence of a functional feature being associated with a particular position, so that there is no reason to assume a functional category such as I. This means that trees like those in (2) are most appropriate for Latin clause structure.

(2)

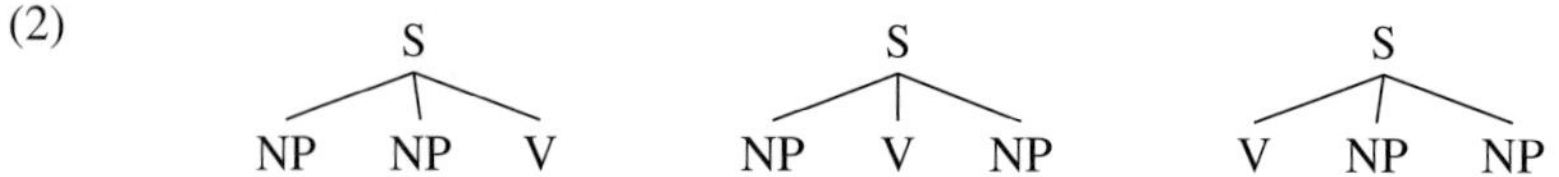

In (3), we provide an annotated version of the c-structure rule introduced in (64f) in Chapter 3 instantiated here for Latin.

(3) S ⟶ V , NP*
↑ = ↓ (↑ GF) = ↓

In (3), the V is marked as the f-structure head of the sentence, and so its f-structure is identified with the f-structure of the sentence as a whole; the verb's PRED feature will be the PRED feature of the sentence. This is ensured by the ↑ = ↓ annotation of V. The Kleene star in the rule in (3) was introduced in Chapter 2 and means 'any number of repetitions of the category, including none'. So the rule in (3) states that a clause will consist of a verb and any number of NPs (including zero), restricted only by the verb's PRED feature and the Coherence and Completeness Conditions (see Chapter 3). As mentioned in Section 2.3.4, the comma between V and NP* in the rule indicates that there are no ordering restrictions; the constituents are free to appear in any possible order. The NP is annotated with (↑ GF) = ↓ to indicate that it has some grammatical function within the clause, but the particular grammatical function is not dictated by the phrase structure position. GF is used here as a generalisation over all possible grammatical functions so it's essentially a shorter way of specifying that NPs can be annotated with (↑ SUBJ) = ↓ or (↑ OBJ) = ↓ or (↑ OBL_θ) = ↓, and so on.

The question then is where does the specific grammatical function information for NPs come from in Latin? How did a speaker of Latin know which noun phrase was the subject and which was the object? The case marking is the clue in a dependent-marking language. In these examples we know which noun phrase is fulfilling which grammatical function because of the case marking: nominative case indicates the subject and accusative case marks the object. There are a number of ways in which this can be done using the LFG formalism. We begin here with a simple way which assumes that the case is selected by the verb, and so the case marking of the arguments is mediated through the verb's lexical entry. In Section 4.4 we will introduce you to another way, using CONSTRUCTIVE CASE, which more accurately captures the fact that it is the case marking directly which contributes information about grammatical relations in productive case systems such as Latin. However, we start with the simpler verb-mediated approach here in order to more clearly introduce some features of LFG.

Assuming a verb-mediated approach to dependent marking, we can assume the lexical entries in (4) to (6) for the Latin words that we need. In the verb's lexical entry we use constraining equations, which we discussed in Chapter 3. The constraining equations here do not define the CASE values for the SUBJ and OBJ f-structures; they just constrain what the values need to be – the feature and its value must be contributed by some other element, namely the argument NPs. We could also use defining equations here, but this would allow an NP that is unmarked for case to appear in an argument position, as we saw in our discussion of *sheep* in Chapter 3. Note that we have simplified these lexical entries in various ways in order to better focus on the features relevant to the current discussion; the full lexical entry for the verb would also include tense/aspect information, for example.

(4) *Caesar* N (↑ PRED) = 'CAESAR'
(↑ NUM) = SG
(↑ PERS) = 3
(↑ CASE) = NOM

(5) *copias* N (↑ PRED) = 'TROOP'
(↑ NUM) = PL
(↑ PERS) = 3
(↑ CASE) = ACC

(6) *subducit* V (↑ PRED) = 'WITHDRAW<SUBJ, OBJ>'
(↑ SUBJ PERS) = 3
(↑ SUBJ NUM) = SG
(↑ SUBJ CASE) $=_c$ NOM
(↑ OBJ CASE) $=_c$ ACC

The c-structure for a simplified version of (1a) generated by the c-structure rule in (3) and the functional equations from the lexical entries above is given in (7). Remember that the c-structure rule adds the very general (↑ GF) = ↓ annotations for the NPs, which should be read as a disjunction of all possible grammatical functions. Since we see no argument for a DP in Latin, we use NPs in (7), but we omit the non-branching N′ node (just for ease of presentation), and we also omit the reflexive possessor *suas*. We will see how agreement within noun phrases is accounted for in Section 4.3.

(7)

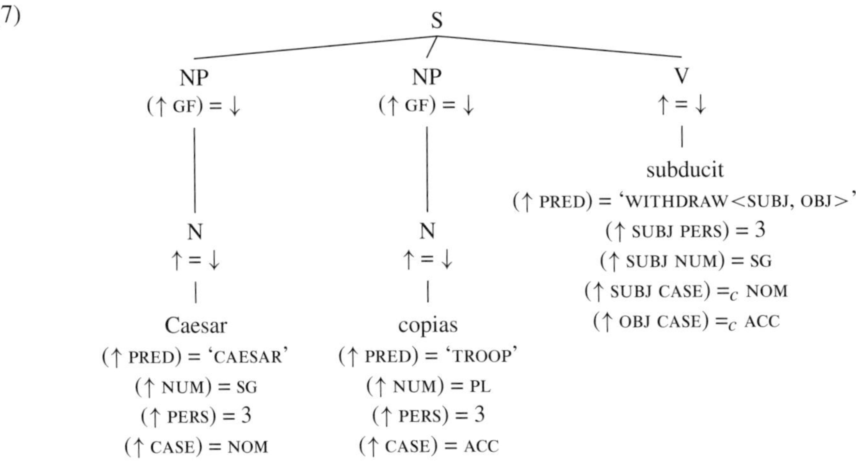

Note that the verb's lexical entry contains information constraining the case values of its arguments, specifying that its subject must have nominative case and its object must have accusative case. We will see how this constrains the mapping to grammatical functions in the f-structure and thus captures the fact that it is the morphological case marking that encodes grammatical functions in Latin, rather than information from the c-structure.

If we now name the f-structures associated with each c-structure node in (7), according to the procedure introduced in Chapter 3, we get the tree in (8).

(8)

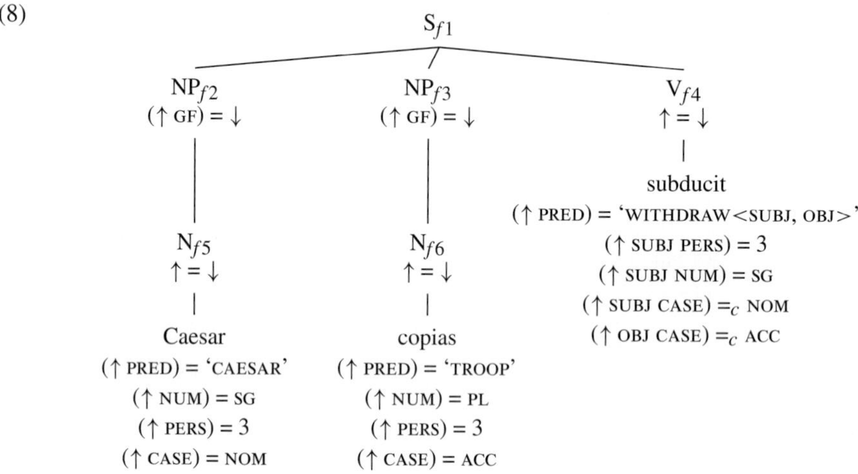

Concentrating on the two NP nodes in the first instance, we can then state the functional equations in (9).

(9)
a. $f_2 = f_5$
b. (f_5 PRED) = 'CAESAR'
c. (f_5 NUM) = SG
d. (f_5 PERS) = 3
e. (f_5 CASE) = NOM
f. $f_3 = f_6$
g. (f_6 PRED) = 'TROOP'
h. (f_6 NUM) = PL
i. (f_6 PERS) = 3
j. (f_6 CASE) = ACC

If we solve the equations in (9), CASE = NOM becomes associated with f_2, because $f_2 = f_5$, and CASE = ACC with f_3, since $f_3 = f_6$. When we expand the f-description for this sentence by also including the functional annotations added from the c-structure and also adding the equations associated with the V node, we get the fuller f-description in (10).

(10)
a. (f_1 GF) $= f_2$
b. $f_2 = f_5$
c. (f_5 PRED) = 'CAESAR'

d. $(f_5$ NUM) = SG
e. $(f_5$ PERS) = 3
f. $(f_5$ CASE) = NOM
g. $(f_1$ GF) $= f_3$
h. $f_3 = f_6$
i. $(f_6$ PRED) = 'TROOP'
j. $(f_6$ NUM) = PL
k. $(f_6$ PERS) = 3
l. $(f_6$ CASE) = ACC
m. $f_1 = f_4$
n. $(f_4$ PRED) = 'WITHDRAW<SUBJ, OBJ>'
o. $(f_4$ SUBJ PERS) = 3
p. $(f_4$ SUBJ NUM) = SG
q. $(f_4$ SUBJ CASE) $=_c$ NOM
r. $(f_4$ OBJ CASE) $=_c$ ACC

If we solve the equations in (10), we get the f-structure in (11). Note that the functional equations $(f_4$ SUBJ CASE) $=_c$ NOM and $(f_4$ OBJ CASE) $=_c$ ACC associated with the verb constrain the GF borne by each of the NPs through the case specifications. Since the verb carries information constraining the case values of its arguments, and since this information relates to the same f-structure as that of the argument itself, the case values must be compatible, ensuring that the nominative NP is the subject and the accusative NP is the object. If 'troops' was made the SUBJ, its case value – ACC – would clash with the verb's SUBJ CASE $=_c$ NOM, and the sentence would be ruled out by Uniqueness.

(11)

$$f1,f4 \begin{bmatrix} \text{PRED} & \text{'WITHDRAW <SUBJ, OBJ>'} \\ \text{SUBJ} & f2,f5 \begin{bmatrix} \text{PRED} & \text{'CAESAR'} \\ \text{NUM} & \text{SG} \\ \text{PERS} & 3 \\ \text{CASE} & \text{NOM} \end{bmatrix} \\ \text{OBJ} & f3,f6 \begin{bmatrix} \text{PRED} & \text{'TROOP'} \\ \text{NUM} & \text{PL} \\ \text{PERS} & 3 \\ \text{CASE} & \text{ACC} \end{bmatrix} \end{bmatrix}$$

In this way we can use case information from the lexical entries of the nouns in combination with the lexical entry of the verb to capture the fact that grammatical relations in Latin are identified morphologically (via case), rather than via fixed positions in the c-structure. In this instance, the nouns are morphologically marked for case, and the verb specifies particular case requirements for its arguments. In fact, while this approach is useful for certain case marking phenomena, particularly those in which verbs idiosyncratically select for unusual case properties of their arguments (we will see such examples from Icelandic in Chapter 5), it fails to capture the intuition that it is the case marking that directly encodes information about grammatical functions in these dependent-marking languages. In Section 4.4 we will see how this can be captured with another approach, known as CONSTRUCTIVE CASE. Now, however, we turn to the other major way in which morphology can be used to identify grammatical relations, namely head marking.

4.2.2 Head Marking

Not all languages which use morphological cues to identify grammatical relations are dependent marking. The marking which is crucial to establishing grammatical functions can also occur on the verb, the head of the clause, and when it does it is called head marking. Verb agreement is then a form of head marking; the verb is marked morphologically to provide information about the features of its subject, for example, and that way the grammatical functions can be identified. Look at the examples from Mbuun, a Bantu language spoken in the Democratic Republic of Congo, in (12) (adapted from Bostoen and Mundeke 2012, 144).

(12) a. ɔ-lwɛŋ á-bwíl bá-an
1-teacher SM1-hit.PRF 2-child
'The teacher has hit the children.'

b. bá-an ɔ-lwɛŋ á-bwíl
2-child 1-teacher SM1-hit.PRF
'**The teacher** has hit the children.'

Mbuun has noun classes which are referred to by numbers. The subject *ɔ-lwɛŋ* belongs to noun class 1 (a singular class), and *bá-an* to noun class 2 (a plural class). The first element of the verb, *á-*, is an agreement marker which indicates that the verb's subject is of noun class 1. Hence this verbal agreement tells us that *ɔ-lwɛŋ* is the subject. Mbuun actually contains structural cues for identifying grammatical relations too (see Section 4.2.5 for further discussion of this), so the verbal agreement would not be the only indication. However, as you can see in (12b), alternative orders are possible under specific information-structural conditions. In (12b), the subject is focused (indicated by boldface in the translation), though this is done by placing the object first. It should be added here that Mbuun also has object markers, but we will return to such elements in Section 4.2.3.

To account for the role of the information contained in the verb in (12), we can assume that the fully inflected verb carries features in its lexical entry that specify information about its subject's noun class, as in (13) (again, this is a simplified lexical entry that omits tense/aspect information).

(13) *á-bwíl* V (↑ PRED) = 'HIT<SUBJ, OBJ>'
(↑ SUBJ NCLASS) = 1

Thus, the verb itself carries information about features of its subject – in this instance specifying that its subject is of noun class 1. This information will be contributed directly into the f-structure of the subject and will therefore have to be consistent with the noun class information marked on the noun phrase. In this way, the marking on the verb ensures that the correct noun phrase is identified as the subject, both in (12a) and (12b). To see how this works consider the c-structure for (12a) given in (14) using the rule in (3) (where we have also given a name to the f-structure associated with each of the c-structure nodes, following our practice in Chapter 3). Here we assume that Mbuun is non-configurational, with sentences of the category S and no canonical positions for the subject and the object. A more thorough study of Mbuun clause structure may suggest a different c-structure from this, with structurally encoded positions for subject and object, but the way the agreement works would be the same.

(14)

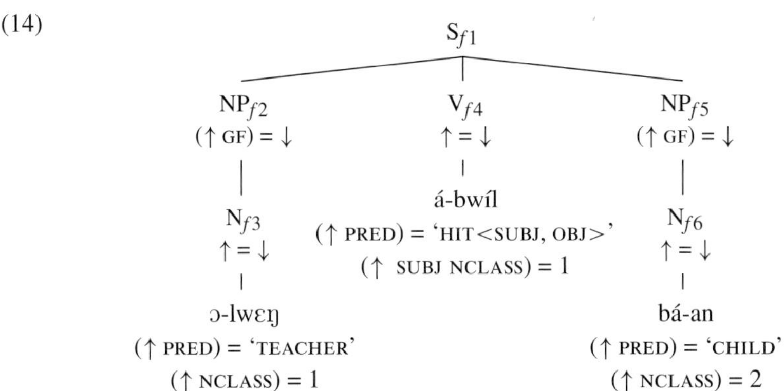

We can now restate the equations associated with the nodes of the tree using these names to give the functional description shown in (15); the f-structure which they define is given in (16).

(15)
a. (f_1 GF) = f_2
b. $f_2 = f_3$
c. (f_3 PRED) = 'TEACHER'
d. (f_3 NCLASS) = 1
e. $f_1 = f_4$
f. (f_4 PRED) = 'HIT<SUBJ, OBJ>'
g. (f_4 SUBJ NCLASS) = 1
h. (f_1 GF) = f_5
i. $f_5 = f_6$
j. (f_6 PRED) = 'CHILD'
k. (f_6 NCLASS) = 2

(16)

$$f1,f4\left[\begin{array}{ll}\text{PRED} & \text{`HIT<SUBJ, OBJ>'}\\ \text{SUBJ} & f2,f3\left[\begin{array}{ll}\text{PRED} & \text{`TEACHER'}\\ \text{NCLASS} & 1\end{array}\right]\\ \text{OBJ} & f5,f6\left[\begin{array}{ll}\text{PRED} & \text{`CHILD'}\\ \text{NCLASS} & 2\end{array}\right]\end{array}\right]$$

Note that the SUBJ NCLASS information comes from two sources: from the verb by virtue of the fact that the verb is a functional co-head of the sentence, so that its f-structure is identical to that of the sentence because $f_1 = f_4$; and from the subject head noun itself because its f-structure f_3 is identical to that of its mother, f_2, and f_2 is identified as a GF of f_1. Crucially, although the verb carries information about the subject's noun class, this information does not end up in the f-structure corresponding to the verb itself (f_4) but rather in the f-structure corresponding to another constituent within the clause, namely the SUBJ. In this way we capture the fact that the noun class information encoded on the verb helps to identify the subject. Since f_2 is annotated as a GF of f_1, it must be either SUBJ or OBJ by virtue of the Coherence Condition, since these are the only two grammatical functions subcategorised for by the verb. If in (12b) *bá-an* was assumed to be the subject, the NCLASS values from the two sources would not be compatible, and hence (correctly) there would be no licit f-structure arising from these constraints. Thus, the only f-structure arising for (12b) is that in which f_2 is subject and f_5 is object.

4.2.3 Pronoun Incorporation

We now turn to a particular type of head marking language, where the marking on the verb provides the true argument of the verb, rather than just agreement. Such languages are often referred to as PRO-DROP languages, but since LFG does not analyse them as having "dropped" a pronoun, but rather as the information associated with the argument being incorporated into the information associated with the verb, we will refer to this as PRONOUN INCORPORATION. Consider the data in (17) to (22); English in the first line, Swedish in the second and Italian in the third. In all examples, we give the present tense forms only. In some cases an ungrammatical version has been added at the end of the example to indicate ungrammaticality for this particular person and number.

(17) a. I eat ice cream. *Eat ice cream.

b. Jag äter glass. *Äter glass.
1SG eat.PRS ice cream

c. Mangio gelato.
eat.1SG.PRS ice cream

(18) a. You eat ice cream. *Eat ice cream.

b. Du äter glass. *Äter glass.
2SG eat.PRS ice cream

c. Mangi gelato.
eat.2SG.PRS ice cream

(19) a. She eats ice cream. *Eats ice cream.

b. Hon äter glass. *Äter glass
3SG.F eat.PRS ice cream

c. Mangia gelato.
eat.3SG.PRS ice cream

(20) a. We eat ice cream. *Eat ice cream.

b. Vi äter glass. *Äter glass
1PL eat.PRS ice cream

c. Mangiamo gelato.
eat.1PL.PRS ice cream

(21) a. You eat ice cream. *Eat ice cream.

b. Ni äter glass. *Äter glass
2PL eat.PRS ice cream

c. Mangiate gelato.
eat.2PL.PRS ice cream

(22) a. They eat ice cream. *Eat ice cream.

b. De äter glass. *Äter glass
3PL eat.PRS ice cream

c. Mangiano gelato.
eat.3PL.PRS ice cream

As you can see, Swedish has the same verb form *äter* for all persons and numbers, and the subject pronoun is obligatory (you could actually use *Äter glass* in what is called "diary Swedish" or "postcard Swedish", but then it is elliptic. You probably know the same kind of thing from English '*Saw the leaning tower. Ate ice cream. Lost luggage. Great holiday!*'). English has the same verb form *eat* for all persons and numbers except 3SG, where it is *eats*. The subject pronoun is always obligatory (though you could use *Eat ice cream!* as an imperative in 2SG/PL). Italian, on the other hand has a different form of the verb for each person and number combination, and you do not need a subject pronoun to be expressed. In fact, if you use the subject pronoun, as in *Io mangio gelato* 'I eat.1SG ice cream', it may sound emphatic, or as if you are contrasting it with someone who isn't eating ice cream. The difference between the three languages lies in whether or not the verb can be used without an overt pronoun as its subject. English and Swedish do not allow this, but Italian does. It seems to be related to whether or not the information about person and number associated with the verb form can fulfil the required grammatical function by itself without an additional pronoun. This is not to say that all languages with many different verb forms allow this; German has a lot of verb forms, but still requires a subject pronoun. There are also languages like Vietnamese, which seem to manage without subject pronouns in some circumstances even though it does not have different verb forms.

Remember that we assume the functional equations in (23) for the English verb *eats*. This was provided in (26) in Chapter 3, and follows our treatment of verbal agreement (head marking) discussed in Section 4.2.2.

(23) *eats* V (↑ PRED) = 'EAT<SUBJ, OBJ>'
(↑ TENSE) = PRES
(↑ SUBJ NUM) = SG
(↑ SUBJ PERS) = 3

The Swedish *äter* would not have the SUBJ NUM and SUBJ PERS features at all since it is the same verb form for all persons and numbers. A first assumption, based on our treatment of 'eats' in English, would then be that a verb like the Italian *mangiano* would have a lexical entry like (24).

(24) *mangiano* V (↑ PRED) = 'EAT<SUBJ, OBJ>'
(↑ TENSE) = PRES
(↑ SUBJ NUM) = PL
(↑ SUBJ PERS) = 3

We can provide the partial lexical entry in (25) for the word *gelato* 'ice cream' and assume that *mangiano* and *gelato* can form a VP together. If we also assume that phrase–structure rules are annotated so as to make *gelato* the OBJ of the sentence, we get the combined f-structure in (26) for *Mangiano gelato*.

(25) *gelato* N (↑ PRED) = 'ICE CREAM'
(↑ NUM) = SG
(↑ PERS) = 3
(↑ GEND) = MASC

(26)

$$\begin{bmatrix} \text{PRED} & \text{`EAT <SUBJ, OBJ>'} \\ \text{TENSE} & \text{PRES} \\ \text{SUBJ} & \begin{bmatrix} \text{NUM} & \text{PL} \\ \text{PERS} & 3 \end{bmatrix} \\ \text{OBJ} & \begin{bmatrix} \text{PRED} & \text{`ICE CREAM'} \\ \text{NUM} & \text{SG} \\ \text{PERS} & 3 \\ \text{GEND} & \text{MASC} \end{bmatrix} \end{bmatrix}$$

Now, this may look like a reasonable f-structure for the sentence in question, but remember the well-formedness conditions that apply to f-structures (see Chapter 2).

Completeness: all governable functions which are part of the value of a PRED feature must be present in the local f-structure. All functions that have a θ-role must themselves have a PRED value.

Coherence: all governable functions present in an f-structure must occur in the value of a local PRED feature. All functions that have a PRED value must have a θ-role.

It is particularly the Completeness Condition that is relevant here. The verb which has the semantics 'EAT' has two argument functions: SUBJ and OBJ, both of which have θ-roles (Agent and Patient, respectively). This means that not only do both functions SUBJ and OBJ have to be present in the f-structure, but they must both have a PRED value. In (26), though the SUBJ has values for the person and number features, there is no PRED feature. In the corresponding English or Swedish sentence (*I eat ice cream* or *Jag äter glass*), the PRED value would come from the subject noun phrase, but the striking thing about these Italian sentences is that they do not need a subject noun phrase to be grammatical.

Now, for the f-structure in (26) to be licit, it must be the case that the verb contributes more than the subject's value for NUM and PERS in Italian; it must also contribute a value for the PRED feature. Since it seems reasonable to assume that it is the nature of the verb's information which allows the sentence to be interpreted correctly without an explicit noun phrase, this is an appropriate formal analysis. We will then expand the lexical entry for *mangiano* as in (27), which takes account of the fact that the verb also contributes a pronominal PRED value.

(27) *mangiano* V ($\uparrow$ PRED) = 'EAT <SUBJ, OBJ>'
($\uparrow$ TENSE) = PRES
($\uparrow$ SUBJ NUM) = PL
($\uparrow$ SUBJ PERS) = 3
($\uparrow$ SUBJ PRED) = 'PRO'

The term pronoun incorporation is then entirely appropriate; we assume that the pronominal meaning has been incorporated into the information associated with the verb. The new lexical entry for *mangiano* in (27) in combination with that for *gelato* in (25) gives us the f-structure in (28), which satisfies the Completeness and Coherence Conditions.

(28)
PRED 'EAT <SUBJ, OBJ>'
TENSE PRES
SUBJ [PRED 'PRO' / NUM PL / PERS 3]
OBJ [PRED 'ICE CREAM' / NUM SG / GEND MASC]

In Italian it is generally only information relating to the subject which can be incorporated into the verb, but in many head marking languages the verb can incorporate information about other arguments as well, meaning that even a transitive sentence can consist solely of a verb (there are some constructions in Italian that complicate the picture somewhat, but this need not concern us here).

These languages are often referred to as POLYSYNTHETIC languages, since the verb is able to morphologically encode all of its arguments, and so a single verb can be used to convey what would be a whole sentence in a language like English (or Italian, or Swedish). Consider the following example from Murrinhpatha, a language of northern Australia spoken by around 2,500 people.

(29) bam-nhi-ngkardu
1SG.SUBJ.NFUT-2SG.OBJ-see
'I saw you.'

In this example we have only a verb, no noun phrases at all. Both the subject and the object are expressed as part of the information associated with the verb, as indicated in the glosses (the NFUT gloss means that the verb is in its 'non-future' tense form, which is used for past and present events). Assuming the approach taken above for Italian, we can treat Murrinhpatha verbs as providing PRED values for both their subjects and their objects, as in the lexical entry for the inflected verb *bamnhingkardu* given in (30).

(30) *bamnhingkardu* V (↑ PRED) = 'SEE <SUBJ, OBJ>'
(↑ TENSE) = NFUT
(↑ SUBJ NUM) = SG
(↑ SUBJ PERS) = 1
(↑ SUBJ PRED) = 'PRO$_i$'
(↑ OBJ NUM) = SG
(↑ OBJ PERS) = 2
(↑ OBJ PRED) = 'PRO$_j$'

We will assume that Murrinhpatha c-structure is generated by a flexible phrase structure rule such as we saw for Latin in (3) above. Thus, the c-structure for the sentence in (29) is shown in (31) and the f-structure in (32). Remember that the value of a PRED feature is always unique (it is a semantic form, that is, a pointer into the semantics), and thus the two instances of 'PRO' we see in (30) are distinct, as indicated informally by the subscripted indices (see the discussion of the uniqueness of PRED values in Section 2.2).

(31)
S
|
V
↑ = ↓
|
bamnhingkardu
(↑ PRED) = 'SEE <SUBJ, OBJ>'
(↑ TENSE) = NFUT
(↑ SUBJ NUM) = SG
(↑ SUBJ PERS) = 1
(↑ SUBJ PRED) = 'PRO$_i$'
(↑ OBJ NUM) = SG
(↑ OBJ PERS) = 2
(↑ OBJ PRED) = 'PRO$_j$'

(32)

$$\begin{bmatrix} \text{PRED} & \text{`SEE <SUBJ, OBJ>'} \\ \text{TENSE} & \text{NFUT} \\ \text{SUBJ} & \begin{bmatrix} \text{PRED} & \text{`PRO}_i\text{'} \\ \text{NUM} & \text{SG} \\ \text{PERS} & 1 \end{bmatrix} \\ \text{OBJ} & \begin{bmatrix} \text{PRED} & \text{`PRO}_j\text{'} \\ \text{NUM} & \text{SG} \\ \text{PERS} & 2 \end{bmatrix} \end{bmatrix}$$

Note that this f-structure looks almost exactly the same as the f-structure would for the English sentence *I saw you*, despite the fact that the c-structures of the two sentences are so different. Of course, there are minor differences between the f-structures that result from slight differences in the grammatical features of the two languages – Murrinhpatha has a 'non-future' tense category where English has a 'past' tense category – or properties of individual lexical items – the English pronoun 'you' is unspecified for number, whereas the Murrinhpatha verbal inflection is unambiguously singular. Note also that we have simplified the representation of English pronouns here.

(33)

(34)

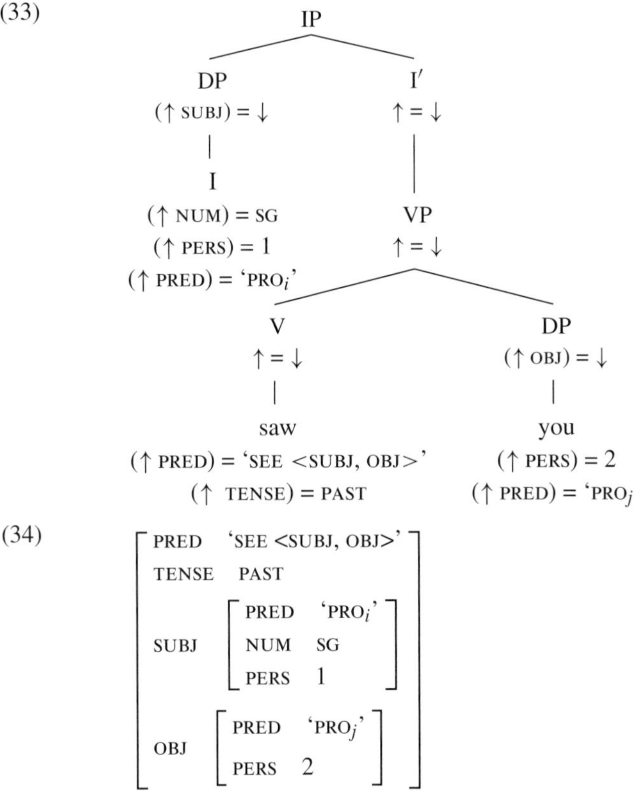

In this way, LFG can capture the fact that languages are able to achieve the same functional meanings in radically different ways; in this case we see that

Murrinhpatha can encode morphologically what English encodes via its syntax (c-structure). We also see how LFG can account for the fact that verbs in some languages are able to incorporate the information associated with their subject and object arguments.

4.2.4 Agreement vs Pronoun Incorporation

We have seen how LFG is able to account for languages in which head marking morphology agrees with the argument noun phrases in the clause (Section 4.2.2), and how it accounts for languages in which head marking morphology can realise the whole argument itself (Section 4.2.3). However, in many head marking languages, both of these options are possible; depending on the clause, the head marking morphology may occur with or without a coreferential noun phrase. In this section we will see how a very minor addition to the analyses presented above accounts for these languages as well.

Consider the Italian verbs discussed in Section 4.2.3. We have shown that these verbs incorporate information about their subjects, as in (27). However these verbs can also co-occur with a subject noun phrase as in (35b) and (35c), in which case the verbal morphology simply functions as verbal agreement.

(35) a. Mangiano gelato
'They eat ice cream.'
b. I bambini mangiano gelato
'The children eat ice cream.'
c. Io mangio gelato
'I eat ice cream.'

In order to account for pronominal incorporation, we assumed that a verb such as *mangiano* specified the PRED of its subject, capturing the fact that no additional noun phrase is required in the clause to encode the subject argument. However, examples such as (35b)–(35c) appear problematic for this approach since there is a subject noun phrase in the clause, with its own PRED value. PRED values are always unique, so even though in (35c) we have a PRED = 'PRO' (contributed by the verb) and a PRED = 'PRO' (contributed by the subject DP), these values are distinct and incompatible (another way of thinking about this is that for a given f-structure, the PRED value can only be contributed *once*) – this is the notion of PRED uniqueness discussed in Chapter 2.

Thus in order to account for languages like Italian and Murrinhpatha (and indeed, virtually all languages with pronominal incorporation), we need to allow the verbal morphology to function sometimes as agreement morphology (as in Section 4.2.2) and sometimes as incorporated pronominals (as in Section 4.2.3). In LFG we can use the optionality of features to do this. We analyse *mangiano* as optionally contributing the pronominal information for its subject. Thus the lexical entry for *mangiano* given in (27) is modified to that in (36), where the parentheses around the feature (↑ SUBJ PRED) = 'PRO' signal optionality.

(36) *mangiano* V (↑ PRED) = 'EAT <SUBJ, OBJ>'
(↑ TENSE) = PRES
(↑ SUBJ NUM) = PL
(↑ SUBJ PERS) = 3
((↑ SUBJ PRED) = 'PRO')

This means that *mangiano*, and by extension all other Italian verbs, will be compatible with coreferential subject noun phrases, but can also form grammatical sentences without them. General principles of LFG ensure that the correct option is realised at all times. Given PRED uniqueness, it won't be possible for the verb to specify a PRED feature for its subject if there is also a subject noun phrase in the clause. Thus in examples such as (35b), the presence of the PRED feature associated with *bambini* 'children' will ensure that the verb does not contribute a PRED for its subject in (37), since otherwise these two conflicting PRED features would clash in the SUBJ f-structure.

(37)

$$\left[\begin{array}{ll} \text{PRED} & \text{'EAT <SUBJ, OBJ>'} \\ \text{TENSE} & \text{PRES} \\ \text{SUBJ} & \left[\begin{array}{ll} \text{PRED} & \text{'CHILDREN'} \\ \text{NUM} & \text{PL} \\ \text{PERS} & 3 \end{array}\right] \\ \text{OBJ} & \left[\begin{array}{ll} \text{PRED} & \text{'ICE CREAM'} \\ \text{NUM} & \text{SG} \\ \text{GEND} & \text{MASC} \end{array}\right] \end{array}\right]$$

Where there is no coreferential subject noun phrase in the c-structure, however, as in (35a), the Completeness Condition will require the SUBJ f-structure to have a PRED. Thus in this case, since there is no external noun phrase to contribute the subject's PRED, it will be contributed by the verb in order to satisfy Completeness and we get (38).

(38)

$$\left[\begin{array}{ll} \text{PRED} & \text{'EAT <SUBJ, OBJ>'} \\ \text{TENSE} & \text{PRES} \\ \text{SUBJ} & \left[\begin{array}{ll} \text{PRED} & \text{'PRO'} \\ \text{NUM} & \text{PL} \\ \text{PERS} & 3 \end{array}\right] \\ \text{OBJ} & \left[\begin{array}{ll} \text{PRED} & \text{'ICE CREAM'} \\ \text{NUM} & \text{SG} \\ \text{GEND} & \text{MASC} \end{array}\right] \end{array}\right]$$

We can take a similar approach to Murrinhpatha verbs, except in this case the optional pronominal specification relates to both the subject and the object. In this way we account for the common flexibility of head marking morphology to function both as agreement markers and as incorporated pronominals. Of course, in head marking languages which don't allow this flexibility we would not assume that the PRED features were optional. In languages in which the head marking morphology cannot co-occur with a coreferential noun phrase we simply assume that the PRED features specified by the verb for these arguments are always present, in which case it cannot combine with a SUBJ noun phrase.

4.2.5 Head and Dependent Marking

In the discussions above we have seen how LFG approaches head marking and dependent marking in languages in order to capture the fact that the information about grammatical relations in these languages comes primarily from the morphology rather than from the c-structure. In fact, while we have so far talked about head marking and dependent marking independently, most languages use a combination of these, as well as configurationality (grammatical relations encoded in the c-structure), with the same values for f-structure features coming from more than one source. So in a given language, for example, there might be a fixed syntactic position for subjects, as well as nominative case and subject agreement marking on the verb. LFG's constraint-based model ensures that all information about the subject will contribute information to the same f-structure, which means that as long as the information is compatible, it doesn't matter how many times it is marked in the structure. In the Italian sentence in (39), information about the SUBJ is coming from the head marking on the verb (40), from the form of the pronoun *io*, which is in the nominative (41), and from the c-structure as well, as shown in (42).

(39) Io mangio gelato.
'I eat ice cream.'

(40) *mangio* V (↑ PRED) = 'EAT <SUBJ, OBJ>'
(↑ TENSE) = PRES
(↑ SUBJ NUM) = SG
(↑ SUBJ PERS) = 1
((↑ SUBJ PRED) = 'PRO')

(41) *io* D (↑ PRED) = 'PRO'
(↑ NUM) = SG
(↑ PERS) = 1
(↑ CASE) = NOM

(42)

IPf_1

DPf_2 (↑ SUBJ) = ↓
Io
(↑ PRED) = 'PRO'
(↑ NUM) = SG
(↑ PERS) = 1
(↑ CASE) = NOM

I′f_3 ↑ = ↓

VPf_4 ↑ = ↓

Vf_5 ↑ = ↓
mangio
(↑ PRED) = 'EAT <SUBJ, OBJ>'
(↑ TENSE) = PRES
(↑ SUBJ NUM) = SG
(↑ SUBJ PERS) = 1

DPf_6 (↑ OBJ) = ↓
gelato
(↑ PRED) = 'ICE CREAM'
(↑ NUM) = SG
(↑ GEND) = MASC

Again using the f-structure names we indicate in the tree in (42), we derive the f-description in (43) from the annotations, as before. Note that the SUBJ PRED information is not contributed by the verb in this case, given the presence of the external subject pronoun as discussed in Section 4.2.4.

(43)

a. (f_1 SUBJ) = f_2
b. (f_2 PRED) = 'PRO'
c. (f_2 NUM) = SG
d. (f_2 PERS) = 1
e. (f_2 CASE) = NOM
f. $f_1 = f_3$
g. $f_3 = f_4$
h. $f_4 = f_5$
i. (f_5 PRED) = 'EAT <SUBJ, OBJ>'
j. (f_5 TENSE) = PRES
k. (f_5 SUBJ NUM) = SG
l. (f_5 SUBJ PERS) = 1
m. (f_4 OBJ) = f_6
n. (f_6 PRED) = 'ICE CREAM'
o. (f_6 NUM) = SG
p. (f_6 GEND) = MASC

This information combines to define the f-structure for the whole sentence.

(44)

$$f1,f3,f4,f5 \begin{bmatrix} \text{PRED} & \text{'EAT} \langle\text{SUBJ, OBJ}\rangle\text{'} \\ \text{TENSE} & \text{PRES} \\ \text{SUBJ} & f2 \begin{bmatrix} \text{PRED} & \text{'PRO'} \\ \text{NUM} & \text{SG} \\ \text{PERS} & 1 \\ \text{CASE} & \text{NOM} \end{bmatrix} \\ \text{OBJ} & f6 \begin{bmatrix} \text{PRED} & \text{'ICE CREAM'} \\ \text{NUM} & \text{SG} \\ \text{GEND} & \text{MASC} \end{bmatrix} \end{bmatrix}$$

In this way LFG is able to capture the fact that many of the world's languages use more than one mechanism for encoding grammatical relations.

The fact that the same information can be distributed across different lexical items and c-structure nodes yet contribute to the same part of the f-structure in LFG is useful beyond accounts of the encoding of grammatical relations. There are many different ways in which morphology interacts with syntax in the languages of the world, and it is this aspect of LFG that we use to account for many of these interactions. For example, it is a common property of languages across the world that the same grammatical feature – such as TENSE or NEGATION – can be marked on many different words in the clause. Since information from many parts of the clause can contribute to one single f-structure in LFG, as we saw above, such data can be accounted for in a similar way. This feature of

LFG is also useful in accounting for agreement phenomena, where modifiers are marked with grammatical features of their heads, since it is possible for information to be encoded on one element of the clause, but be contributed to a different part of the f-structure. In the following sections we explore some of these more complex morphology–syntax interactions, and show how they can be accounted for within LFG. We begin in Section 4.3 with a discussion of agreement and concord within noun phrases, and introduce the mechanism of INSIDE-OUT FUNCTION APPLICATION to allow modifiers to carry information that contributes to the f-structure of the phrases that contain them. In Section 4.4, we show how this mechanism provides us with an alternative way of dealing with dependent-marking languages. It allows the case morphology to contribute grammatical function information to the clause directly, without having to be mediated by the lexical entry of the verb as in Section 4.2.1. This means it captures the nature of dependent marking better than the verb-mediated approach we used earlier. In Section 4.5 we see how this constructive approach to morphology is useful for accounting for examples where the morphology seems to be 'in the wrong place', such as in languages that allow tense marking on noun phrases. Finally, in Sections 4.6 and 4.7 we look at some more complex agreement patterns, including agreement in coordinate structures.

4.3 Concord and Agreement

Above we have talked about verbal agreement, also referred to as PREDICATE–ARGUMENT AGREEMENT, whereby verbs agree with features of their arguments, and we saw how this is captured in LFG by allowing verbs to carry information about the f-structure features of their arguments. We have not yet, however, talked about how LFG handles other types of agreement, such as agreement within noun phrases, also called HEAD–MODIFIER AGREEMENT or CONCORD. We turn to this type of agreement in this section.

In many languages of the world adjectives and other modifiers within a noun phrase must agree with the head noun in features such as number, gender or definiteness. In (45) are some examples from Wambaya (showing agreement in gender), in (46) from English (showing agreement in number) and in (47) from Swedish (showing agreement in definiteness – there is also some marking for number and gender, but we ignore that here).

(45) a. bulyungurna alanga
little.F child.F
'small girl'

b. bulyungi alaji
little.M child.M
'small boy'

(46) a. this dog

b. these dogs

(47) a. en fin bil
a nice-looking.INDF car.INDF
'a nice-looking car'

b. den fin-a bil-en
the nice-looking-DEF car-DEF
'the nice-looking car'

There is a sense in which an adjective like *bulyungu-* in (45a) is not itself categorised for gender, but is carrying the FEM gender feature only to signal that the **noun** it is modifying has this feature. Following the approach we took for verbal agreement above, we can treat the gender feature on the modifier as being contributed directly to the f-structure of the head noun, rather than to the f-structure of the modifier itself. Thus, the phrase in (45a) would correspond to the f-structure in (48).

(48)
$$f_1\begin{bmatrix} \text{PRED} & \text{`CHILD'} \\ \text{GEND} & \text{FEM} \\ \text{ADJ} & \{f_2[\text{PRED} \quad \text{`LITTLE'}]\} \end{bmatrix}$$

In order to do this, we need to allow words to contribute information to f-structures outside of their own f-structures; in (48) we see that the modifier has not contributed GEND FEM to its own f-structure (f_2), but to the outer f-structure (f_1), where it agrees with the feature provided by the noun itself. We achieve this by using a mechanism referred to as INSIDE-OUT FUNCTION APPLICATION. To understand how this works, let's revisit the function application that we have seen in practice so far, which we can call OUTSIDE-IN FUNCTION APPLICATION. In a functional description such as (49), we begin by identifying an f-structure (designated by ↑) and then define a constraint on embedded structures within it, namely that it will contain a SUBJ and that this SUBJ will contain a NUM attribute, the value of which is SG. These constraints define a path through the f-structure starting from the outermost f-structure (↑), the path in this case being SUBJ NUM.

(49) $(\uparrow \text{SUBJ NUM}) = \text{SG}$

The constraint in (49) thus defines the f-structure given in (50), where f_1 is the f-structure designated by ↑.

(50)
$$f_1\begin{bmatrix} \text{SUBJ} & f_2[\text{NUM} \quad \text{SG}] \end{bmatrix}$$

We can see that the function application here proceeds from the 'outside-in': we start with f_1 and define constraints that apply to structures within it, namely the number value of f_2.

It is also possible for constraints to work in the opposite way, whereby they are defined on enclosing structures, structures that are outside of the f-structure we start with. This is inside-out function application. To see how it works, consider the functional description in (51), which, as we will see, can be read as 'my f-structure is the value of SUBJ in a higher f-structure which has the value SG for the attribute NUM'.

(51) $((\text{SUBJ}\uparrow)\ \text{NUM}) = \text{SG}$

Here we begin by identifying an f-structure (again, designated by ↑) and state that it is the value of a SUBJ attribute in the immediately higher f-structure; this higher f-structure is designated by the string (SUBJ ↑). This part of the functional description defines the f-structure given in (52), where f_2 is the f-structure designated by ↑ and f_1 the f-structure designated by (SUBJ ↑), i.e. the f-structure within which f_2 is the value of SUBJ.

(52) $f_1\Big[\text{SUBJ}\quad f_2[\cdots\ ]\Big]$

Since (SUBJ ↑) designates the outer f-structure to which ↑ belongs, i.e. f_1, the functional description in (51) then specifies that this outer f-structure has a NUM attribute whose value is SG. Thus the full f-structure denoted by this functional description is that given in (53).

(53) $f_1\begin{bmatrix}\text{SUBJ} & f_2[\cdots\ ]\\ \text{NUM} & \text{SG}\end{bmatrix}$

Note that the NUM information in this case is associated with the outer f-structure, f_1, rather than the inner f-structure as it was in (50). This is due to the fact that inside-out function application defines constraints on enclosing (outer) f-structures, whereas outside-in function application defines constraints on embedded (inner) f-structures. In (51) we begin by identifying an f-structure (here instantiated as f_2) and then define constraints that hold of its enclosing f-structures; in (49), as we saw, this happens the other way around. Inside-out function application can be used in a variety of ways in LFG, including in analyses of anaphora, as we will see in Chapter 7.

Returning now to the issue of agreement within noun phrases, since inside-out function application allows us to specify information about enclosing levels of f-structure, we can use it to capture the gender agreement in examples such as (45). We do this by ensuring that the gender feature associated with the adjective *bulyungurna* ends up in the outer f-structure, namely f_1 in (48), and therefore contributes directly to the f-structure of the noun. To do this, we assume the following lexical entry for *bulyungurna*. Note that Wambaya, like many Australian languages, does not treat adjectives or pronouns as a different part of speech from nouns, so we consider them all to be N.

(54) *bulyungurna* N (↑ PRED) = 'LITTLE'
$((\text{ADJ} \in \uparrow)\ \text{GEND}) = \text{FEM}$

The second line in this lexical entry is slightly complicated by the fact that ADJ is a set-valued feature. The equation should be read as follows 'my f-structure (↑) is a member of a set of f-structures which form the value of an ADJ attribute in a higher f-structure (ADJ ∈ ↑), and this higher f-structure has a GEND feature whose value is FEM'. Thus (ADJ ∈ ↑) refers to the outer f-structure (f_1 in the f-structure for (45a), repeated as (55)), which contains an ADJ whose value is a set containing an f-structure corresponding to *bulyungurna* (f_2). The complete f-description ((ADJ ∈ ↑) GEND) = FEM says that the outer f-structure, f_1, contains the information GEND = FEM, thus contributing this gender information directly into the f-structure of the head nominal.

(55)

$$f_1 \begin{bmatrix} \text{PRED} & \text{`CHILD'} \\ \text{GEND} & \text{FEM} \\ \text{ADJ} & f_2 \left\{ \begin{bmatrix} \text{PRED} & \text{`LITTLE'} \end{bmatrix} \right\} \end{bmatrix}$$

The benefit of treating agreement in this way is clear when we consider pronominal possessors which show agreement, as in the following Wambaya example.

(56)

Ngajbi	ng-a	nangi-marnda-rna	alalangmiminya
see	1SG.SUBJ-PST	3SG.M.POSS-PL-F(ACC)	daughter.PL.F(ACC)

'I saw his daughters.'

In this example the pronominal possessor *nangi-marnda-rna* 'his' carries two different gender and number features: one set referring to the possessor itself (masculine, singular), and another agreeing with the head nominal (feminine, plural). If both gender and number features were unified into the f-structure associated with the pronominal possessor itself, it would result in an illicit f-structure since the two sets of features would violate the Uniqueness Condition, as shown in (57).

(57)

$$\begin{bmatrix} \text{PRED} & \text{`PRO'} \\ \text{PERS} & 3 \\ \text{GEND} & {*}\text{MASC/FEM} \\ \text{NUM} & {*}\text{SG/PL} \end{bmatrix}$$

However, intuitively it is only the features associated with the possessor that belong in this f-structure; the others are agreement features associated with the outer f-structure, as we saw in (55). Following this approach, we assume that the lexical entry associated with *nangi-marnda-rna* is that given in (58), producing the f-structure in (59). In this f-structure, the agreement features have all contributed to the outer f-structure, that associated with the head nominal *alalangmiminya* 'daughters', and there is no violation of Uniqueness.

(58) *nangimarndarna* N (↑ PRED) = 'PRO'
(↑ PERS) = 3
(↑ NUM) = SG
(↑ GEND) = MASC
((POSS ↑) NUM) = PL
((POSS ↑) GEND) = FEM

(59)

$$\begin{bmatrix} \text{NUM} & \text{PL} \\ \text{GEND} & \text{FEM} \\ \text{POSS} & \begin{bmatrix} \text{PRED} & \text{`PRO'} \\ \text{PERS} & 3 \\ \text{NUM} & \text{SG} \\ \text{GEND} & \text{MASC} \end{bmatrix} \end{bmatrix}$$

In this way, we capture the fact that agreement morphology such as gender and number agreement on noun phrase modifiers can provide information about outer levels of f-structure, by indicating that the head nominal has particular gender and number features. In the next section, we will see how this idea can be extended to case marking, and thus provide a more comprehensive analysis of dependent marking in LFG.

4.4 Constructive Case

The approach to noun phrase modifier agreement exemplified in (48) and (59) can also be used for case agreement, and thus it provides an alternative way of handling dependent-marking morphology from that which we discussed in Section 4.2.1. This approach uses inside-out function application to capture the fact that it is the case morphology which encodes the grammatical function of the nominal to which it is attached. Inflecting a nominal with accusative case, for example, doesn't just mark the nominal as having accusative case, but also encodes the fact that the nominal is functioning as the object of the larger clause. Thus, on this view, case markers do not just **reflect** grammatical relations, but actually play a central role in **constructing** them.

As a simple illustration of the model, consider the Latin accusative nominal *copias* 'troops.ACC' from the example given in (1a) and repeated as (60).

(60) Caesar suas copias in proximum
Caesar.NOM REFL.ACC.F.PL troop.ACC.F.PL in nearest.ACC.M.SG
collem subducit
hill.ACC.M.SG withdraw.PRS.3SG
'Caesar withdraws his (own) forces to the nearest hill.' [*De bello Gallico* 1.22]

A traditional approach to case might assume that the accusative case here contributes the case information $(\uparrow \text{CASE}) = \text{ACC}$, and that elsewhere in the grammar this information will interact with the argument structure of the verb to ensure that the nominal is only licensed as the object. This was the approach that we took to Latin case in Section 4.2.1. On the constructive case approach, however, the accusative case describes the outer f-structure within which this nominal's f-structure belongs, specifying that the nominal's f-structure is the value of the grammatical function OBJ. The information associated with the accusative nominal is shown in (61), and the f-structure constructed by the whole nominal *copias* is shown in (62).

(61) *copias* N (↑ PRED) = 'TROOP'
(↑ NUM) = PL
(↑ PERS) = 3
(↑ CASE) = ACC
(OBJ ↑)

(62)

$$f_1\left[\text{OBJ}\quad f_2\begin{bmatrix}\text{PRED} & \text{'TROOP'}\\ \text{NUM} & \text{PL}\\ \text{PERS} & 3\\ \text{CASE} & \text{ACC}\end{bmatrix}\right]$$

The crucial difference between this approach and that presented in Section 4.2.1 is the f-description (OBJ ↑) in (61), which states that the f-structure to which the nominal belongs (indicated by ↑) is the value of an OBJ function in a higher f-structure (as we saw in Section 4.3). This is shown in the f-structure in (62), where the information associated with the accusative-marked nominal is contained within f_2, which is the value of the OBJ attribute inside the higher f-structure, f_1, which is the f-structure of the clause. Thus, the case-inflected nominal carries information about the grammatical function that it holds in the higher clausal f-structure. This analysis then captures the essence of dependent marking more accurately than the verb-mediated approach presented in Section 4.2.1.

To see how this approach interacts with the c-structure of Latin and the rest of the sentence, let's work through the full analysis of example (1a) (repeated above as (60)), as we did in Section 4.2.1, but this time with constructive case. The relevant lexical entries required are given in (63)–(65). The crucial differences from those that we assumed in Section 4.2.1 are the presence of grammatical function information in the lexical entries of the nominals, and the absence of case specifications in the lexical entry of the verb. This is no longer required to ensure that the nominals are correctly associated with their grammatical functions since this job is now done by the case morphology itself.

(63) *Caesar* N (↑ PRED) = 'CAESAR'
(↑ NUM) = SG
(↑ PERS) = 3
(↑ CASE) = NOM
(SUBJ ↑)

(64) *copias* N (↑ PRED) = 'TROOP'
(↑ NUM) = PL
(↑ PERS) = 3
(↑ CASE) = ACC
(OBJ ↑)

(65) *subducit* V (↑ PRED) = 'WITHDRAW <SUBJ, OBJ>'
(↑ SUBJ PERS) = 3
(↑ SUBJ NUM) = SG

Recall the c-structure generated by our non-configurational rules for Latin (again, we have added unique names for the f-structures associated with the nodes).

(66)

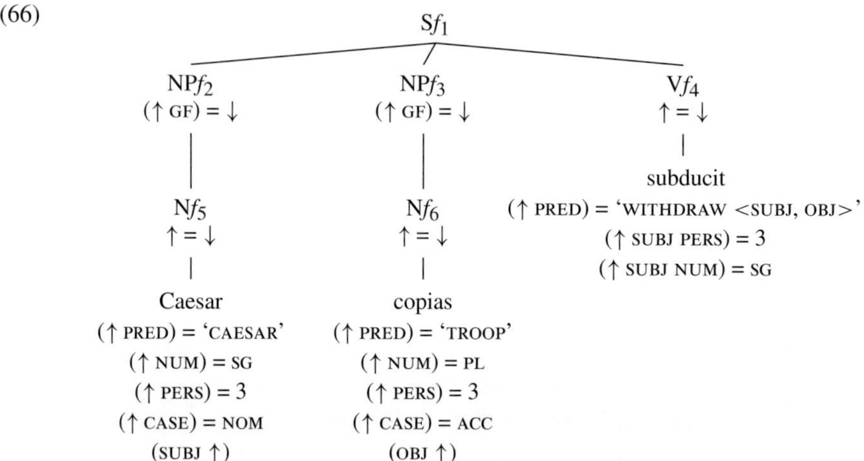

The functional equations for the two NP nodes are shown in (67).

(67)
a. $f_2 = f_5$
b. (f_5 PRED) = 'CAESAR'
c. (f_5 NUM) = SG
d. (f_5 PERS) = 3
e. (f_5 CASE) = NOM
f. (SUBJ f_5)
g. $f_3 = f_6$
h. (f_6 PRED) = 'TROOP'
i. (f_6 NUM) = PL
j. (f_6 PERS) = 3
k. (f_6 CASE) = ACC
l. (OBJ f_6)

When we expand the f-description for this sentence by including the functional annotations added from the c-structure and also adding the equations associated with the V node, we get the fuller f-description in (68).

(68)
a. (f_1 GF) $= f_2$
b. $f_2 = f_5$
c. (f_5 PRED) = 'CAESAR'
d. (f_5 NUM) = SG
e. (f_5 PERS) = 3
f. (f_5 CASE) = NOM
g. (SUBJ f_5)

h. $(f_1 \text{ GF}) = f_3$

i. $f_3 = f_6$

j. $(f_6 \text{ PRED}) = \text{`TROOP'}$

k. $(f_6 \text{ NUM}) = \text{PL}$

l. $(f_6 \text{ PERS}) = 3$

m. $(f_6 \text{ CASE}) = \text{ACC}$

n. $(\text{OBJ}\, f_6)$

o. $f_1 = f_4$

p. $(f_4 \text{ PRED}) = \text{`WITHDRAW <SUBJ, OBJ>'}$

q. $(f_4 \text{ SUBJ PERS}) = 3$

r. $(f_4 \text{ SUBJ NUM}) = \text{SG}$

Solving the equations in (68) then provides the f-structure in (69).

(69)

$$f1,f4 \begin{bmatrix} \text{PRED} & \text{`WITHDRAW <SUBJ, OBJ>'} \\ \text{SUBJ} & f2,f5 \begin{bmatrix} \text{PRED} & \text{`CAESAR'} \\ \text{NUM} & \text{SG} \\ \text{PERS} & 3 \\ \text{CASE} & \text{NOM} \end{bmatrix} \\ \text{OBJ} & f3,f6 \begin{bmatrix} \text{PRED} & \text{`TROOP'} \\ \text{NUM} & \text{PL} \\ \text{PERS} & 3 \\ \text{CASE} & \text{ACC} \end{bmatrix} \end{bmatrix}$$

Note that the functional descriptions (SUBJ f_5) and (OBJ f_6) associated with the case morphology borne by each of the nominals ensure that the f-structure of the NP is associated with the correct grammatical function in the clausal f-structure. This no longer needs to be mediated through the lexical entry of the verb, as in the analysis given in Section 4.2.1, and thus we directly capture the fact that it is the case morphology in (non-configurational) dependent-marking languages which determines grammatical function.

4.5 Tense on Noun Phrases

The idea that case morphology can contribute information to the larger (clausal) f-structures within which case-marked nominals are contained opens up possibilities for nominal morphology to encode information about other aspects of the clause as well. Thus, we can extend the idea of constructive case to CONSTRUCTIVE MORPHOLOGY more generally and account for other types of morphology–syntax interactions beyond just case encoding grammatical function. For example, we can use this approach to account for languages which encode tense information on noun phrases. Although we don't usually expect noun phrases to encode information about the tense of the clause, in some languages this is exactly what happens. Consider the example from Lardil (a language from Mornington Island in northern Australia).

(70) a. Ngada bilaa wu-thur ngimbenthar diin-kur
1SG.NOM tomorrow give-FUT 2SG.FOBJ this-FOBJ
wangalk-ur.
boomerang-FOBJ
'I'll give you this boomerang tomorrow.' (Klokeid, 1976, 493)

b. Ngada niwentharr maarn-arr wu-tharr.
1SG.NOM 3SG.NFOBJ spear-NFOBJ give-NFUT
'I gave him a spear.' (Klokeid, 1976, 476, 56b)

As is shown in these examples, the object case morphology in Lardil also encodes a distinction between future and non-future tense. In (70a) the object nominal 'boomerang' is marked with the future tense object case marker *-ur* (FOBJ) while in (70b) the object nominal 'spear' is marked with the non-future form *-arr* (NFOBJ). In each example, the case marker agrees in tense with the tense of the verb and thus the tense of the clause as a whole. We can capture this in LFG by using inside-out function application, once again, therefore assuming that these two inflected nominals carry the information shown in (71) and (72) respectively.

(71) *wangalk-ur* N (↑ PRED) = 'BOOMERANG'
(↑ PERS) = 3
(↑ CASE) = ACC
((OBJ ↑) TENSE) $=_c$ FUT

(72) *maarn-arr* N (↑ PRED) = 'SPEAR'
(↑ PERS) = 3
(↑ CASE) = ACC
((OBJ ↑) TENSE) ≠ FUT

In the final line of these lexical entries we see that the inflected nominal carries the information that it is contained within the OBJ of a higher (clausal) f-structure (OBJ ↑), as we saw in Section 4.4, but in this case the nominal also specifies information about that higher f-structure, namely a requirement that it have a particular value for TENSE (or **not** have a particular value for tense, in the case of (72)). Thus, ((OBJ ↑) TENSE) $=_c$ FUT in (71) can be read as 'my f-structure is the value of OBJ in a higher f-structure which must have the value FUT for the attribute TENSE'. Note that (TENSE) $=_c$ FUT is a constraining equation. The constraining equation here does not define TENSE for the higher f-structure, it just constrains what its value has to be; the feature and its value must be contributed by some other element, in this example the verb. The negative equation in (72) is not specified as constraining, though it functions in the same way as a constraining equation. A negative equation is by its nature constraining, since a defining equation could not define the absence of a feature.

The f-structure associated with the inflected nominal in (71) is given in (73). The tense constraint on the clausal f-structure is represented informally here with the notation TENSE FUT_c but in fact the feature–value pair [TENSE FUT] is contributed to the f-structure by the verb, not by the nominal itself. The use of the constraining equation ensures that the verb cannot be unmarked for tense, but must carry an appropriate tense marker for the structure to be grammatical.

(73)
$$f_1\begin{bmatrix} \text{TENSE} & \text{FUT}_c \\ \text{OBJ} & f_2\begin{bmatrix} \text{PRED} & \text{`BOOMERANG'} \\ \text{PERS} & 3 \\ \text{CASE} & \text{ACC} \end{bmatrix} \end{bmatrix}$$

Tense marking on nominals, although unusual, is found in a number of languages of the world. In fact, we can take a similar approach to some reduced auxiliaries in English in order to account for the differences shown in (74) and (75). These examples use the auxiliary *will*; analogous facts are also found with *would*, and tensed forms of *be* and *have*. Here we add a representation indicating the difference in pronunciation between the syllabic /əl/ and the non-syllabic /l/.

(74)
a. Mary's flu'll (*/l/, /əl/) be gone by tomorrow.
b. John and Sue'll (*/l/, /əl/) be singing all day long.
c. The boy who's laughing'll (*/l/, /əl/) go to the party.

(75)
a. You'll (/l/) be able to go home at two o'clock.
b. I'll (/l/) be leaving tomorrow.

The syllabic reduced forms in (74) form their own syllables and do not allow complete contraction with the preceding word. They can also attach to any word that appears at the end of the noun phrase they follow. The non-syllabic forms in (75), however, are quite different. They can be completely reduced so that they don't form their own syllable, and they only appear attached to a pronoun. Thus, they can be shown to behave like inflectional affixes rather than syntactically independent words or clitics.

We can account for these differences if we treat the subject pronouns in (75) as tense-inflected pronominals. These can be given a straightforward account within LFG using inside-out function application, as we saw in the discussion of Lardil case above. On this approach, the inflected pronoun *you'll*, as in (75a), has the lexical entry shown in (76), corresponding to the f-structure information shown in (77). As shown in this f-structure, the inflected pronoun contributes both information about the subject of the clause, and tense information to the clause itself. Here the equation is not constraining, it actually **defines** the value for TENSE for the clause.

(76) *you'll* D $(\uparrow \text{PRED}) = \text{`PRO'}$
$(\uparrow \text{PERS}) = 2$
$((\text{SUBJ} \uparrow)\ \text{TENSE}) = \text{FUT}$

(77)
$$\begin{bmatrix} \text{TENSE} & \text{FUT} \\ \text{SUBJ} & \begin{bmatrix} \text{PRED} & \text{'PRO'} \\ \text{PERS} & 2 \end{bmatrix} \end{bmatrix}$$

Thus, the constructive approach to morphology, which makes use of inside-out function application to allow words to contribute information to f-structures outside of their own, provides an account of a range of morphology–syntax interactions across languages of the world, from noun phrase agreement to dependent marking to the appearance of clausal information like tense on noun phrases. In the next section we turn again to issues of noun phrase agreement, and look in more detail at the set of agreement features involved. Until now, we have assumed that noun phrases have a single set of agreement features (PERS, NUM, GEND, etc.). As we will see, in some languages there are good reasons to assume that noun phrases have **two** different sets of agreement features which interact with the syntax in different ways.

4.6 More on Agreement: INDEX and CONCORD

In this chapter we have discussed two types of agreement. Predicate–argument agreement involves the verb agreeing with its arguments, usually subject, but possibly also object and other arguments as well, as we saw in Section 4.2.2. Head–modifier agreement is when modifiers agree with the head of their noun phrase, as discussed in Section 4.3. In these discussions, we have assumed that nouns have a single set of agreement features that verbs (in predicate–argument agreement) or nominal modifiers (in head–modifier agreement) agree with. So in the French example in (78) we would assume that the nominal *filles* has the agreement features PERS = 3, NUM = PL, GEND = FEM, and that both the verb and the modifying adjective agree with this single set of features: the verb *partent* agreeing with PERS and NUM; and the adjective *jeunes* agreeing with NUM and GEND.

(78) Les vieilles femmes partent demain.
the.PL old.F.PL woman.PL leave.PRS.3PL tomorrow
'The old women leave tomorrow.'

However, as we will see in this section, there is good evidence from some languages that these assumptions are oversimplified. In fact, in many languages we find phenomena which seem to suggest that more than one set of syntactic agreement features might be associated with a single noun phrase. One piece of evidence comes from so-called MIXED or HYBRID AGREEMENT, where we find that a single noun is agreed with differently by the verb than by its modifiers. For example, there is a class of nouns in Serbo-Croatian which appear to trigger two different sorts of agreement. In the examples in (79) and (80) we see that the nouns *braća* 'brothers' and *deca* 'children' are agreed with by F.SG modifiers within the noun phrase, while the auxiliary verb shows 3PL neuter agreement (the participle verb form is syncretic and could in fact be either N.PL or F.SG as indicated in the glossing). Thus, the relevant agreement features within the noun phrase are different from those involved in predicate–argument agreement with the auxiliary verb; in particular, we have singular agreement within the noun phrase but plural agreement on the verbal auxiliary.

(79) Starija braća su puno vikala.
old.F.SG brother.PL AUX.3PL much shout.PPTCP-N.PL/F.SG
'Older brothers shouted a lot.' (Alsina and Arsenijević 2012, 9)

(80) Ta dobra deca su došla
that.F.SG good.F.SG child.PL AUX.3PL come.PPTCP-N.PL/F.SG
'Those good children came.' (Wechsler and Zlatić 2003, 51)

Examples such as these, where a single noun appears to trigger mutually incompatible agreement (singular on the one hand, and plural on the other), motivate the introduction of two distinct sets of agreement features – CONCORD and INDEX features – which may interact differently in agreement with other parts of the clause. It is generally assumed that the set of CONCORD features includes NUM, GEND (but not PERS) while the set of INDEX features include NUM, PERS and GEND. In the Serbo-Croatian examples above we see that the CONCORD features of the noun control agreement within the noun phrase while the INDEX features control agreement on the finite auxiliary verb. (Since the participle forms are syncretic, we can't tell whether agreement between the participle and the subject reflects the INDEX or the CONCORD features.) If we use these two sets of features, a noun such as *deca* would have the description shown in (81), with 'mismatched' NUM and GEND features.

(81)
$$\left[\begin{array}{ll} \text{PRED} & \text{`CHILD'} \\ \text{INDEX} & \left[\begin{array}{ll} \text{PERS} & 3 \\ \text{NUM} & \text{PL} \\ \text{GEND} & \text{NEUT} \end{array}\right] \\ \text{CONCORD} & \left[\begin{array}{ll} \text{NUM} & \text{SG} \\ \text{GEND} & \text{FEM} \end{array}\right] \end{array}\right]$$

So within the noun phrase in (80) the attributive adjective *dobra* 'good.F.SG' specifies that the noun it modifies has the CONCORD features GEND = FEM and NUM = SG. As we saw in Section 4.3, an inside-out path such as (82) points to the f-structure of the noun *deca*, which the adjective modifies, so these CONCORD features are features of the noun, not of the adjective itself.

(82) *dobra* Adj $((\text{ADJ} \in \uparrow)\ \text{CONCORD GEND}) = \text{FEM}$
$((\text{ADJ} \in \uparrow)\ \text{CONCORD NUM}) = \text{SG}$

On the other hand, the auxiliary verb *su* specifies that the SUBJ has the INDEX features NUM = PL and GEND = NEUT, as shown in (83).

(83) $(\uparrow \text{SUBJ INDEX GEND}) = \text{NEUT}$
$(\uparrow \text{SUBJ INDEX NUM}) = \text{PL}$

Now that we have proposed that there are two sets of agreement features – CONCORD and INDEX – we must revisit our treatment of verb-subject agreement in languages more generally and reformulate it in terms of INDEX agreement. Thus, the lexical entry for the verb in the French example (78) is given in (84), and the f-structure for the whole sentence in (85). Likewise, the lexical entry for the English verb *eats* given in (23) above is reformulated as in (86).

(84) *partent* V (↑ PRED) = 'LEAVE<SUBJ>'
(↑ TENSE) = PRES
(↑ SUBJ INDEX PERS) = 3
(↑ SUBJ INDEX NUM) = PL

(85)

$$\left[\begin{array}{ll} \text{PRED} & \text{`LEAVE<SUBJ>'} \\ \text{TENSE} & \text{PRES} \\ \text{SUBJ} & \left[\begin{array}{ll} \text{PRED} & \text{`WOMAN'} \\ \text{INDEX} & \left[\begin{array}{ll} \text{PERS} & 3 \\ \text{NUM} & \text{PL} \\ \text{GEND} & \text{FEM} \end{array}\right] \\ \text{CONCORD} & \left[\begin{array}{ll} \text{NUM} & \text{PL} \\ \text{GEND} & \text{FEM} \end{array}\right] \\ \text{ADJ} & \left\{\left[\text{PRED} \;\; \text{`OLD'}\right]\right\} \end{array}\right] \\ \text{ADJ} & \left\{\left[\text{PRED} \;\; \text{`TOMORROW'}\right]\right\} \end{array}\right]$$

(86) *eats* V (↑ PRED) = 'EAT <SUBJ, OBJ>'
(↑ TENSE) = PRES
(↑ SUBJ INDEX NUM) = SG
(↑ SUBJ INDEX PERS) = 3

Although it is very often the case that CONCORD features are relevant to noun phrase internal agreement and INDEX features are relevant to subject–verb agreement and other cases of predicate–argument agreement, this is not always the case, as we discuss in the reading section at the end of the chapter. In the following section, we will look at the role and place of the INDEX features in coordinate structures.

4.7 Agreement and Coordinate Structures

In Section 3.1 we said that coordinate structures are represented as sets at f-structure. We will not develop a full analysis of coordinate structures in this book, but here we will take a brief look at the interaction of predicate–argument agreement with coordinate arguments and the role of the INDEX features. The schematic f-structure in (88) illustrates the representation of a coordinate argument, like that in (87).

(87) I saw Peter and Mary.

(88)

$$\left[\begin{array}{ll} \text{PRED} & \text{`SEE}<\text{SUBJ, OBJ}>\text{'} \\ \text{OBJ} & \left[\begin{array}{l} \text{CONJ} \quad \text{AND} \\ \left\{\begin{array}{l} \left[\text{PRED} \quad \text{`PETER'}\right] \\ \left[\text{PRED} \quad \text{`MARY'}\right] \end{array}\right\} \end{array}\right] \\ \text{SUBJ} & \left[\begin{array}{ll} \text{PRED} & \text{`PRO'} \\ \text{PERS} & 1 \\ \text{NUM} & \text{SG} \end{array}\right] \end{array}\right]$$

Consider now the two French examples in (89). Here we see that the coordinated subject *Jean et moi* 'Jean and I' determines precisely the same 1PL agreement on the verb as the first person plural pronoun *nous* 'we'. We provide the lexical entry for *partons* in (90). This means that the coordinate subject as a whole in (89) has an INDEX with NUM = PL and PERS = 1 values, since it is this that the verb agrees with, as we discussed in Section 4.6. However, the individual conjuncts *Jean* and *moi* have their own INDEX values as well, 3SG and 1SG, respectively. The schematic f-structure in (91) illustrates the crucial point (since we are concerned only with INDEX values here, we omit CONCORD and many other features from the f-structures).

(89) a. Nous partons demain.
1PL leave.PRS.1PL tomorrow
'We are leaving tomorrow.'

b. Jean et moi partons demain.
Jean and 1SG leave.PRS.1PL tomorrow
'Jean and I are leaving tomorrow.'

(90) *partons* V (↑ PRED) = 'LEAVE <SUBJ>'
(↑ SUBJ INDEX PERS) = 1
(↑ SUBJ INDEX NUM) = PL

(91)

$$\left[\begin{array}{ll} \text{PRED} & \text{`LEAVE}<\text{SUBJ}>\text{'} \\ \text{SUBJ} & \left[\begin{array}{l} \text{INDEX} \left[\begin{array}{ll} \text{NUM} & \text{PL} \\ \text{PERS} & 1 \end{array}\right] \\ \left\{\begin{array}{l} \left[\begin{array}{ll} \text{PRED} & \text{`PRO'} \\ \text{INDEX} & \left[\begin{array}{ll} \text{NUM} & \text{SG} \\ \text{PERS} & 1 \end{array}\right] \end{array}\right] \\ \left[\begin{array}{ll} \text{PRED} & \text{`JEAN'} \\ \text{INDEX} & \left[\begin{array}{ll} \text{NUM} & \text{SG} \\ \text{PERS} & 3 \end{array}\right] \end{array}\right] \end{array}\right\} \end{array}\right] \\ \text{ADJ} & \left\{\left[\text{PRED} \quad \text{`TOMORROW'}\right]\right\} \end{array}\right]$$

The issue, then, is how the INDEX for the coordinate structure as a whole is determined, and how it relates to the INDEX features of the individual conjuncts within it. In fact, the relationship between the INDEX of the coordinate structure and those of the conjuncts themselves is systematic and subject to principles or generalisations known as SYNTACTIC RESOLUTION. We will not show here how these are formalised in LFG but will just briefly discuss some of the resolution principles which operate in various languages.

Consider the PERS feature now: (89b) shows that the combination of a first person conjunct with a third person conjunct gives a resolved person value of first person. This is shown by the fact that when we have two coordinated noun phrases, one third person (*Jean*) and the other first person (*moi*), the verb agreement is first person (plural). Thus, when a third person noun phrase is coordinated with a first person noun phrase, the first person value 'wins out' and becomes the person value for the coordinated structure as a whole. In fact, there is a systematic person hierarchy that determines the value of the person feature of the coordinated structure, which holds across many languages. The verb agreement in the French examples in (92) shows us the rest of this hierarchy, namely that: first person wins out over second person (92a) and third person (89b); and second person wins out over third person (92b). When two third person noun phrases are coordinated, naturally the coordinated structure as a whole is third person, as shown in (92c). The hierarchy is therefore 1> 2 > 3, as schematised in (93).

(92) a. Toi et moi partons demain.
2SG and 1SG leave.PRS.1PL tomorrow
'You and I are leaving tomorrow.'

b. Toi et lui partez demain.
2SG and 3SG.M leave.PRS.2PL tomorrow
'You and he are leaving tomorrow.'

c. Jean et Marie partent demain.
Jean and Marie leave.PRS.3PL tomorrow
'Jean and Marie are leaving tomorrow.'

(93) Person Resolution:
1 & 2 = 1
1 & 3 = 1
2 & 3 = 2
3 & 3 = 3

In the same sort of way, a syntactic resolution process governs the values of the gender feature. The following examples show that in French, when the two conjuncts have different genders, one FEM and one MASC, then the INDEX GEND value of the coordinate structure as a whole is MASC; when both conjuncts have the same gender, then there is no mismatch and the gender of the whole coordinate structure is the same as that of the conjuncts. In the first two examples in (94), we can see that the resolved gender, as shown by the adjectival agreement is the same as that of the conjuncts. In (94c), however, the two conjuncts have different genders, but the adjective has MASC agreement. The corresponding f-structure for the coordinated subject in (94c) is given in (95).

(94) a. Josephine et Marie sont intelligentes.
Josephine(F) and Marie(F) be.PRS.3PL intelligent.F.PL
'Josephine and Marie are intelligent.'

b. Louis et Claude sont intelligents.
Louis(M) and Claude(M) be.PRS.3PL intelligent.M.PL
'Louis and Claude are intelligent.'

c. Louis et Marie sont intelligents.
Louis(M) and Marie(F) be.PRS.3PL intelligent.M.PL
'Louis and Marie are intelligent.'

(95)
$$\left[\begin{array}{l} \text{INDEX} \ \left[\text{GEND} \quad \text{MASC}\right] \\ \left\{ \begin{array}{l} \left[\begin{array}{ll} \text{PRED} & \text{`LOUIS'} \\ \text{INDEX} & \left[\text{GEND} \quad \text{MASC}\right] \end{array}\right] \\ \left[\begin{array}{ll} \text{PRED} & \text{`MARIE'} \\ \text{INDEX} & \left[\text{GEND} \quad \text{FEM}\right] \end{array}\right] \end{array} \right\} \end{array}\right]$$

Of course other languages have different resolution principles, and indeed more than two genders. We won't go into the details of how the resolved feature values are calculated in such cases, but see the next section for references to the literature where this is discussed. For our purposes, the important point is that coordinate structures have their own INDEX feature which controls predicate–agreement phenomena, and that the INDEX feature of the coordinate structure is determined from the INDEX features of the conjuncts through systematic resolution principles.

Reading

For a detailed typological discussion of head marking and dependent marking across languages see Nichols (1986), and for more detailed discussion of pronominal incorporation and its development across languages see Givón (1976). For further discussion of pronominal incorporation and agreement within the LFG framework, see Bresnan and Mchombo (1987); Austin and Bresnan (1996); Toivonen (2000) and the discussions in Bresnan et al. (2016), sections 6.3, 6.4 and chapter 8 (although note that the approach discussed in these sections is different in some respects from ours). Issues related to LFG's approach to non-configurationality and the morphological encoding of grammatical relations are also discussed in Dalrymple (2001, pages 125–38 and 275–8).

Dependent marking and non-configurationality in LFG has been discussed in most detail with respect to the Australian non-configurational languages Warlpiri, Jiwarli and Wambaya; see Simpson (1991); Nordlinger (1998); Austin and Bresnan (1996) and Austin (2001). The constructive case approach to case marking in dependent-marking languages was developed in Nordlinger's (1998) analysis of case stacking in Australian languages. Nordlinger (1998) shows how the constructive case approach can provide a straightforward account for a range of complex morphological phenomena in Australian languages that are challenging for other theoretical frameworks, such as multiple case marking (case stacking) and the use of case morphology to encode clausal tense/aspect/mood (TAM).

Interactions between morphology and syntax are discussed in detail by Andrews (1990b) and in a number of papers by Joan Bresnan using the Optimality Theoretic Framework such as Bresnan (2001b) and Bresnan (1998). Nordlinger and Bresnan (2011) provide an introduction to the LFG framework focusing particularly on the interactions between morphology and syntax.

Since LFG is essentially a syntactic framework, it has not traditionally assumed a particular view of the morphology. In fact, given the Principle of Lexical Integrity and the separation assumed between the morphology and the syntax, such that the terminal leaves of the c-structure trees are fully inflected words, LFG is compatible with most theoretical models of the morphological component. Nonetheless, various researchers have put forward proposals as to what it should look like. A number of researchers have proposed a level of m-structure, although the proposals differ in terms of how this structure is integrated with the LFG architecture – see Butt et al. (1996) and Frank and Zaenen (2002) for two such proposals as well as Dalrymple (2001, 178–82) for discussion. In recent work Dalrymple (2015a) has shown how a realisational approach to morphology can be integrated with the LFG architecture. Nordlinger and Sadler (2019) provide an overview of approaches to a range of morphological phenomena in LFG.

Nordlinger and Sadler (2004a) provide a typological overview of tense-aspect-mood (TAM) marking on nominals cross-linguistically, and Nordlinger and Sadler (2004b) show how such facts are accounted for within the LFG framework. The Lardil data presented in Section 4.5 are taken from Klokeid (1976). The analysis of English reduced auxiliaries presented in Section 4.5 is due to an empirical observation by Spencer (1991), and work by Sadler (1998) showing how the framework of LFG can be used to capture Spencer's (1991) insight that *non-syllabic* reduced auxiliaries in English are more appropriately treated as affixes, while the *syllabic* reduced auxiliaries are clitics.

The distinction between two types of agreement as reflected in the INDEX and CONCORD features is well known – a traditional view (see, for example, Corbett 1983) is that this reflects a distinction between morphosyntactic agreement (CONCORD) and agreement based on semantic properties (INDEX). The distinction between two sets of syntactic agreement features is discussed in detail in Wechsler and Zlatić (2000, 2003); King and Dalrymple (2004); Sadler (2016). Bresnan et al. (2016, 187–9) claim that the existence of these two features reflects different diachronic sources of agreement.

While it is generally true that CONCORD features control head–modifier agreement, and INDEX features control predicate–argument agreement, this need not always be the case. Mittendorf and Sadler (2005) provide an analysis of agreement within the Welsh noun phrase that shows that both CONCORD and

INDEX features are relevant for noun–phrase internal agreement in Welsh, in different ways.

The approach to feature resolution presented here is proposed in Dalrymple and Kaplan (2000). As mentioned above, languages differ in the syntactic resolution principles that apply in coordinate structures. For example, Corbett (1983) discusses agreement in Icelandic, which has three genders with different resolution principles from those we saw for French above: MASC agreement only appears if **all** conjuncts are MASC, and FEM agreement is similarly restricted, with NEUT agreement occurring in all other cases. Interestingly, this means that we see NEUT agreement even when there are **no** neuter conjuncts, such as when a MASC noun phrase is coordinated with a FEM noun phrase. See Corbett (1983) for details and examples.

Exercises

4.1 Provide the lexical entry for the Murrinhpatha verb *bamnhingkardu* that accounts for the following examples, and the f-structures for each sentence. Explain how the lexical entry you have given for the verb ensures that the Completeness and Coherence Conditions are satisfied in all cases.

(96)
a. bam-nhi-ngkardu
1SG.SUBJ.NFUT-2SG.OBJ-see
'I saw you.'

b. ngay-ka bam-nhi-ngkardu
1SG-TOP 1SG.SUBJ.NFUT-2SG.OBJ-see
'I saw you.'

c. nhinhi-ka bam-nhi-ngkardu
2SG-TOP 1SG.SUBJ.NFUT-2SG.OBJ-see
'I saw you.'

How does LFG account for the differences between the Murrinhpatha verb in the examples above, and the English verb *saw* in the examples below?

(97)
a. I saw you.
b. *Saw.
c. *I saw.
d. *Saw you.

4.2 What are the f-structures that correspond to the following (hypothetical) lexical entries?

(98)
a. $(\uparrow \text{PRED}) = \text{`CHILD'}$
$(\uparrow \text{NUM}) = \text{SG}$
$(\uparrow \text{CASE}) = \text{NOM}$
$(\text{SUBJ} \uparrow)$

b. (↑ PRED) = 'CHILD'
(↑ NUM) = SG
(↑ POSS GEND) = FEM

c. (↑ PRED) = 'CHILD'
(↑ NUM) = SG
((POSS ↑) GEND) = FEM

d. (↑ PRED) = 'YOUNG'
((ADJ ∈ ↑) GEND) = FEM
((ADJ ∈ ↑) NUM) = SG

4.3 Martuthunira is a Pama-Nyungan language from the Pilbara region of Western Australia. Like many other languages of Australia, it is dependent-marking and makes extensive use of case agreement, although it is different in having a nominative–accusative case system, rather than an ergative–absolutive case system like Jiwarli and Wambaya. The data for this exercise comes from Dench (1995).

Consider the simple Martuthunira sentences in (99) and (100).

(99) Ngayu panyi-lalha kanparr-yu.
1SG.NOM step.on-PST spider-ACC
'I stepped on a spider.' (Dench 1995: 67)

(100) Muyi yanga-lalha tharnta-a.
dog.NOM chase-PST euro-ACC
'The dog chased the euro.' (Dench 1995:68)[1]

Using constructive case as discussed in Section 4.4, provide the lexical entries for the nouns and verbs in these two sentences. Assume that nominals marked for NOM and ACC case construct the SUBJ and OBJ grammatical functions, respectively.

Unlike some of the other Australian languages we have discussed in this chapter, Martuthunira does not have free word order, but has a basic word order of Subject–Verb–Object. For present purposes, let's assume the simple c-structure for basic Martuthunira sentences as given in (101).

(101)	S	⟶	NP	V	NP
			(↑ SUBJ) = ↓	↑ = ↓	(↑ OBJ) = ↓

Using this c-structure rule and your lexical entries from above, provide c-structures and f-structures for (99) and (100) showing how the grammatical function information from the case-marked nominals interacts with that from the c-structure to construct a complete and coherent f-structure.

4.4 Consider the following (modified) examples from Chamicuro (Peru, based on data from Parker (1999)). Provide a lexical entry for each determiner (glossed THE) which accounts for its function and which will allow for an LFG analysis of the examples. Show how your analysis works in LFG by providing c-structures and f-structures for (102b) and (102c).

[1] A euro is a type of macropod (like a kangaroo), also known as a hill wallaroo.

(102) a. I-nis na camálo
3-see THE bat
'He/she sees the bat.'

b. P-askalaht-ís ka camálo
2-kill-2PL THE bat
'You (plural) killed the bat.'

c. I-mak-yeh-kana na wáhni
3-sleep-FUT-PL THE tomorrow
'They are going to sleep tomorrow (lit: the tomorrow).'

d. Y-alíyo ka ké:ni
3-fall THE rain
'It rained (lit: the rain fell).'

4.5 Provide f-structures for the French examples in (92b) and (92c) above and provide f-structures and c-structures for the following English examples:

(103) Peter and Mary saw me.

(104) Peter and I saw Mary.

(105) Mary saw Peter and me.

5 Complementation and Predication

5.1 Clauses as Complements

Predicates of different kinds can take clauses as their complements. We illustrate this in (1), where the *that*-clause is the complement of a verb in (1a), of the adjective *afraid* in (1b) and of the noun *fact* in (1c).

(1) a. Oscar [thinks [that Sarah likes musicals]].
b. John was [afraid [that Sarah would like musicals]].
c. The [fact [that Sarah likes musicals]] is an issue for Oscar.

In Section 2.2, we said that these clausal complements have the function COMP, and in Section 2.3.2, we argued that they are of the c-structure category CP. In this chapter we will take a closer look at clausal complementation, focusing on complements of verbs. Although we don't discuss complements of adjectives and nouns in any detail here, the analysis we present for verbal complements can be extended to these other complement types.Verbs that take clausal complements are referred to as MATRIX VERBS.

The example in (1a) involves a finite declarative complement clause. In English, a finite verb is one which can inflect for present or past tense; other languages may have more extended inflectional systems. The subclause in (1a) is finite because *likes* is present tense and could have been past tense, *liked*. DECLARATIVE is a clause type which is associated with a statement, and it contrasts with INTERROGATIVE, which is associated with a question. In (2a), we provide an example of a finite interrogative complement clause and in (2b) of a non-finite declarative complement clause.

(2) a. Ingrid enquired [whether Fred liked musicals].
b. Oscar arranged [for Sarah to see the abbey].

The subordinate clauses in (1) and (2) (indicated by the square brackets) all contain a COMPLEMENTISER – *that*, *whether* and *for* – respectively – which fills the C position of the CP. This CP is the c-structure complement of the matrix verb in all examples in (1) and (2), much like a DP object would be. In (3a), we provide the c-structure tree for (1a), but the structure would be the same for the example in (2a). The structure for (2b) is provided in (3b).

(3) a.

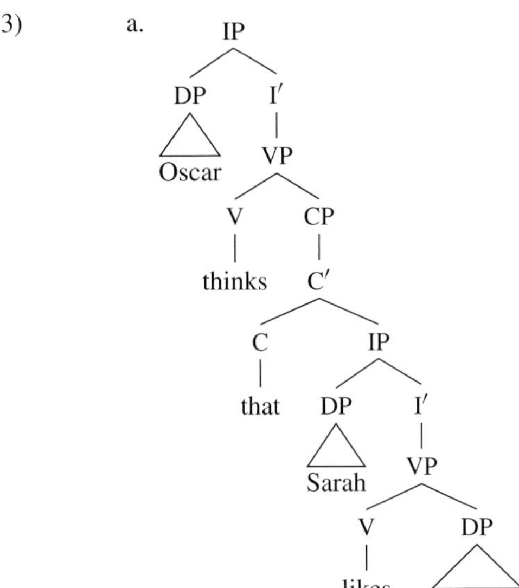

b.

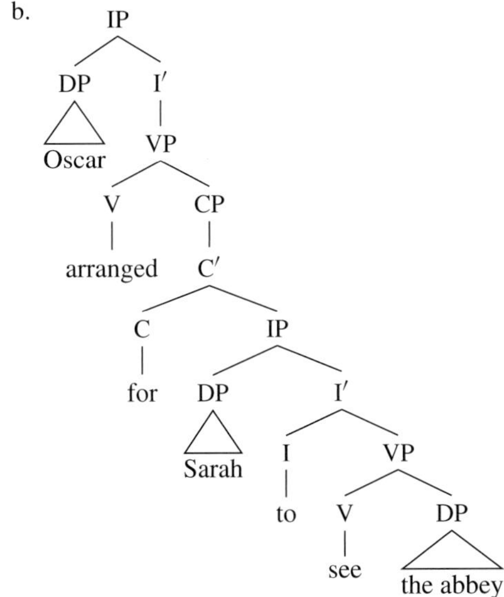

The verbs *think*, *enquire* and *arrange* then subcategorise for a SUBJ and a COMP, giving the PRED values in (4).

(4)
a. *thinks* V (↑ PRED) = 'THINK <SUBJ, COMP>'
b. *enquired* V (↑ PRED) = 'ENQUIRE <SUBJ, COMP>'
c. *arranged* V (↑ PRED) = 'ARRANGE <SUBJ, COMP>'

For a full analysis of these verbs, we need to add information relating to finiteness and clause type to the verb's lexical entry. In (1a), *thinks* combines with a finite declarative clause; as (5a) shows, it cannot combine with a non-finite complement clause. In (2a) *enquired* selects a finite interrogative complement, and cannot combine with a finite declarative complement as illustrated in (5b). Similarly, in (2b), *arranged* takes a non-finite declarative complement clause, and as (5c) shows, it cannot combine with an interrogative non-finite clause.

(5)
a. *Oscar thinks for Sarah to like musicals.
b. *Ingrid enquired that Fred liked musicals.
c. *Oscar arranged whether Sarah to see the abbey.

In order to capture these restrictions, we can introduce a clause-type feature, CLTYPE, with the values DECLarative and INTERrogative, and a VFORM feature with values FINite and INFinitive. The feature TENSE is dependent on VFORM having the value FIN. Both CLTYPE and VFORM can have other values, but these are the only relevant values for these examples. The lexical entries need to contain constraints on the features of COMP, so that we can expand the lexical entries in (4) to give the f-descriptions (6)–(8).

(6)
$(\uparrow \text{PRED}) = \text{`THINK}\langle\text{SUBJ, COMP}\rangle\text{'}$
$(\uparrow \text{COMP CLTYPE}) = \text{DECL}$
$(\uparrow \text{COMP VFORM}) =_c \text{FIN}$

(7)
$(\uparrow \text{PRED}) = \text{`ENQUIRE}\langle\text{SUBJ, COMP}\rangle\text{'}$
$(\uparrow \text{COMP CLTYPE}) =_c \text{INTER}$
$(\uparrow \text{COMP VFORM}) =_c \text{FIN}$

(8)
$(\uparrow \text{PRED}) = \text{`ARRANGE}\langle\text{SUBJ, COMP}\rangle\text{'}$
$(\uparrow \text{COMP CLTYPE}) = \text{DECL}$
$(\uparrow \text{COMP VFORM}) =_c \text{INF}$

In order to generate the trees in (3), we need to add a further category to the right-hand side of the phrase-structure rule for a VP in English, which we provided in (6b) in Section 3.1 and expanded with PP in (38b) in Section 3.3. Indeed we will see that this rule needs to be expanded further, and we will provide further categories to be included on the right-hand side of this rule in (15) and (63b). With annotations, this addition gives (9) – recall that we interpret everything on the right-hand side of a phrase-structure rule as optional, but omit the optionality brackets as a simplifying convention. Of course there is no verb in English which can combine with all these complements at the same time, but the rule expanding VP allows for all of these possibilities. The PRED feature of the verb, combined with the well-formedness conditions, the Completeness Condition and the Coherence Condition, will ensure that the only constituents present in a given VP are those licensed by the predicate.

(9)
$$\begin{array}{llllll} \text{VP} \longrightarrow & \text{V} & \text{DP} & \text{DP} & \text{PP} & \text{CP} \\ & \uparrow = \downarrow & (\uparrow \text{OBJ}) = \downarrow & (\uparrow \text{OBJ}_\theta) = \downarrow & (\uparrow (\downarrow \text{PCASE})) = \text{OBL}_\theta & (\uparrow \text{COMP}) = \downarrow \end{array}$$

The f-structures of (1a) and (2b) are shown in (10) and (11), respectively. Here we have included CLTYPE and VFORM for both clauses, but in what follows, we will generally use simplified f-structures without some of these features.

(10)

$$\begin{bmatrix} \text{PRED} & \text{‘THINK<SUBJ, COMP>’} \\ \text{CLTYPE} & \text{DECL} \\ \text{VFORM} & \text{FIN} \\ \text{TENSE} & \text{PRES} \\ \text{SUBJ} & \begin{bmatrix} \text{PRED} & \text{‘OSCAR’} \end{bmatrix} \\ \text{COMP} & \begin{bmatrix} \text{PRED} & \text{‘LIKE <SUBJ, OBJ>’} \\ \text{CLTYPE} & \text{DECL} \\ \text{VFORM} & \text{FIN} \\ \text{TENSE} & \text{PRES} \\ \text{SUBJ} & \begin{bmatrix} \text{PRED} & \text{‘SARAH’} \end{bmatrix} \\ \text{OBJ} & \begin{bmatrix} \text{PRED} & \text{‘MUSICAL’} \\ \text{INDEX} & \begin{bmatrix} \text{NUM} & \text{PL} \end{bmatrix} \end{bmatrix} \end{bmatrix} \end{bmatrix}$$

(11)

$$\begin{bmatrix} \text{PRED} & \text{‘ARRANGE<SUBJ, COMP>’} \\ \text{CLTYPE} & \text{DECL} \\ \text{VFORM} & \text{FIN} \\ \text{TENSE} & \text{PAST} \\ \text{SUBJ} & \begin{bmatrix} \text{PRED} & \text{‘OSCAR’} \end{bmatrix} \\ \text{COMP} & \begin{bmatrix} \text{PRED} & \text{‘SEE <SUBJ, OBJ>’} \\ \text{CLTYPE} & \text{DECL} \\ \text{VFORM} & \text{INF} \\ \text{SUBJ} & \begin{bmatrix} \text{PRED} & \text{‘SARAH’} \end{bmatrix} \\ \text{OBJ} & \begin{bmatrix} \text{PRED} & \text{‘ABBEY’} \\ \text{INDEX} & \begin{bmatrix} \text{NUM} & \text{SG} \end{bmatrix} \\ \text{DEF} & + \end{bmatrix} \end{bmatrix} \end{bmatrix}$$

Notice that a verb like *arrange* may also take a complement which does not contain an overtly expressed subject, as in (12b).

(12) a. Oscar arranged [for Sarah to visit the abbey].

b. Oscar arranged [to visit the abbey].

Subject-less subordinate clauses of the type illustrated in (12b) are referred to as CONTROL complements because the interpretation of the subject missing in the c-structure is "controlled" by an element in the matrix clause, in this case *Oscar*. Control complements are common cross-linguistically, but we will start here by illustrating with English sentences. We will return to the c-structure and f-structure of the specific type of control illustrated in (12b) in Section 5.3.

5.2 Functional Control and XCOMP

5.2.1 Subject Control

We will now consider in some detail two types of control constructions illustrated in (13) with the English verbs *try* and *seem*.

(13) a. Ingrid tried [to buy olives].
b. Oscar seemed [to like olives].

In these cases, the bracketed material is the c-structure complement of the finite verbs *tried* and *seemed* respectively. One question is whether the c-structure category of the bracketed material is a CP, as in (3) above, or some other phrasal category. The subordinate clause is non-finite, and it cannot contain a complementiser in these cases, as shown in (14) – or indeed any of the other elements associated with a CP projection that we will introduce in Chapter 6.

(14) a. *Ingrid tried [for (Oscar) to buy olives].
b. *Oscar seemed [for (Ingrid) to like olives].

We will assume then that the complements of *seem* and *try* in (13) are not of the category CP and differ in this respect from the complements of verbs like *think* or *ask*. In Section 2.3.2, we argued that the infinitival *to* is of category I, and since the complements in (13) contain *to*, we will assume that they are of the category IP, even though there is no subject in the specifier of IP. This means that, in English at least, we need to allow for the possibility that verbs can take IPs as complements, not just DPs, PPs and CPs. Therefore, the VP rule in (9) needs to be expanded further as in (15). In order to fit it onto the page, we have used … to replace some of the categories found in (9). The crucial point is that we have added the category IP.

(15)
$$\text{VP} \longrightarrow \underset{\uparrow=\downarrow}{\text{V}} \quad \underset{(\uparrow\,\text{OBJ})=\downarrow}{\text{DP}} \quad \ldots \quad \underset{(\uparrow\,\text{COMP})=\downarrow}{\text{CP}} \quad \underset{(\uparrow\,\text{XCOMP})=\downarrow}{\text{IP}}$$

The absence of a subject in the c-structure of the complements in (13) is puzzling since the PRED features for *buy* and *like* require a SUBJ and an OBJ. Hence the f-structure associated with the subordinate clauses in (13) might be expected to be ruled out by the Completeness Condition; *buy* and *like* require a SUBJ, but do not have an overtly expressed subject in (13). However, these sentences are obviously grammatical, and we can find a referent for the SUBJ of the complement clause; the non-finite complements are interpreted as being predicated of the SUBJ of the whole sentence, i.e. the subject of *to buy* and *to like olives* is understood as *Ingrid* and *Oscar*, respectively.

The clausal complements in (13) are then OPEN in the sense that the SUBJ function is left open, to be "filled in" by something outside the non-finite clause itself. In Section 2.2, we referred to such open complements as XCOMP. So the verb *try* takes a SUBJ and an XCOMP and also establishes that its SUBJ is to be understood as the SUBJ of the XCOMP. Though the relationship between *seem* and its complement appears to be identical to that between *try* and its complement, there are crucial differences, and we will return to *seem* once we have looked at *try* in a little more detail.

The lexical entry for *try* then specifies the equations shown in (16). To keep the main point clear, we ignore CLTYPE and VFORM features in these lexical entries. This lexical entry contains a type of equation (in the second line) we have not yet encountered, called a FUNCTIONAL CONTROL EQUATION, which states that the SUBJ of *try* is also the SUBJ of the XCOMP of *try*.

(16) *try* V (↑ PRED) = 'TRY<SUBJ, XCOMP>'
(↑ SUBJ) = (↑ XCOMP SUBJ)

Informally, the control equation in (16) states that 'the f-structure of my mother's SUBJ is the same as that of my mother's XCOMP's SUBJ'. Since these structures are defined to be the same, the two attributes – the SUBJ and the XCOMP SUBJ – share the same value, a specific f-structure (in this case the one for *Ingrid*). This sharing is referred to as STRUCTURE SHARING, and it is indicated in an f-structure by a line between the shared structures. This is illustrated for (13a) in (17), where we have named some of the f-structures to make it easier to refer to them.

(17)

$$f:\left[\begin{array}{ll} \text{PRED} & \text{`TRY <SUBJ, XCOMP>'} \\ \text{TENSE} & \text{PAST} \\ \text{SUBJ} & g:\left[\text{PRED}\quad \text{`INGRID'}\right] \\ \text{XCOMP} & \left[\begin{array}{ll} \text{PRED} & \text{`BUY <SUBJ, OBJ>'} \\ \text{SUBJ} & \rule{3cm}{0.4pt} \\ \text{OBJ} & \left[\begin{array}{ll}\text{PRED} & \text{`OLIVE'} \\ \text{INDEX} & \left[\text{NUM}\quad \text{PL}\right]\end{array}\right]\end{array}\right]\end{array}\right]$$

It is important to understand that in a structure such as this, the f-structure *g* is shared – it is both the value of *f* SUBJ and *f* XCOMP SUBJ. This means that any f-structure information contributed about either the matrix SUBJ or the SUBJ of the complement clause holds of both, for example if the matrix SUBJ is the subject of a verb which gives it the feature value CASE = ACC, then this will also hold of the XCOMP SUBJ. We will see some examples of this in Icelandic in Section 5.4.

Coherence and Completeness are satisfied in (17) – every governable grammatical function in the f-structure is required by the PRED of the f-structure in which it appears, and every grammatical function required by the PRED of a predicate – *try* and *buy* – is present in the f-structure and has a PRED value. The SUBJ of the XCOMP is then present in the f-structure, but absent in the c-structure.

Anticipating our discussion of *seem* shortly, we want to point to a few of *try*'s properties. The SUBJ of *try* is on its list of arguments, as indicated by the fact that it occurs within the angle brackets in the PRED value. A predicate can place selectional restrictions on its arguments by requiring that the argument has a particular θ-role. We will return to the mapping between a-structure and f-structure in Chapter 8, but here we need to know that the SUBJ of *try* has to be an Agent, capable of 'trying'. For this reason, a sentence such as (18) sounds odd, unless it occurs in what we may refer to as a "Disney context" with a cartoon stone. When a sentence is not ungrammatical, but rather infelicitous, just plain odd, if you like, then we mark it with # rather than *.

(18) #The stone tried to move.

In order to assess whether a particular function has a θ-role, we can use expletives, which we introduced in Section 2.2 in connection with the definitions of Coherence and Completeness. These are elements that are semantically empty and incapable of having a θ-role. In English there are two expletives: *it* and *there* as illustrated in (19).

(19) a. It is snowing.
b. There is a man in the wardrobe.

It follows from the fact that *try* assigns a θ-role to its SUBJ that these expletive elements cannot be the subject of verbs like *try*, and indeed, examples such as (20) are ungrammatical. Again, (20a) may possibly be acceptable in a "Disney reading", if we imagine a cloud trying to snow, but then we would have a referential (i.e. non-expletive) *it*, referring to the cloud. (Some speakers can use a sentence like (20a), and, for them, this might involve treating the weather as an autonomous agent, or it may be some sort of special collocation. If you are such a speaker, see if you can use *it is misty* or *it thundered loudly* instead of *it is snowing* to get the same grammaticality judgements in all the examples that follow.)

(20) a. *It tried to snow.
b. *There tried to be a man in the wardrobe.

A second important point to note is that it is never possible to have a subject present in the c-structure of the infinitival complement of *try* – that is, functional control for this class of predicates is obligatory. This means that a sentence such as (21) is completely ungrammatical.

(21) *Ingrid tried [(for) Oscar to like olives].

Verbs like *try* have traditionally been called EQUI verbs in the literature – the term comes from the idea that there are "underlyingly" two instances of 'Ingrid' in the sentence "Ingrid tried Ingrid to like olives", and one of them gets deleted because they are equivalent. However, in the LFG analysis outlined above, these verbs are treated as FUNCTIONAL CONTROL PREDICATES. The key property of such predicates is that their lexical description contains a control equation as shown in (16). This equation ensures that the SUBJ of the matrix verb and the SUBJ of the complement share the same f-structure. Other predicates in this class in English include verbs such as *manage* and *refuse*, but also adjectives such as *ready* and *eager* in sentences like (22).

(22) a. Oscar is ready to give up.
b. Oscar is eager to see the musical.

We are now in a position to consider *seem*, and we return to the sentence in (13b), repeated here as (23).

(23) Oscar seemed [to like olives].

Oscar is an argument of the lower verb *like* in (23), just like *Ingrid* is an argument of *buy* in (13a), and we will show that like *tried* in (13a), *seemed* in (23) involves functional control. However, despite their superficial similarity, there is a key difference between the two sentences in (13). We saw that *try* puts restrictions on its subject; it must be capable of trying, and hence (18) was infelicitous. With *seem* things are different; *seem* does not put restrictions on its subject, as the contrast between (24) and (18) illustrates.

(24) The stone seemed to move.

The subject of *seem* does not have a semantic role with respect to *seem*; whereas Ingrid does some 'trying' in (13a), we cannot really say that Oscar does some 'seeming' in (23). Further evidence that the subject of *seem* is not an argument of the verb, and hence that *seem* does not assign a θ-role to its subject, comes from examples such as (25), where the subject of *seem* is an expletive. This can be compared with the behaviour of *try* in (20).

(25) a. It seems to be snowing.
b. There seems to be a man in the wardrobe.

The construction in (13b) is traditionally referred to as SUBJECT TO SUBJECT RAISING, since it looks as if *Oscar* has been "raised" from the position in the lower clause, where it gets its θ-role, to the higher clause, where it does not have any separate θ-role in relation to *seem*. However, in LFG, as we will see, nothing has been raised. Rather, verbs like *seem* just illustrate another type of functional control construction where the main verb does not assign a θ-role to its subject (see Chapter 8 for further discussion). The semantic relationship involved can be described as a predicate 'seem' holding over a proposition 'Oscar to like olives'. In connection with this, notice that an alternative to (23) is (26), where the lower clause is a finite clause which clearly forms a unit, and the subject position of *seems* is filled by an expletive.

(26) It seems that Oscar likes olives.

In summary, the empirical observations made in this section indicate that the "raised" subject of verbs like *seem* in (13b) is an argument of the embedded predicate, and hence must satisfy any syntactic or semantic constraints placed by that predicate, but is not a semantic argument of *seem*. Another verb that behaves in the same way is *appear*, as do adjectives such as *likely* and *certain* in (27). Here, *likely* and *certain* are predicated over the propositions 'Fred to buy olives' and 'Ingrid to like olives', respectively.

(27) a. Fred is likely to buy olives.
b. Ingrid is certain to like olives.

The functions inside the angle brackets in a PRED value are the arguments of the predicate, so since the SUBJ of a raising verb like *seem* is not an argument of the verb, it is placed outside the brackets in the PRED value. The lexical entry for *seem* in (13b) is provided in (28).

(28) *seem* V (↑ PRED) = ‘SEEM<XCOMP> SUBJ’
(↑ SUBJ) = (↑XCOMP SUBJ)

The f-structure for (13b) is provided in (29), which should be compared with (17).

(29)

$$\begin{bmatrix} \text{PRED} & \text{‘SEEM <XCOMP> SUBJ’} \\ \text{TENSE} & \text{PAST} \\ \text{SUBJ} & \begin{bmatrix} \text{PRED} & \text{‘OSCAR’} \end{bmatrix} \\ \text{XCOMP} & \begin{bmatrix} \text{PRED} & \text{‘LIKE <SUBJ, OBJ>’} \\ \text{SUBJ} & \text{———} \\ \text{OBJ} & \begin{bmatrix} \text{PRED} & \text{‘OLIVE’} \\ \text{INDEX} & \begin{bmatrix} \text{NUM} & \text{PL} \end{bmatrix} \end{bmatrix} \end{bmatrix} \end{bmatrix}$$

Completeness and Coherence are satisfied as follows. Every governable grammatical function which is specified in the argument list of a PRED feature is present in the local f-structure, satisfying Completeness. The Coherence Condition is also satisfied, since every PRED-bearing, that is, non-expletive, function is an argument of the local predicate. The fact that *Oscar* is not an argument of *seem* does not cause a violation of Coherence, since it is an argument of *like* in the lower clause.

The infinitival clause that forms the complement of *seem* is of the category IP and has the function XCOMP, just like the complement of *try*, and the c-structure tree for the two sentences in (13) is the same, as shown in (30).

(30)

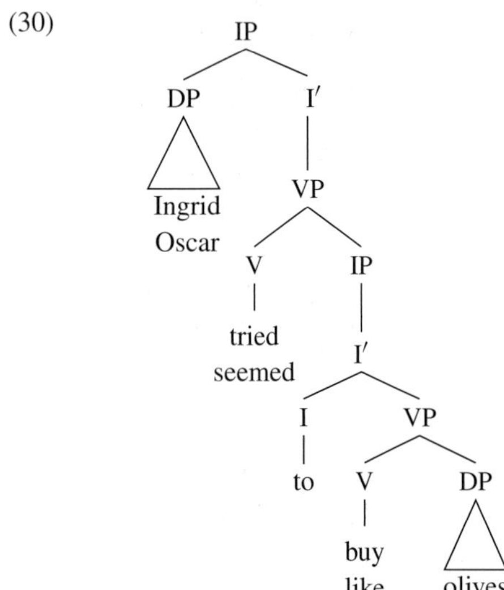

The difference between the two types of verb then lies in the fact that in one case (*try*) the SUBJ of the sentence is an argument of the matrix verb, but in the other case (*seem*) it is not. In both cases a functional control equation links the SUBJ of the lower clause with that of the matrix clause. We return later to the PRED value for examples such as (26), where the complement of *seem* is a finite clause.

Returning now to the properties of *seem*, because it does not subcategorise for a thematic subject, *seem* can take a range of expletive subjects provided the requirements of the embedded predicate are satisfied. As long as the verb of the complement can combine with an expletive SUBJ, *seem* can have an expletive SUBJ. This was illustrated in (25). We will use (25a) to illustrate how Completeness and Coherence are satisfied in this case. The verb *snow*, and other so-called meteorological verbs, do not take any arguments, so they have an empty list between the angle brackets in their PRED value. These verbs do require a SUBJ, but that is a non-argument, and so occurs outside the brackets. This gives the lexical entry in (31). Since there are two different expletive subjects in English, and *snow* can only occur with one of them, we can assume an explicit feature SUBJ FORM. There may be a more principled way of accounting for the difference between the two expletives, but this is not our concern here.

(31) *snow* V ($\uparrow$ PRED) = 'SNOW< > SUBJ'
($\uparrow$ SUBJ FORM) $=_c$ IT

For a simple sentence like (32a), this gives us the f-structure in (32b).

(32) a. It snowed.

b. [PRED 'SNOW < > SUBJ'
TENSE PAST
SUBJ [FORM IT]]

Remember from the definitions of Completeness and Coherence in Section 2.2 that only grammatical functions which are assigned a θ-role require a PRED feature, and only those grammatical functions which have a PRED feature have to be assigned a θ-role. The predicate *snow* has no element in its argument list, and hence does not assign any θ-roles. The SUBJ lacks a PRED feature in (32b), but this does not violate Completeness since *snow* does not assign a θ-role to it. Similarly (32b) is coherent because the SUBJ required by *snow* is not an argument of any predicate, hence is not assigned a θ-role and so is not required to have a PRED feature.

We turn now to an example with *seem* such as (33a), and the associated f-structure in (33b).

(33) a. It seemed to snow.

b.

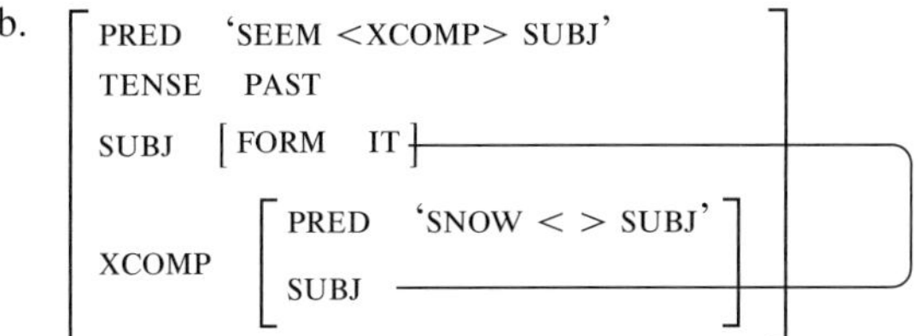

Since neither *seem* nor *snow* assigns a θ-role to their subjects, the fact that the shared SUBJ lacks a PRED feature does not cause a violation of either Completeness or Coherence.

Before leaving this discussion, we need to return to (26), repeated here as (34a). This use of *seem* has a different PRED value. It is still the case that 'seem' takes only one argument in (34a), but it is a finite clause that contains a subject, and hence it is not an XCOMP, but a COMP. The subject is not an argument of 'seem', so is not assigned a θ-role, and is therefore outside the angle brackets. As in the use with a non-finite complement, the non-thematic subject is required to be *it*, rather than *there*. This gives the lexical entry in (34b).

(34) a. It seems that Oscar likes olives.

b. *seem* V (↑ PRED) = 'SEEM <COMP> SUBJ'
(↑ SUBJ FORM) $=_c$ IT

In this section we have introduced the notion of functional control and shown how it can account for clausal complements with "missing" subjects. Functional control predicates like *seem* and *try* select an XCOMP and share their SUBJ with the SUBJ of the XCOMP in the f-structure. The SUBJ of the complement is then missing only at c-structure. We saw that functional control in English involves two different types of predicate – those that assign a thematic role to their subject, and those that do not. A number of important differences in the behaviour of these two types of predicate follows from whether or not they assign a θ-role to their subject: predicates like *try* do, but predicates like *seem* do not. The lexical entries of predicates of both types introduce what we call a functional control equation specifying structure-sharing between the matrix and embedded SUBJ: (↑ SUBJ) = (↑ XCOMP SUBJ). The embedded subject is therefore interpreted as referentially identical to the subject of the controlling predicate.

In the next section, we will turn to cases in which "missing subjects" in subordinate clauses are controlled by a non-subject argument of the matrix predicate – cases of what we will call OBJECT FUNCTIONAL CONTROL. Eventually we will see that there are two classes of object control predicates, which correspond to the two classes of subject control predicates discussed above.

5.2.2 Object Control

Here we will consider the superficially very similar examples in (35).

(35) a. Oscar persuaded **Sarah** to move.

b. Oscar expected **Sarah** to move.

Starting with verbs such as *persuade* in (35a), we need to establish what the role is of the noun phrase in boldface. In principle, it could be the OBJ of the matrix verb or it could be the SUBJ of the non-finite clause. That is, in principle the structure of (35a) could be as in (36a) or as in (36b).

(36) a. Oscar persuaded [Sarah] [to move].

b. Oscar persuaded [Sarah to move].

How would we be able to tell? Well, we can ask whether there is evidence that the noun phrase in bold fills a θ-role with respect to the matrix verb. If it does, then we know that it is a semantic argument of the matrix verb, and hence a syntactic argument of the matrix verb, in this case, an OBJ. The meaning of *persuade* is such that it requires a participant that does the persuading, one that is persuaded and then a course of action or a proposition of which the persuaded participant becomes persuaded – semantically, it is a three-place predicate. This means that there need to be two noun phrases, one to represent the persuader and one the "persuadee", as well as a clausal argument to represent the action or proposition. In (35a) *Sarah* fills the role of "persuadee"; if (35a) is true, then it is also true that 'Oscar persuaded Sarah'.

(37) a. Oscar persuaded Sarah to move. *entails*
b. Oscar persuaded Sarah.

This means that we can conclude that *Sarah* in (35a) is an argument of *persuaded* and is assigned a θ-role by it.

Since the verb *persuade* assigns a θ-role to the OBJ, it can put restrictions on it, it must for instance be an entity that is capable of being persuaded – and of resisting such persuasion. Hence sentences such as (38) are anomalous or at least require a very specific context.

(38) #Kevin persuaded the building to collapse.

Another relevant observation is that verbs such as *persuade* also allow finite complement clauses, and in such examples the object is equally obligatory as a separate argument, as shown in (39a). Moreover they also permit an alternative three-argument frame in which the 'content' of the persuasion is represented not by a clause but by a PP, as in (39b). All these examples make it clear that semantically, *persuade* requires three participants, supporting our conclusion that *Sarah* in (35a) is an argument of *persuade*.

(39) a. Oscar persuaded Sarah that she should move.
b. Oscar persuaded Sarah of the truth of this unhappy fact.

The arguments we have used so far have indicated that the DP *Sarah* that immediately follows *persuade* in (35a) is an argument of the verb. This means that it must be an OBJ. There is in fact further evidence from passivisation to indicate that the postverbal DP is the OBJ. Like other objects of active clauses, the object of *persuade* may be the subject of a corresponding passive clause, as shown in (40), which is the passive version of (35a), in which *Sarah* is now the subject.

(40) Sarah was persuaded to move (by Oscar).

From the fact that the postverbal DP is an argument of *persuade* in (35a) it follows that the verb assigns a θ-role to that DP. As in Section 5.2.1, we can use the non-thematic (i.e. expletive) pronouns *it* and *there* to test this. If the postverbal DP is assigned a θ-role, these two elements should not be able to occur in this position. The examples in (41) show that this is indeed the case, with the caveat about "Disney readings" as before.

(41) a. *Ingrid persuaded it to snow.
 b. *Oscar persuaded there to be a man in the wardrobe.

All in all, we have strong evidence to conclude that *persuade* has three semantic arguments, and that in the use exemplified in (35a), their f-structure functions are SUBJ, OBJ and XCOMP respectively. It is also clear that the SUBJ of the subordinate non-finite clause is interpreted as identical to the OBJ of *persuade* since in (35a), it is *Sarah* who moves. *Sarah* is then an argument of the verb *move* and the SUBJ of the lower clause. These facts are captured in the lexical entry of the verb, as shown in (42), which involves a control equation of the type we saw in Section 5.2.1.

(42) *persuade* V (↑ PRED) = ‘PERSUADE<SUBJ, OBJ, XCOMP>’
 (↑ OBJ) = (↑ XCOMP SUBJ)

(43) shows the f-structure which will arise for (35a) from (42) (and other relevant f-descriptions).

(43)

$$\begin{bmatrix} \text{PRED} & \text{‘PERSUADE <SUBJ, OBJ, XCOMP>’} \\ \text{TENSE} & \text{PAST} \\ \text{SUBJ} & \begin{bmatrix}\text{PRED} & \text{‘OSCAR’}\end{bmatrix} \\ \text{OBJ} & \begin{bmatrix}\text{PRED} & \text{‘SARAH’}\end{bmatrix} \\ \text{XCOMP} & \begin{bmatrix}\text{PRED} & \text{‘MOVE <SUBJ>’} \\ \text{SUBJ} & \text{———} \end{bmatrix}\end{bmatrix}$$

Of course, because *persuade* also permits a finite complement, as in (39a), it will also have an alternative lexical description, as shown in (44). Since functional control is not involved in this construction, there is no control equation in the lexical entry.

(44) *persuade* V (↑ PRED) = ‘PERSUADE <SUBJ, OBJ, COMP>’

We are now in a position to consider more closely an example like (35b), repeated as (45).

(45) Oscar expected Sarah to move.

Though superficially identical to the sentences with *persuade* that we have just discussed, we will see that there are a number of crucial differences between constructions with *persuade* and those with *expect*, and that a different analysis is called for.

When we considered *persuade*, we used passivisation as evidence of object status in the active sentence, and as (46) shows, this applies also to *expect*.

(46) Sarah was expected to move.

The grammaticality of (46) indicates that the postverbal DP in (45) is indeed the OBJ of the matrix verb in the active example, but this does not necessarily mean that it is an argument of the verb; it could be a non-thematic OBJ, similar to the non-thematic SUBJ of *seem*. To establish this, we can use the same test that we applied to *persuade*. We argued that the use with a finite clause in (39a) showed that *persuade* takes three semantic arguments. If we compare this with (47), we can conclude that *expect* only needs two semantic arguments, in this case the subject argument and the finite clausal complement. Semantically, *expect* just needs someone to do the expecting and a situation that is expected.

(47) Oscar expected that Sarah would move.

From this, it follows that *Sarah* is not an argument of *expect* in (45), so that the entailment that we saw for *persuade* in (37) does not hold for *expect*.

(48) a. Oscar expected Sarah to move. *does not entail*
b. Oscar expected Sarah.

Furthermore, we can use the non-thematic pronouns *it* and *there* and compare the outcome for *expect* with that of *persuade* in (41). As (49) shows, this gives two perfectly acceptable sentences, which indicates that the OBJ of *expect* is indeed not a thematic argument of *expect*.

(49) a. Ingrid expected it to snow.
b. Oscar expected there to be a man in the wardrobe.

If our conclusion is that the OBJ of *expect* is not an argument of the verb, it also holds that the OBJ is not assigned a θ-role by that verb and hence *expect* cannot place any restrictions on the OBJ, the way we saw that *persuade* does in (38). Again, our predictions turn out to be correct as illustrated by (50).

(50) Kevin expected the building to collapse.

We conclude then that *expect* in (45) takes a non-thematic object and a non-finite open complement. The "missing subject" of the embedded clause is interpreted as referentially identical to the object of *expect*. The lexical entry of the verb therefore contains the functional description in (51).

(51) *expect* V (↑ PRED) = 'EXPECT <SUBJ, XCOMP> OBJ'
(↑ OBJ) = (↑ XCOMP SUBJ)

This specifies that the verb has two thematic arguments, placed inside the angled brackets, which correspond to the SUBJ and XCOMP grammatical functions, and a non-thematic OBJ, outside the angled brackets. A functional control equation specifies that the OBJ and the XCOMP SUBJ are one and the same f-structure. The f-structure which results for example (45) is shown in (52).

(52)

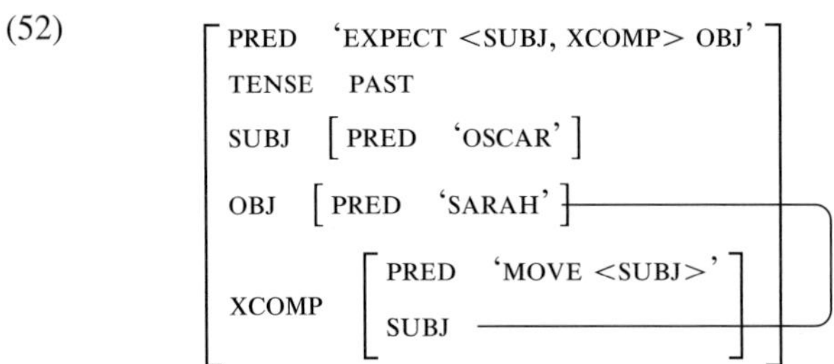

As in the case of the pair of examples of subject control which we compared to each other in Section 5.2.1, the c-structure for the two sentences in (35) is identical, and is provided in (53). The distinction between the two sentences lies in whether or not the matrix verb assigns a θ-role to the OBJ, and all the differences we have seen between the two sentences follow from this.

(53)

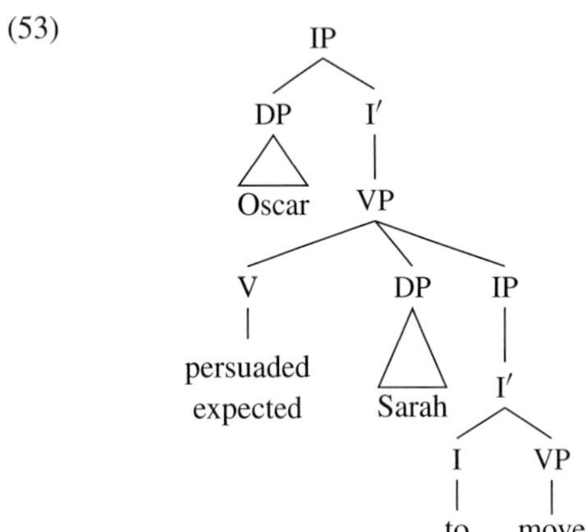

A consequence of the differences between *persuade* and *expect* can be seen when we passivise the lower clause. Compare the pairs of sentences in (54) and (55), where the lower clause has been passivised in the (b) examples and the OBJ of the matrix verb is in bold.

(54) a. Kevin persuaded **the doctor** to examine Eve.
b. Kevin persuaded **Eve** to be examined by the doctor.

(55) a. Kevin expected **the doctor** to examine Eve.
b. Kevin expected **Eve** to be examined by the doctor.

In (54), the meaning has changed between the two; in the active example, Kevin is exercising persuasion on the doctor, whereas in the second he is trying to influence Eve, though the situation Kevin is trying to bring about through persuasion is the same; that of 'the doctor to examine Eve'. This meaning difference follows because the object **is** a thematic argument of the matrix verb. This contrasts with the pair in (55), where Kevin's relation to the doctor and Eve has not changed between the (a) and the (b) sentences, nor has his expectation. This is because in this pair of sentences the object is not an argument of the matrix verb, is not assigned a θ-role by it and hence does not have a direct semantic relation with the verb.

5.2.3 The Category–Function Correspondence and XCOMP

So far, the c-structure category of the function XCOMP has always been IP, specifically a non-finite IP. In English, verbal XCOMPs will always be non-finite, but this is not the case for all languages. However, even in English, the open complement grammatical function XCOMP may correspond to a wide range of different c-structure categories. This is unlike COMP, which is generally thought to be restricted to clausal arguments (that is, arguments headed by verbs). Consider the example in (56a). This is what is known as a RESULTATIVE construction; if this sentence is true, then the wall **is** red and that is as a result of Khaled's painting activity. In this example, *the wall* is an OBJ of the verb *paint*, as indicated by the grammaticality of the passive version in (56b).

(56) a. Khaled painted the wall red.
b. The wall was painted red (by Khaled).

The adjective phrase *red* in (56a) is known as a SECONDARY PREDICATION. It provides information about the OBJ of the matrix verb (*the wall*), while itself occurring as a constituent part of the matrix sentence. We can assume that adjectives like *red* take a SUBJ, since the adjective needs to predicate over something (here *the wall*). This means that the lexical entry contains the information shown in (57).

(57) *red* A (↑ PRED) = 'RED <SUBJ>'

So, we have now seen that in (56a), *the wall* is an OBJ in the matrix clause, *red* needs a SUBJ at f-structure, and that *the wall* serves as the SUBJ of *red*. In LFG secondary predicates like those in (56) are analysed as control constructions. We can assume that there is a resultative use of *paint* (as well as the use where *paint* combines with just an OBJ, as in *paint the house*), with the lexical entry in (58a), which involves a control equation. This conversion of a verb to a resultative construction is not unique to *paint*, but is an example of a systematic alternation that can apply to verbs of an appropriate kind. We will return to a discussion of resultatives in Section 8.4. This analysis of (56a) gives the f-structure in (58b). Since the secondary predicate is an adjective phrase, the associated c-structure tree is (59), where the XCOMP has the category AP. In order to make the category–function correspondence clear, we have included the annotations in the tree.

(58)

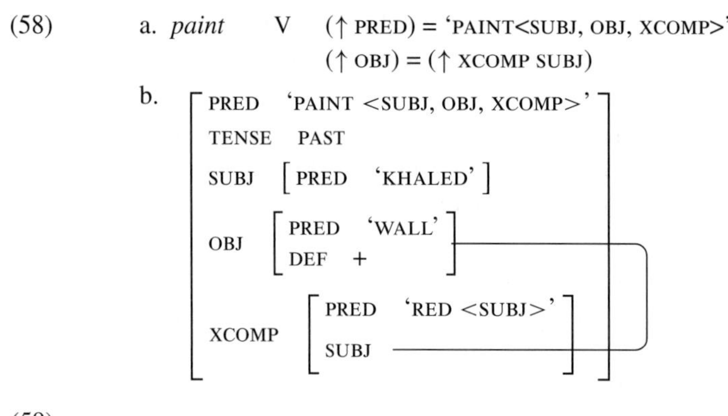

a. paint V (↑ PRED) = ‘PAINT<SUBJ, OBJ, XCOMP>’
(↑ OBJ) = (↑ XCOMP SUBJ)
b.
PRED ‘PAINT <SUBJ, OBJ, XCOMP>’
TENSE PAST
SUBJ PRED ‘KHALED’
OBJ PRED ‘WALL’
DEF +
XCOMP PRED ‘RED <SUBJ>’
SUBJ

(59)

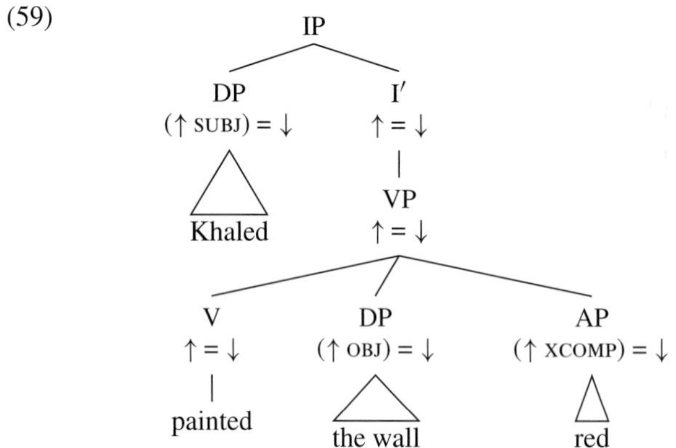

The control predicate *seem*, which we considered in some detail in Section 5.2.1 can take XCOMP arguments which correspond to a range of different c-structure categories, as illustrated in (60). Here *unhappy* requires a SUBJ just like *red* does in (57). In Section 3.3, we showed that semantic prepositions like *in* require an OBJ, and now we see in (60b) that in some uses they can also take a SUBJ, for the same reasons that *red* and *unhappy* do.

(60) a. Deema seems [unhappy]$_{AP}$ this morning.
b. Deema seems [in a bad mood]$_{PP}$ this morning.

There are many other places in which we find non-verbal categories heading XCOMP functions. The verbs *consider* and *keep* in (61) and (62) respectively are also control verbs, where the postverbal DP is the OBJ of the matrix verb, but it is also interpreted as the SUBJ of the lower predicate.

(61) a. Kim considers Oscar [to be an unlikely candidate]$_{IP}$.
b. Fred considers Sarah [a fool]$_{DP}$.
c. Ingrid considers Oscar [foolish]$_{AP}$.

(62) a. Oscar kept the fridge [empty]$_{AP}$.
b. Fred kept the car [running quietly]$_{VP}$.
c. Fred kept his flat [in a filthy state]$_{PP}$.

Note that *running quietly* in (62b) is of category VP rather than IP since there is no evidence of an IP projection; no SUBJ in c-structure and nothing that could occur under I.

When we consider a wider range of examples such as these, we see that in English we have not just IP XCOMPs, but also AP, VP, DP and PP XCOMPs. This means that our previous c-structure rule in (15) should be altered to allow for this. We can achieve this simply by using an abbreviation to represent the set of categories that can map to an XCOMP as in (63a) and by using this in the c-structure rule, as shown in an abbreviated form in (63b).

(63) a. $XP_{xcomp} \equiv \{DP, IP, VP, AP, PP\}$.

b.
$$\begin{array}{lccc} VP \longrightarrow & V & \ldots & XP_{xcomp} \\ & \uparrow = \downarrow & & (\uparrow \text{XCOMP}) = \downarrow \end{array}$$

The discussion in this section has also told us that predicative DPs, PPs, VPs and APs have subjects, as the illustrative f-structure for (60b) in (64) shows.

(64)
$$\begin{bmatrix} \text{PRED} & \text{'SEEM <XCOMP> SUBJ'} \\ \text{TENSE} & \text{PAST} \\ \text{SUBJ} & \begin{bmatrix} \text{PRED} & \text{'DEEMA'} \end{bmatrix} \\ \text{XCOMP} & \begin{bmatrix} \text{PRED} & \text{'IN <SUBJ, OBJ>'} \\ \text{SUBJ} & \text{———} \\ \text{OBJ} & \begin{bmatrix} \text{PRED} & \text{'MOOD'} \\ \text{ADJ} & \left\{ \begin{bmatrix} \text{PRED} & \text{'BAD'} \end{bmatrix} \right\} \end{bmatrix} \end{bmatrix} \end{bmatrix}$$

Given that a range of non-verbal categories can have subjects, as we have just established, we might wonder about the analysis of copula sentences such as those in (65), in which the property denoted by the constituent in boldface is predicated of the subject.

(65) a. Leila is **angry**.

b. Pete was **in a filthy state**.

c. Ingrid is **a doctor**.

These can also be analysed as cases of functional control, in which the verb *be* takes a non-thematic SUBJ, as shown in (66). The resultant f-structure is shown in (68).

(66) *be* V (↑ PRED) = 'BE <XCOMP> SUBJ'
(↑ SUBJ) = (↑ XCOMP SUBJ)

(67) *angry* A (↑ PRED) = 'ANGRY <SUBJ>'

(68)

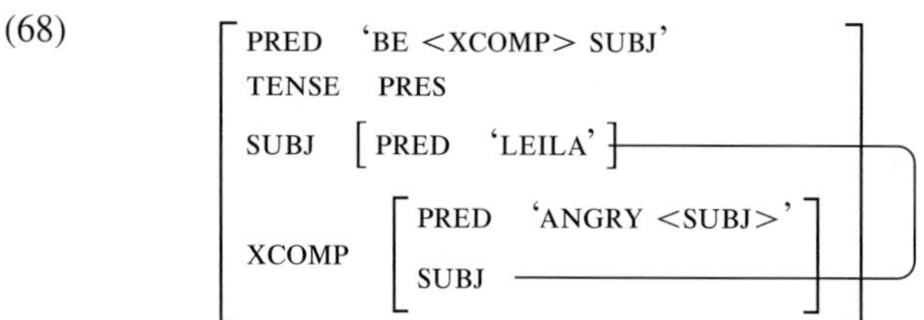

In some languages, the non-verbal element can be directly predicated of the overt subject, and hence there are "copula" constructions like those illustrated for English in (65) which do not contain a verbal element. Sentences in which a non-verbal constituent provides the main predicate for the sentence are found in a wide range of languages including Japanese, Russian and Hebrew, as well as other Semitic languages including Arabic and Maltese. For example, in the Hebrew example in (69a) we see that there is no copula verb when the sentence is interpreted in the present, and hence the adjective serves as the main PRED. On the other hand, a copula is used to express the past, in (69b).

In this case we might want to adopt a uniform analysis for the sentences in (69a) and (69b) by treating the copula verb *haya* 'be' in Hebrew as lacking a PRED value and serving only to contribute a tense value. On this analysis, the f-structure of (69b) would be along the lines shown in (70).

(69)

a. Pnina nora xamuda.
Pnina awfully cute.SG.F
'Pnina is awfully cute.'

b. Pnina hayta nora xamuda.
Pnina be.PST.F.SG awfully cute.SG.F
'Pnina was awfully cute.'

(70)

[TENSE PAST
SUBJ [PRED 'PNINA']
PRED 'CUTE <SUBJ>'
ADJ {[PRED 'AWFULLY']}]

Another possibility is that both the copula-less construction such as the Hebrew example in (69a), and its past tense counterpart (69b) with an overt copula, **do** actually have a PRED value 'BE <XCOMP> SUBJ' as the clausal predicate, giving rise to a two-tier f-structure like the one we saw in (68). It is possible to adopt such an analysis for copula-less constructions in LFG without postulating a null copula V in the c-structure itself, but outlining this type of analysis, which may be appropriate for some languages, takes us too far afield. We have suggested some further reading at the end of the chapter for those who are interested in finding out more.

5.3 Anaphoric Control

Consider now sentences like those in (71).

(71) a. **To eat unripe apples** would be stupid.
b. **Eating unripe apples** makes Mary feel sick.

The clauses in bold in (71) function as the subjects of their respective sentences. In both cases, the SUBJ of the non-finite verb is missing in the c-structure. In (71a), the subject of *eat* is understood to be something like 'anyone' and in (71b) it would normally be assumed to be *Mary*. These constructions differ from those discussed in the previous sections in a number of ways. First, there is no particular predicate to which we can attribute these special properties. We said in Section 5.2 that it is part of the lexical entry for a control verb like *seem* or *persuade* that a SUBJ that is not present in the c-structure is equated in f-structure with a function in the matrix clause. However, in these examples we cannot assume that it is somehow part of the lexical entry of the matrix predicates that the subordinate SUBJ has a particular interpretation, because there is no specific set of verbs that allow subjects like these. Hence the explanation for the interpretation of the subject of the subordinate clause cannot be defined as a control equation in a lexical entry the way we did for the verbs in the previous sections. Second, there is an option with an explicit subject, as in (72). As the examples in (73) show, this is not possible with the functional control constructions we considered in Section 5.2.

(72) a. For anyone to eat unripe apples would be stupid.
b. For Oscar to eat unripe apples would be stupid.
c. Her eating unripe apples makes Mary feel sick.

(73) a. *Oscar tried Oscar/Sarah to eat unripe apples.
b. *Oscar seemed Oscar/Mary to like apples.

Note that it is possible to get a specific interpretation of (71a) by inserting an overt subject in c-structure, as in (72b). Similarly, in principle, *her* in (72c) could refer to any female referent, much like *she* could in a sentence like *She feels sick.* For instance, if Mary is very sensitive, just watching, say, her sister, eat unripe apples might make her feel sick. Then under the right context, (72c) could be interpreted the same way as (74).

(74) Her sister's eating unripe apples makes Mary feel sick.

Another big difference then is that the referent of the missing subject need not occur inside the sentence, whereas for functional control the controller will always occur inside the sentence. In (71a), it is understood as 'anybody', but in a different context it could be understood as referring to someone who is not mentioned in the same sentence. For instance, if (71a) was preceded by *Oscar looked at the very green apples in the bowl and thought for a while*, then the subject of *to eat unripe apples* is most likely interpreted as referring to *Oscar*. In many ways, this is similar to the way ordinary pronouns behave. Consider (75).

(75) Peter$_i$ told Oscar$_j$ that he$_{i/j/k}$ had won the tournament.

Here we have used the indices *i*, *j* and *k* to show that *he* could refer to *Peter*, *Oscar* or to a third male person. It is maybe easy enough to think of a context in which Peter tells Oscar that he, Peter, has won the tournament, or that a third person, say Tom, has won it. However, if you imagine a scenario in which Oscar leaves the venue before all the matches are finished, but Peter stays until the results are announced, then Peter may well be in a position to tell Oscar that he, Oscar, has won. This relation is referred to as ANAPHORIC BINDING, and we will return to it in Chapter 7. Since the SUBJ that is missing in c-structure finds a referent in essentially the same way that an overt pronoun may find a referent, we will refer to the kind of control we see in (71) as ANAPHORIC CONTROL.

Turning now to the analysis of the examples in (71), we have seen that when the non-finite verb occurs without an explicit overt subject, the range of interpretations which we find corresponds to that of a pronoun, and so our analysis will posit a pronominal subject in the corresponding f-structure. Note that this is similar in some ways to the analysis of pronoun incorporation that we introduced in Section 4.2.3. One difference, however, is that in the case of pronominal incorporation the choice of a particular morphological form of the finite verb determines (or constrains) the interpretation of the pronoun, but here we have a general option available for (all) non-finite verb forms. We will assume that the lexical entries of verbs provide an optional f-description introducing a pronominal subject. In English, this option is only available for non-finite verb forms, such as *eat* in (71a) and *eating* in (71b) – these verb forms are therefore associated with the following additional f-description, in which the round brackets denote optionality.

(76) $((\uparrow \text{SUBJ PRED}) = \text{`PRO'})$ where $\text{VFORM} \neq \text{FIN}$

Consider now the analysis of examples such as (77). In each of these sentences the subject of the matrix clause is *Eating unripe apples*. The f-structure is shown as the value of the SUBJ attribute in (78).

(77) a. Eating unripe apples made Mary ill.

b. Eating unripe apples is inadvisable.

(78)

$$\left[\begin{array}{ll} \text{PRED} & \ldots \\ \text{SUBJ} & f\left[\begin{array}{ll} \text{PRED} & \text{`EAT<SUBJ, OBJ>'} \\ \text{VFORM} & \text{ING} \\ \text{SUBJ} & \left[\text{PRED} \ \ \text{`PRO'}\right] \\ \text{OBJ} & \left[\begin{array}{ll} \text{ADJ} & \left\{\left[\text{PRED} \ \ \text{`UNRIPE'}\right]\right\} \\ \text{PRED} & \text{`APPLE'} \\ \text{INDEX} & \left[\text{NUM} \ \ \text{PL}\right] \end{array}\right] \end{array}\right] \\ \ldots & \end{array}\right]$$

In (78) the f-structure *f* is complete and coherent. The verb is non-finite and hence the equation in (76) allows us to insert a pronominal as the value for SUBJ. The interpretation of the pronominal subject is *arbitrary* in the context of the sentence in (77b), while in the case of (77a) it is typically understood as referring to *Mary*, that is, as anaphoric to a particular syntactic antecedent (these terms will be explained in Chapter 7).

The examples of anaphoric control that we have considered so far involve subject clauses; we turn now to complements of verbs and consider a verb that is superficially similar to verbs like *try* and *seem* in (13), namely *want* as illustrated in (79).

(79) Oscar wants to buy olives.

As was the case with *try* and *seem*, the subject of *buy* in (79) is interpreted as being the same as the matrix subject, that is, *Oscar*. There are, however, a number of differences between *try* and *seem*, on the one hand, and *want*, on the other; for one thing *want* can occur with a noun phrase immediately following it as illustrated in (80), and in this, it resembles *expect* in (35b).

(80) a. Oscar wants Fred to buy olives.
b. *Oscar tries/seems Fred to buy olives.

By the criteria we used in Section 5.2, this noun phrase is not assigned a θ-role by *want*; there is no entailment pattern of the sort we would expect if it was, as shown in (81). This is similar to the behaviour of *expect*.

(81) a. Oscar wants Fred to buy olives. *does not entail*
b. Oscar wants Fred.

Furthermore, given the arguments we used in Section 5.2, sentences such as those in (82) provide evidence that *want* does not assign a θ-role to the following noun phrase.

(82) a. Oscar wants there to be more nuts in his muesli.
b. Oscar wants it to rain.

In all these respects *want* resembles *expect*, which might lead us to think that what we have in the case of *want* is a non-thematic object control verb. However, we will see that this would not be the correct conclusion.

In the case of *expect*, since the postverbal noun phrase could become the subject of a corresponding passive in (46), we concluded that it was an object of the verb, albeit a non-thematic one. However, this argument does not hold for *want*, since the passive version of (80a) is ungrammatical (at least in standard English) as shown in (83).

(83) *Fred is wanted to buy olives (by Oscar).

From this it follows that the postverbal noun phrase is neither an argument of *want* nor its non-thematic OBJ, but only SUBJ of the complement clause and an argument of the lower verb, *buy* in (80a).

We return now to the example in (79), where there is no postverbal noun phrase, and hence the structure resembles those of *try* and *seem*. The analysis we provided for these two verbs involved structure sharing between the matrix SUBJ and the embedded SUBJ enforced by a functional control equation. This cannot be the solution for *want* even when there is no postverbal noun phrase in c-structure, as in (79), because there is a crucial difference between the SUBJ of the complement of verbs like *want* and that of verbs like *try* (and *seem*). When a functional control equation is involved, the two functions involved have to be completely identical. This is not the case with *want*. Consider the sentences in (84a) and (85a) and contrast them with (84b) and (85b).

(84) a. The chairman wanted to meet at 3.
b. #The chairman tried to meet at 3.

(85) a. Oscar wants to invade the country that has been threatening the government.
b. Oscar tries to invade the country that has been threatening the government.

In (84a), the interpretation cannot be that the subject of *meet* is *the chairman*, because the sentence does not mean that the chairman wants to meet himself at 3. Rather, it means that chairman wants himself **and** some other people to meet; this is referred to as PARTIAL CONTROL. It is for this reason that (84b) is ungrammatical or at least very odd; with *try*, the lower subject has to be interpreted as identical to the matrix subject. Turning to (85a), the natural interpretation is that *Oscar* wants his country's army to do the invading, so here the interpretation of the lower subject is distinct from the matrix subject. This would not be predicted under functional control. In (85b), on the other hand, the lower subject has to be interpreted as identical to the matrix subject, and the sentence has to mean that Oscar is trying to invade the country all on his own.

The conclusion we can draw from the data is that with *want*, we do not have functional control, which would predict complete identity between the subject of the matrix clause and the subject of the subordinate clause. Instead the interpretation depends on the context, much like it does in example (75). This means that we analyse *want* as involving anaphoric control rather than functional control. When there is no overt subject in the lower clause, we assume there is a PRO in the f-structure. This pronominal SUBJ shows the range of interpretations we find with overt pronouns: it may be coreferential to something else in the clause or outside it, or it may have arbitrary reference. Unlike the functional control predicates *try*, *persuade*, *seem* and *expect*, the complement of *want* is not an XCOMP, but a COMP; though it lacks a SUBJ at c-structure, at f-structure it has an anaphorically controlled PRO subject. The resulting lexical entry for *want* is (86) and the f-structure for (79) is the one provided in (87). The interpretation of the PRO is regulated by the generalisations captured in the theory of anaphoric binding, which we turn to in Chapter 7.

(86) *want* V (↑ PRED) = 'WANT <SUBJ, COMP>'

(87)

```
[ PRED    'WANT <SUBJ, COMP>'                            ]
[ TENSE   PRES                                           ]
[ SUBJ    [ PRED  'OSCAR' ]                              ]
[         [ PRED  'EAT <SUBJ, OBJ>'       ]              ]
[ COMP    [ SUBJ  [ PRED  'PRO' ]         ]              ]
[         [ OBJ   [ PRED  'OLIVES' ]      ]              ]
```

5.4 Contrasting Functional and Anaphoric Control

Icelandic has two properties that make a comparison of functional and anaphoric control particularly interesting. Specifically, it illustrates the difference between structure sharing, where a grammatical function in the lower clause is identical to one in the matrix clause, and the use of an unexpressed pronoun subject to principles of anaphoric binding. This is illustrated in the schematic f-structures in (88) and (89), where F is a variable over (i.e. stands for) functional control verbs and G is a variable over anaphoric control verbs.

(88)

```
[ PRED    'F <SUBJ, XCOMP>'                  ]
[ SUBJ    [ PRED  'OSCAR' ] ------------------]---+
[         [ PRED  'YAWN<SUBJ>' ]             ]   |
[ XCOMP   [ SUBJ  --------------------------]]---+
```

(89)

```
[ PRED    'G<SUBJ, COMP>'                    ]
[ SUBJ    [ PRED  'OSCAR' ]                  ]
[         [ PRED  'YAWN <SUBJ>'      ]       ]
[ COMP    [ SUBJ  [ PRED  'PRO' ]    ]       ]
```

The first of the relevant properties of Icelandic is that it has case marking on its noun phrases. The regular case marking pattern in Icelandic is that the subject bears nominative case and the object bears accusative case. This is illustrated by the example in (90). (Many verbal and nominal forms are actually ambiguous in Icelandic, but here we simplify the glossing somewhat, following the glossing practice of the source of these examples, which is Andrews (1982).)

(90) Hann elskar hana
3SG.M.NOM love.PRS 3SG.F.ACC
'He loves her.'

However Icelandic also has a number of predicates which lexically select a particular, non-nominative case on their subjects – the examples in (91) illustrate this with ACC, DAT and GEN subjects selected by different predicates.

(91) a. Drengina vantar mat.
boy.PL.DEF.ACC lack.PRS food.ACC
'The boys lack food.'

b. Barninu batnaði veikin.
child.SG.DEF.DAT recovered.from.PST disease.SG.DEF.NOM
'The child recovered from the disease.'

c. Verkjanna gætir ekki
pain.PL.DEF.GEN be.noticeable.PRS NEG
'The pains are not noticeable.'

The regular case marking pattern illustrated in (90) is often referred to as STRUCTURAL CASE and the lexically selected patterns in (91) as LEXICAL CASE or QUIRKY CASE. Let's see now what happens when we embed a verb which lexically selects a non-nominative subject under a functional control verb. In (92) a verb taking a SUBJ with the structurally determined nominative case is embedded under a functional control verb ('seem'), and we see that the subject of the matrix verb appears in nominative case.

(92) Hann virðist elska hana.
3SG.M.NOM seem.PRS love.INF 3SG.F.ACC
'He seems to love her.'

This contrasts with what we see when the embedded predicate imposes lexical case requirements on the subject – in this case, the subject of the matrix verb appears in whatever case the embedded predicate lexically specifies for **its** subject, as in (93). This behaviour is often called CASE PRESERVATION or QUIRKY CASE PRESERVATION.

(93) a. Hana virðist vanta peninga.
3.SG.F.ACC seem.PRS lack.INF money.PL.ACC
'She seems to lack money.'

b. Barninu virðist hafa batnað
child.SG.DEF.DAT seem.PRS have.INF recover.from.PPTCP
veikin.
disease.SG.DEF.NOM
'The child seems to have recovered from the disease.'

c. Verkjanna virðist ekki gæta.
pain.PL.GEN seem.PRS NEG be.noticeable.INF
'The pains don't seem to be noticeable.'

The pattern in (93) follows from the analysis of these examples as involving functional control with structure sharing between the matrix SUBJ and the lower clause SUBJ. Consider (93a). The embedded predicate *vanta* specifies that its SUBJ bears ACC case as in (94). The matrix predicate subcategorises for an XCOMP and defines a functional control predicate, as shown in (95). The shared SUBJ f-structure will have ACC case, as required by the embedded predicate; the lexically specified quirky case (ACC) "wins out" over the structural NOM case that the subject of *virðast* 'seem.INF' would normally take and we get (93a).

(94) *vanta* V (↑ PRED) = 'LACK <SUBJ, OBJ>'
(↑ SUBJ CASE) = ACC

(95) *virðast* V (↑ PRED) = 'SEEM <XCOMP> SUBJ'
(↑ SUBJ) = (↑ XCOMP SUBJ)

(96)

$$\left[\begin{array}{ll} \text{PRED} & \text{`SEEM} \langle \text{XCOMP} \rangle \text{ SUBJ'} \\ \text{SUBJ} & \left[\begin{array}{ll} \text{PRED} & \text{`PRO'} \\ \text{INDEX} & \left[\begin{array}{ll} \text{NUM} & \text{SG} \\ \text{PERS} & 3 \\ \text{GEND} & \text{FEM} \end{array}\right] \\ \text{CASE} & \text{ACC} \end{array}\right] \\ \text{XCOMP} & \left[\begin{array}{ll} \text{PRED} & \text{`LACK} \langle \text{SUBJ, OBJ} \rangle \text{'} \\ \text{SUBJ} & \text{———} \\ \text{OBJ} & \left[\text{PRED} \quad \text{`MONEY'}\right] \end{array}\right] \end{array}\right]$$

Now let's consider what happens when a predicate which lexically selects a non-nominative subject is embedded under a control predicate that can be shown to involve anaphoric control, such as *vona* 'to hope'. The example in (91a) showed that the verb *vanta* takes an accusative subject, and in (93a), we saw that this accusative case was preserved with the raising verb *virðast*. However, in (97), we see that the matrix subject occurs in its standard structural nominative case.

(97) Ég vonast að vanta ekki efni í ritgerðina.
I.NOM hope.PRS INF lack.INF NEG material for thesis.DEF
'I hope not to lack material for the thesis.'

This pattern follows from the anaphoric control analysis in which the embedded infinitival clause has a PRED = 'PRO' subject. Since the embedded SUBJ and the matrix SUBJ are distinct f-structures, the matrix subject appears in the regular, nominative case.

(98)

$$\left[\begin{array}{ll} \text{PRED} & \text{`HOPE} \langle \text{SUBJ, COMP} \rangle \text{'} \\ \text{SUBJ} & \left[\begin{array}{ll} \text{PRED} & \text{`PRO'} \\ \text{CASE} & \text{NOM} \end{array}\right] \\ \text{COMP} & \left[\begin{array}{ll} \text{PRED} & \text{`LACK} \langle \text{SUBJ, OBJ} \rangle \text{'} \\ \text{SUBJ} & \left[\begin{array}{ll} \text{PRED} & \text{`PRO'} \\ \text{CASE} & \text{ACC} \end{array}\right] \\ \text{OBJ} & \left[\text{PRED} \quad \text{`MATERIAL'}\right] \end{array}\right] \end{array}\right]$$

5.5 Control into Adjuncts

Our discussion of functional control up to this point has been concerned with the subcategorised (governable) grammatical function XCOMP. We have seen that verbs such as *seem* and *persuade* are associated with functional control equations in the lexicon. In Section 2.2 we showed that optional adjuncts can also be open, that is, we have a function XADJ, and the SUBJ of these XADJs can also be functionally controlled. In many such cases in English, the controller can have one of a number of different grammatical relations in the main clause, though certain choices of controller may be strongly favoured by the context. Consider the examples in (99).

(99) a. Fred fell off his chair, drunk as usual.

b. Fred bumped into Oscar, drunk as usual.

c. Fred served Ingrid the curry, spicier than ever.

In these examples, *drunk as usual* and *spicier than ever* are adjective phrases functioning as XADJs. As modifiers, they are introduced by a recursive rule like (100). As we said in Section 2.2 and showed in rule (6e) in Section 3.1, adjuncts are attached at phrasal level in English and have a set-valued feature in the f-structure. This is the case also at IP level, as indicated in (100). However, in order to keep things simpler, we will not make this explicit in the discussion that follows here.

(100) IP $\longrightarrow$ IP AP

$\uparrow = \downarrow$ $\downarrow \in (\uparrow$ XADJ)

In Section 5.2.3, we showed that adjectives may take a SUBJ argument, and it is this argument that is missing in these XADJs. In (99a), the SUBJ of the adjective *drunk* is controlled by the SUBJ of the sentence, *Fred*. However, in (99b) *Oscar* is at least an equally plausible controller for the SUBJ of the adjective *drunk*; in principle, given the right context, either *Oscar* or *Fred* could be the controller. In (99c), the SUBJ of *spicier* is controlled by the OBJ$_\theta$ *the curry*.

In these examples, there is no specific lexical item with which a functional control equation can be associated, as there was for predicates that select an XCOMP, because XADJs appear freely with predicates, and are not subcategorised grammatical functions. Since a range of grammatical functions can serve as controllers, we can assume a general mechanism for identifying the XADJ SUBJ with some function in the main clause, the clausal SUBJ, OBJ or OBJ$_\theta$ as formalised in (101):

(101) If ($\uparrow$ XADJ) = $\downarrow$ is a syntactically encoded functional annotation, then add ($\uparrow$ G) = ($\downarrow$ SUBJ) to it, where G is one of {SUBJ, OBJ, OBJ$_\theta$}

In (99a) and (99b) *drunk as usual* has the functional annotation ($\uparrow$ XADJ) = $\downarrow$, so by (101) we can add ($\uparrow$ G) = ($\downarrow$ SUBJ) to it and instantiate G as SUBJ in (99a) and SUBJ or OBJ in (99b). In this way, the SUBJ of *drunk as usual* is the same as the SUBJ of the sentence in (99a), and it is understood as *Fred* being drunk. By the same process, either *Fred* or *Oscar* is interpreted as the SUBJ of *drunk as usual* in (99b); G is instantiated either as SUBJ or OBJ depending on the context.

Notice that although in principle any one of the term functions (SUBJ, OBJ and OBJ$_\theta$) can control the SUBJ, these cases bear the hallmarks of **functional** control rather than **anaphoric** control and hence correspond to open XADJs rather than closed ADJ functions with PRO in SUBJ at f-structure. Two pieces of evidence support this conclusion. The first is that we cannot simply "spell out" the SUBJ of the adjective, as we would expect if this were a case of anaphoric control: (102) is ungrammatical.

(102) *Fred fell off his chair, him drunk as usual.

The second is that we do not find cases of arbitrary reference or partial control. Remember that in the case of functional control, the controller and the controlled function share the same structure and hence have to be identical, whereas this is not the case for anaphoric control. Consider the contrast between the examples in (103).

(103) a. Fred and Sarah elegantly executed a perfect tango, very pleased with themselves.
b. Fred elegantly executed a perfect tango with Sarah, very pleased with himself/*themselves.

Fred and Sarah is the SUBJ in (103a) and can control the SUBJ of the adjunct *very pleased with themselves*, and hence the SUBJ of the adjunct is also plural. This in turn allows the plural reflexive *themselves* as OBJ of the preposition within the adjunct. In (103b), even though it is still *Fred* and *Sarah* who are dancing, and they may well both be very pleased with themselves, notice that *themselves* is ungrammatical in the adjunct in (103b). If we have here a case of functional control into the adjunct, then we have an explanation for this contrast; in (103b) the SUBJ in the adjunct is controlled by the SUBJ of the sentence, which is just *Fred*, and hence it is singular. Therefore it cannot serve as an antecedent for the plural reflexive *themselves*. If this was instead a case of anaphoric control, we would expect (103b) to be fine with the plural reflexive since there is no structure sharing, and hence no need for the controlled SUBJ to be identical to a function in the main clause.

In other cases of control into adjuncts, only one specific grammatical function may serve as controller of the XADJ SUBJ. There is a class of AP adjuncts in English which occur immediately before the main clause and can only have their SUBJ controlled by the SUBJ of the clause they modify. The examples in (104) illustrate this. In these examples, only *Mary*, *Tom* and *Kim* can control the SUBJ of the ADJ.

(104) a. Sure of winning, Mary hit an easy ball to her opponent.
b. Woebegone and haggard, Tom went over every detail of it with his friends a hundred times.
c. Upset by the enormous fuss, Kim left Eve to deal with the situation.

This obligatory subject control into ADJ depends on a particular construction, and for such cases, the functional control equation can be introduced as part of the c-structure rule. This may be achieved by means of a rule (specific to English) like the one in (105). The f-description (↑ SUBJ) = (↓ SUBJ) states that the SUBJ of the IP is the same f-structure as the SUBJ of the AP which is its daughter in the c-structure.

(105) IP ⟶ AP IP
(↑ XADJ) = ↓ ↑ = ↓
(↑ SUBJ) = (↓ SUBJ)

As well as the open adjunct function XADJ, we also have a closed ADJ function among our set of grammatical functions. Some English examples are shown in (106).

(106) a. **With Oscar in a really bad mood**, Amina went out for a long walk.
b. **The train being crowded**, Eve was forced to stand all the way.

We can now ask whether closed ADJS can also have "missing" subjects – that is, do we find cases of anaphoric control into adjuncts?

To answer this question, we turn to Warlpiri, an indigenous language spoken in the Northern Territory, Australia by a few thousand speakers. There is evidence that control into adjuncts in Warlpiri is indeed anaphoric, so the grammatical function of the adjuncts is ADJ rather than XADJ. Furthermore, Warlpiri is interesting because it has a way of avoiding ambiguity in control into adjuncts. The data is rather complex, but we think it is worth the effort to follow the argument. Like Wambaya, which we looked at in Section 2.3.4, Warlpiri has an ergative case-marking system, so that generally the SUBJ of a transitive clause has ergative case, and the SUBJ of an intransitive clause and the OBJ of a transitive clause have absolutive case. As we will see, there are also some verbs that take an absolutive SUBJ and dative OBJ. For those who are interested in knowing more, some relevant reading is provided at the end of the chapter.

The clauses we will consider here are described as NONFINITE CLAUSES OF CONTEMPORANEOUS ACTION, which means that the nonfinite clause refers to an action that happens at the same time as that described by the matrix clause. In such Warlpiri clauses, the subject can be controlled by the SUBJ, the OBJ or the dative-marked OBL_θ of the clause it modifies. In principle, this may lead to ambiguities, but Warlpiri has a set of suffixes which attach to the nonfinite verb and determine which function is the controller. The three suffixes we will be concerned with here are: *-karra* denoting control by the SUBJ, *-kurra* denoting control by the OBJ and *-rlarni* denoting control by the dative OBL_θ. These markers will be glossed as C for complementiser. Consider (107) and (108) first (from Simpson and Bresnan, 1983, 51).

(107) Ngarrka ka wirnpirli-mi [karli jarnti-rninja-**karra**].
man.ABS PRS whistle-NPST boomerang-.ABS trim-INF-C
'The man is whistling, while trimming a boomerang.'

(108) Ngarrka-ngku ka purlapa yunpa-rni, [karli
man-ERG PRS corroboree.ABS sing-NPST boomerang.ABS
jarnti-rninja-**karra**-rlu].
trim-INF-C-ERG
'The man is singing a corroboree, while trimming a boomerang.'

The element *ka* in both examples is similar to an auxiliary, indicating tense. The SUBJ of the matrix clause in (107), 'man', is marked as absolutive, since it is the SUBJ of an intransitive verb, whereas in (108) it has ergative case marking because the verb is transitive. The adjunct clause in both (107) and (108) consists of a nonfinite transitive verb 'trim' and an OBJ 'boomerang', marked with absolutive as expected. In spite of the case difference between the two sentences, it is 'man' that controls the SUBJ of the nonfinite clause in both cases. Note that in both cases, the nonfinite verb has the suffix *karra*, forcing a SUBJ controller. We will return to the ergative case marking on the verb in (108) shortly.

We turn now to the examples in (109) and (110) (Simpson and Bresnan, 1983, 53 and 61).

(109) Kurdu-ngku ka karnta nya-nyi, [ngurlu
child-ERG PRS woman.ABS see-NPST seed.ABS
yurrpa-rninja-**kurra**].
grind-INF-C
'The child sees the woman grind mulga seed.'

(110) Ngarrka-ngku ka-rla kurdu-ku karli kaji-jarnti-rni,
man-ERG PRS-DAT child-DAT boomerang.ABS BEN-trim-NPST
[nguna-nja-**rlarni**-(ki)].
lie-INF-C-(DAT)
'The man is trimming a boomerang for the child lying down.'

In (109), the understood SUBJ of the lower verb, 'grind', is 'woman', which is the OBJ of the matrix clause, and we see that the suffix on the nonfinite verb is the control marker for an OBJ, *kurra*. The sentence cannot mean that it was the child who was grinding the mulga seed. The matrix clause in (110) is a little more complex in that a dative marker has been added to the auxiliary *ka*, and the verb 'trim' has a benefactive marker. However, the functions of the noun phrases in the matrix clause are clear; SUBJ 'man', OBJ 'boomerang' and OBL_{Ben} 'child'. The missing SUBJ of the verb 'lie' in the nonfinite clause is controlled by the OBL_{Ben}, and the verb has the marker *rlarni* ensuring control by the dative oblique in the matrix clause.

You might argue that in these examples the context has largely been enough to identify the controller; in (110), for instance, you would not expect the man doing the trimming to be the one lying down. However, consider now the example in (111) (Simpson and Bresnan, 1983, 54).

(111) Karnta ka-rla wangka-mi ngarrka-ku
woman.ABS PRS-DAT speak-NPST man-DAT
[jarnti-rninja-**kurra**-(ku)].
trim-INF-C-(DAT)
'The woman is speaking to the man trimming it.'

In principle, the meaning of a sentence like this could have been 'The woman is speaking to the man, while (she is) trimming it', but the marker *kurra* ensures that the OBJ, 'man', is interpreted as the SUBJ of the nonfinite verb. Note that the object of 'trim' is unexpressed here because it has previously been mentioned and is recoverable from the discourse.

We turn now to the issue of whether this is functional or anaphoric control. In the case of functional control, there is a functional control equation that ensures there is just one f-structure that is the value of both the controller and the controllee. Hence the two must be identical. When we considered Icelandic in Section 5.4, we saw that case marking could be used to distinguish functional control from anaphoric control. We can do the same for Warlpiri, though the data is a little more complex.

In Warlpiri, adjuncts modifying nominal arguments agree in case with those nominals. We see an example of this in (112) (Simpson and Bresnan, 1983, 57).

(112) Ngarrka-ngku ka jarnti-rni karli ngurra-ngka-rlu.
man-ERG PRS trim-NPST boomerang-ABS camp-LOC-ERG
'The man is trimming the boomerang in camp.'

In (112) 'camp' has locative case to make up the adjunct 'in camp'. This adjunct modifies 'man' and since 'man' carries ergative case, so does the adjunct. The adjunct then has two cases, one that is "its own", so to speak, to indicate that it is a location and one to show agreement with the ergative noun it modifies to indicate who it is that is in the camp. Now let's turn this sentence into a nonfinite adjunct clause, and have its SUBJ be controlled by a noun phrase that is not ergative and see what happens. If the adjunct 'in camp' has to have the case of the controller, then we have functional control. However, if 'in camp' can have a different case from the controller, specifically the ergative case that the SUBJ in (112) has, then we have anaphoric control. The example we need can be found in (113) (Simpson and Bresnan, 1983, 57).

(113) Karnta ka-rla wangka-mi ngarrka-ku, [ngurra-ngka-rlu
woman.-ABS PRS-DAT speak-NPST man-DAT camp-LOC-ERG
jarnti-rninja-**kurra**-(ku)].
trim-INF-C-(DAT)
'The woman is speaking to the man (while he is) trimming it in camp.'

Here we see that 'camp' has its local case and ergative, just like it did in (112) when there was an overt SUBJ. This in spite of the fact that the controller 'man' in the matrix clause has dative case. This must then be anaphoric control. Note that the control marker *kurra* demands object control, but in this case the OBJ is marked by dative, rather than absolutive, case. This is a regular property of Warlpiri; when the SUBJ of a particular verb is required to have absolutive case, the OBJ of the verb appears in dative case.

We would then also expect any adjunct modifying the 'silent' subject of nonfinite clauses to show case agreement and carry the same case as the silent subject would have if it wasn't silent. If the SUBJ of these nonfinite clauses in Warlpiri exemplified functional control, then this would always have to be the same case as that of the controller. If it is anaphoric control, on the other hand, the SUBJ of the nonfinite verb is a PRO, and we would expect it to be possible for the adjunct that modifies that PRO to have a different case from that of the controller, and this is indeed what we find; in (113), the controller 'man' in the main clause is dative, but 'in camp' is ergative, which is what the case of the subject of 'trimming' would be if it was overt, as indicated in (112).

We have seen here how Warlpiri uses a set of markers for nonfinite adjunct clauses which code the function of the controller. These markers determine what controls the "missing" subject. Then, we have seen evidence from adjunct agreement that the controller and the controlled SUBJ can have different case, and hence that this is anaphoric control into the nonfinite adjunct, rather than functional control. This in turn means we have an ADJ, rather than an XADJ.

Reading

Control and complementation played a central role in the development of LFG, and a key article is still Bresnan (1982a), also published as Bresnan (1982b). The material presented in Section 5.2 relies heavily on this text.

Following the analysis in Bresnan (1982c); Falk (2001); Bresnan et al. (2016) we have treated English equi verbs such as *try* and *persuade* as thematic functional control. However, Dalrymple (2001, 323–30) proposes an alternative analysis of these verbs as obligatory anaphoric control. Kroeger (1993, 71–107) provides an extensive discussion of control in Tagalog and argues that the language has equi verbs involving both functional and anaphoric control. In this chapter, we have discussed control only in the context of non-finite complementation; discussion and analysis of functional control in finite clauses can be found in Asudeh (2005). The discussion of anaphoric and functional control in Icelandic in Section 5.4 draws mainly on Andrews (1982) and Andrews (1990a). The discussion of anaphoric control in adjuncts in Warlpiri is based on Simpson and Bresnan (1983). A further core reference on Warlpiri is Simpson (1983, 1991).

We assume here that the infinitival marker *to* in English is found in I, and this is a common assumption in the LFG literature and more broadly. Falk (2001) assumes it is in C, and hence the infinitival complements are CPs. We introduced a feature VFORM in this chapter and introduced a couple of simple values, but did not discuss it in full. There are a number of proposals for what the values of VFORM should be, and for this we refer to discussion in Falk (2001, 84–9) and Payne and Börjars (2015).

There are different views on the SUBJ function of adjectives, especially differences between attributive and predicative adjectives. We have assumed that predicative adjectives subcategorise a SUBJ function but that attributive adjectives do not. For a view that adjectives should be analysed as selecting a SUBJ not just in predicative use, but also when used attributively, see for instance Zweigenbaum (1988).

The issue of how to analyse copula constructions like (65) has been discussed quite extensively in the LFG literature. We proposed an analysis of AP, PP and NP complements in copula constructions as open predicates, that is, as XCOMPs. An alternative analysis in terms of an additional closed function PREDLINK has been proposed by Butt et al. (1999). Dalrymple et al. (2004) compares the two analyses and suggests that the XCOMP analysis may be the most appropriate one in some circumstances, and that the use of a closed function may be appropriate in other circumstances. The Hebrew copula is discussed in Falk (2004).

Exercises

5.1 Section 5.2.1 gives (114) as an example of an adjective showing subject functional control.

(114) Oscar is **eager** to see the musical.

Provide a lexical entry for *eager* in (114).

Now using the lexical entry suggested for predicative *be* in Section 5.2.3, repeated here as (115), give the f-structure for the sentence in (114).

(115) *be* V (↑ PRED) = 'BE <XCOMP> SUBJ'
(↑ SUBJ) = (↑ XCOMP SUBJ)

Now provide the annotated c-structure for (114).

5.2 Look back at (33) and say why **Oscar seemed to snow* is ruled out.

5.3 Review the differences between the sentences in (116) discussed in Section 5.2.

(116) a. Ingrid tried to buy olives.
b. Oscar seemed to like olives.

Using the diagnostics which we have discussed in this chapter, decide whether each of the verbs in (117) is a subject control verb like *try* (an EQUI verb) or like *seem* (a RAISING verb), when it appears with a *to*-infinitive or other subjectless complement.

(117) *continue, happen, tend, appear, start, fail, ought, begin, keep, become, manage, condescend, attempt, prepare*

5.4 This exercise looks at the interaction of non-thematic functional control (RAISING) with the EXTRAPOSITION construction in English. To do this we need to explain what we mean by extraposition. The verb *bother* can take a finite clause as SUBJ, as shown in (118a). However *bother* also permits an alternative, extraposition, structure, in which the finite clause occurs (or is 'extraposed' to a position) after the predicate, and the expletive pronoun *it* appears as SUBJ, as in (118b).

(118) a. That Deema missed the train really bothers John.
b. It really bothers John that Deema missed the train.

We want to say that *bother* is a two-place predicate in both (118a) and (118b), that is, it has only two thematic arguments (although in (118b) it has three syntactic arguments). The (partial) lexical entry in (119) captures the extraposition use of *bother*.

(119) *bother* V (↑ PRED) = 'BOTHER<OBJ, COMP> SUBJ'
(↑ SUBJ FORM) $=_c$ IT

The f-structure for the 'extraposition *it*' use of *bother* in example (118b) is shown in (120), suppressing details which are not relevant to the point at hand.

(120)

$$\begin{bmatrix} \text{PRED} & \text{`BOTHER <OBJ, COMP> SUBJ'} \\ \text{TENSE} & \text{PRES} \\ \text{SUBJ} & \begin{bmatrix} \text{FORM} & \text{IT} \end{bmatrix} \\ \text{OBJ} & \begin{bmatrix} \text{PRED} & \text{`JOHN'} \end{bmatrix} \\ \text{COMP} & \begin{bmatrix} \text{PRED} & \text{`MISS<SUBJ, OBJ>'} \\ \text{TENSE} & \text{PAST} \\ \text{SUBJ} & \begin{bmatrix} \text{PRED} & \text{`DEEMA'} \end{bmatrix} \\ \text{OBJ} & \begin{bmatrix} \text{PRED} & \text{`TRAIN'} \end{bmatrix} \end{bmatrix} \end{bmatrix}$$

Completeness and Coherence are satisfied in this structure, because every governable grammatical function which is specified in the argument list of a semantic form is present in the local f-structure (Completeness) and every PRED-bearing governable grammatical function is governed by a local predicate which assigns it a semantic role (Coherence).

Now review the analysis of *seem* and *expect* and then provide f-structures for the sentences in (121) and explain how Completeness and Coherence are satisfied in these f-structures.

(121) a. It seems to bother John that Deema missed the train.
b. I expected it to bother John that Deema missed the train.

Building on your understanding of extraposition, now provide lexical entries for the two uses of *obvious* illustrated in (122).

(122) a. That Eve made a mistake is obvious.
b. It is obvious that Eve made a mistake.

6 Long-Distance Dependencies

6.1 TOPIC and FOCUS Fronting in English

We introduced the concept of grammaticalised discourse functions in Section 2.2. These are warranted when a language has a particular position reserved for information-structurally special constituents. English has relatively little room for manoeuvre when it comes to reorganising constituents for reasons related to information structure. However, there is a sentence-initial position where constituents that have the discourse functions FOCUS or TOPIC can be placed. This is exemplified in (1).

(1) a. *Sausages*, the dog can eat very quickly (but the healthy stuff goes down more slowly).
b. *On that shelf*, Ingrid only puts the cat's food.

In both examples, a grammatical function precedes the subject – in (1a) it is the OBJ of *eat* and in (1b) it is the OBL_{Loc} of *put*, and the effect is that emphasis is put on the fronted constituent. In Section 6.2, we will look in more detail at this phenomenon by considering constituent questions in English, and we will see how they are analysed in LFG. However, before we move on, we should point out that fronting is not the only way of adding focus to a constituent in English; frequently prosodic means are used, and there is extra stress on the constituent and/or a particular intonational contour is used. This is exemplified in (2), where we have used boldface to indicate emphasis on the SUBJ in (2a) and the OBJ in (2b).

(2) a. **Ingrid** patted the big dog, but her brother was too scared.
b. Ingrid patted **the small dog**, but she was too afraid of the big one.

6.2 Constituent Questions in English

At a general level, two kinds of question can be distinguished: POLAR QUESTIONS – in the literature on English frequently referred to as *yes/no* questions – and CONSTITUENT QUESTIONS also referred to as *wh*-questions (though one of the words that can introduce such a question, *how*, does not begin with *wh*). For simplicity, we will occasionally use English-centric terms such as *wh*-question and *wh*-phrase also for languages other than English. Examples are provided in

(3) and (4); in each case a corresponding sentence with canonical word order is provided.

(3) a. Will Ingrid pat the big dog?
b. Ingrid will pat the big dog.

(4) a. Which dog will Ingrid pat?
b. Ingrid will pat which dog!?

The polar question in (3a) differs from the declarative counterpart in (3b) only in that the auxiliary *will* precedes the subject. We saw in Section 3.2 that in a highly configurational language like English, we can define the subject as the phrase that occurs as the daughter of IP and the sister of I′, which is captured by the annotated rule in (5).

(5) IP $\longrightarrow$ DP $(\uparrow \text{SUBJ}) = \downarrow$ I′ $\uparrow = \downarrow$

This means that *Ingrid pat the big dog* in (3a) is an IP and *will* is outside that IP. In Section 2.3.2, we introduced a category above IP, namely CP, and it seems reasonable then to assume that the fronted auxiliary in (3a) heads a CP that takes the IP *Ingrid pat the big dog* as its complement, giving the tree in (6). As we said in Section 2.3.2, by convention, in LFG phrase structure rules, all nodes are optional, so we do not need to include parentheses around them. In the same spirit, pre-terminal nodes must dominate some overt material; in (6), there is no I since the finite auxiliary occurs in C and only finite auxiliaries can occur in I (and *to*, but that is not relevant here). Hence I does not dominate any overt material and so it does not appear in the tree.

(6)

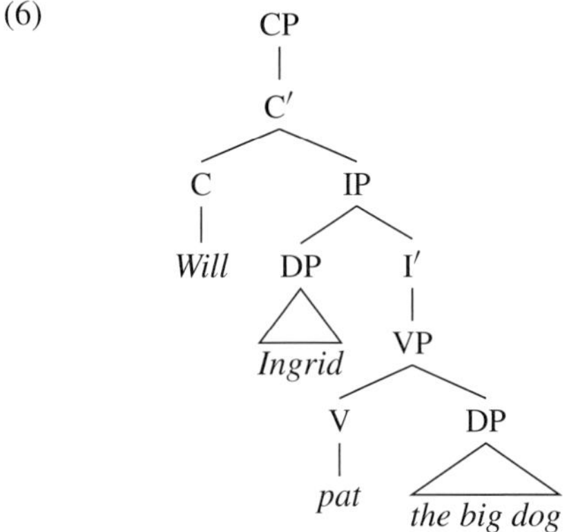

There is empirical evidence for this structure in that a fronted finite auxiliary and a complementiser such as *whether*, which also occurs in C, cannot co-occur. If Fred asked the question in (7a), then we can relate this to someone either in the form of a direct quotation as in (7b) or in a subordinate clause with a complementiser as in (7c). What we cannot do, as is shown by the ungrammaticality of (7d), is have a subordinate clause with a complementiser and an inverted auxiliary. Under our assumptions, this would be explained by the fact that we cannot have two elements in C at the same time.

(7)
a. Would the dog eat the sausages?
b. Fred asked: "Would the dog eat the sausages?"
c. Fred asked whether the dog would eat the sausages.
d. *Fred asked whether would the dog eat the sausages.

We return now to the constituent question in (4a), where we also have an auxiliary preceding the subject, but in addition, the phrase *which dog* precedes the fronted auxiliary. In an English constituent question, it is obligatory to front the questioned phrase, the *wh*-phrase. If it is left where it would occur if it was not a *wh*-phrase, as in (4b), we get an ECHO-QUESTION instead of a regular question. We will return to the motivation for the fronting of the *wh*-phrase in just a moment; we will just consider the structure first. In (4a), the *wh*-phrase precedes the inverted auxiliary, which we have said is found in C. Looking back at the tree in (6), there is nothing in the specifier of CP position, and hence it is available. Positioning the *wh*-phrase there would make the correct predictions about its distribution. This results in the tree in (8), where V has no sister since the object we would expect to follow a verb like *pat* is not found there.

(8)

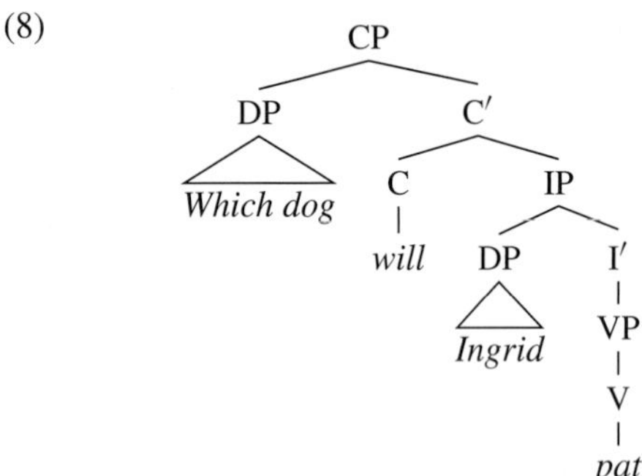

Since the *wh*-phrase is in the specifier position, which is a unique position, not introduced by a recursive rule (see Section 2.3.1), we would expect there to be room for just one such phrase, and this is indeed what we find in English, though we will see below that there is cross-linguistic variation in how constituent questions are formed. In (9), where we have more than one *wh*-phrase, only one of them can occur at the front.

(9)
a. What did Ingrid give to whom?
b. *What to whom did Ingrid give?

The fronted *wh*-phrase can be quite complex and can be of a range of different categories. In (4a) it is a DP, in (10a) a PP and in (10b) an AP. In fact, it can be any lexical category, except VP, as illustrated by (11).

(10)
a. *In which basket* does the dog sleep?
b. *How hungry* does the dog seem?

(11) **Pat which dog* did Ingrid?

The *wh*-phrase is fronted in order to put focus on it. In the case of *wh*-questions, the specifier of CP position is associated with the discourse function FOCUS, but in other constructions, like relative clauses, it can be a TOPIC. Since this discourse function is associated with a specific structural position, it is a grammaticalised discourse function (see Section 2.2 for a definition of (grammaticalised) discourse functions). The rule in (12) captures the connection between the specifier of CP position and the FOCUS status of that constituent. Since a range of categories can be fronted, we will use a metacategory XP_{wh} as an abbreviation to stand for the set of categories which can appear in this position. We define XP_{wh} (which excludes VP) as in (13). The rule in (12) is just a first attempt; we will develop it in steps and consider data as we go along. If you want to jump straight to the final version of our rule for English, you can find it in (26).

(12) C-structure rule for long-distance dependencies in English (first attempt)

$$\text{CP} \longrightarrow \underset{(\uparrow \text{FOCUS}) = \downarrow}{\text{XP}_{wh}} \quad \underset{\uparrow = \downarrow}{\text{C}'}$$

(13) $XP_{wh} \equiv \{DP \mid AP \mid PP \mid AdvP\}$

However, this is not enough. If all that *which dog* in (4a) contributes is a discourse function, then *pat* in this example would not have an object, and since the PRED feature of *pat* requires both a SUBJ and an OBJ, this would mean that the resulting f-structure would be incomplete. Since (4a) is grammatical, we can assume that the fronted phrase also functions as the OBJ. We could then expand the rule in (12) as in (14), where an equation is added that ensures that the fronted element, the FOCUS, also functions as the OBJ of the sentence. This equating of two functions is similar to what we saw used in control constructions in Chapter 5, and like those equations it gives rise to structure sharing.

(14) C-structure rule for long-distance dependencies in English (second attempt)

$$\text{CP} \longrightarrow \underset{\substack{(\uparrow \text{FOCUS}) = \downarrow \\ (\uparrow \text{FOCUS}) = (\uparrow \text{OBJ})}}{\text{XP}_{wh}} \quad \underset{\uparrow = \downarrow}{\text{C}'}$$

This still isn't quite right though, since the fronted phrase can have different functions in the sentence; in (10a) it is an ADJ, in (10b) it is an XCOMP, as we saw in Chapter 5, in (15a) it is an OBJ_θ and in (15b) an OBL_θ.

(15) a. What did Sarah give Fred?
b. Where did Ingrid put the book?

Since the focused element in the specifier position of CP can have a range of grammatical functions within the sentence, we use GF to generalise over grammatical functions and revise the rule in (14) as in (16), which states that the fronted phrase has the discourse function FOCUS within the sentence and also some unspecified grammatical function.

(16) C-structure rule for long-distance dependencies in English (third attempt)

$$\text{CP} \longrightarrow \underset{\substack{(\uparrow \text{FOCUS}) = \downarrow \\ (\uparrow \text{FOCUS}) = (\uparrow \text{GF})}}{\text{XP}_{wh}} \quad \underset{\uparrow = \downarrow}{\text{C}'}$$

However, we are still not quite capturing the facts of English. As the examples in (17) show, the "missing" GF_{wh} can be embedded within a clause, finite or non-finite. In fact, it can be deeply embedded. This is why these constructions are usually referred to as LONG-DISTANCE DEPENDENCIES or UNBOUNDED DEPENDENCIES.

(17)
a. Which dog did Fred say that Sarah bought?
b. Which dog did Ingrid think that Fred had said that Sarah bought?
c. Which dog did Ingrid manage to train?
d. Which dog did Ingrid seem to manage to train?

In both (17a) and (17b), *which dog* is the OBJ of *bought*, which is inside the COMP *that Sarah bought*. In (17b) this COMP is in turn inside another COMP *that Fred had said that Sarah bought*. This means that for (17b) we can specify a path – a notion introduced in Section 3.2 – from the fronted position: COMP COMP OBJ. Similarly for (17c) and (17d), except that the verb that *which dog* is the OBJ of, *train*, is inside the XCOMP *to train*, and in (17d), that XCOMP is inside another XCOMP *to manage to train*. The path here would then be XCOMP XCOMP OBJ. This means that we need to refine the rule in (16) to capture the fact that the GF_{wh} can be embedded inside zero or more COMPS or XCOMPS. This is captured in (18), where * is the Kleene star we introduced in Section 2.3.4, which means 'zero or more', and | indicates 'or'. The second annotation under the XP then states that the discourse function FOCUS that fills this position also functions as some grammatical function in the rest of the sentence and that this grammatical function could be embedded inside some COMPS or XCOMPS.

(18) C-structure rule for long-distance dependencies in English (fourth attempt)

$$\text{CP} \longrightarrow \underset{\substack{(\uparrow \text{FOCUS}) = \downarrow \\ (\uparrow \text{FOCUS}) = (\uparrow \{\text{COMP}|\text{XCOMP}\}^* \text{ GF})}}{\text{XP}_{wh}} \quad \underset{\uparrow = \downarrow}{\text{C}'}$$

We turn our attention now to GF at the bottom of the path. In English, it is actually not true that all GFS introduced in Section 2.2 can be fronted in *wh*-interrogatives. Consider the examples in (19).

(19)
a. *Whose did Ingrid feed dog?
b. *Whose did Fred put the oranges in bag?

In both (19a) and (19b), *whose* functions as POSS – of *dog* and *bag*, respectively – and it cannot be fronted on its own, instead the whole phrase *whose dog* or *whose bag* would have to occur initially. We can conclude that GF in (16) cannot include POSS. Therefore we need to specify a set of GFS for the rule in (16), much like we did for categories in (13). We introduce GF_{wh} into the rule as in (20a), and define it as in (20b). We have also left COMP off this list; if you can think of an example in which a COMP has been fronted in a *wh*-question, it would need to be added to the list in (20b). As the values of ADJ and XADJ are sets of f-structures, we need the symbol $\in$ for them.

(20) a. C-structure rule for long-distance dependencies in English (fifth attempt)

$$\text{CP} \longrightarrow \underset{\substack{(\uparrow \text{FOCUS}) = \downarrow \\ (\uparrow \text{FOCUS}) = (\uparrow \{\text{COMP}|\text{XCOMP}\}^* \ \text{GF}_{wh})}}{\text{XP}_{wh}} \quad \underset{\uparrow = \downarrow}{\text{C}'}$$

b. $\text{GF}_{wh} \equiv \{\text{SUBJ}|\text{OBJ}|\text{OBJ}_\theta|\text{OBL}_\theta|\text{XCOMP}|\text{ADJ} \in|\text{XADJ} \in\}$

Though our aim here is not to give a full analysis of constituent questions in English, we will add one more possibility here. Consider the data in (21).

(21) a. Which bin did Fred put the bottles in?
b. Who did Ingrid give the book to?

In both examples in (21), the fronted phrase – *which bin* and *who*, respectively – functions as the OBJ of an OBL_θ. In order to allow for this, we can extend (20b) to include OBL_θ OBJ, replacing (20) by (22).

(22) a. C-structure rule for long-distance dependencies in English (sixth attempt)

$$\text{CP} \longrightarrow \underset{\substack{(\uparrow \text{FOCUS}) = \downarrow \\ (\uparrow \text{FOCUS}) = (\uparrow \{\text{COMP}|\text{XCOMP}\}^* \ \text{GF}_{wh})}}{\text{XP}_{wh}} \quad \underset{\uparrow = \downarrow}{\text{C}'}$$

b. $\text{GF}_{wh} \equiv \{\text{SUBJ}|\text{OBJ}|\text{OBJ}_\theta|\text{OBL}_\theta|\text{OBL}_\theta \ \text{OBJ}|\text{XCOMP}|\text{ADJ} \in | \ \text{XADJ} \in\}$

Fronted *wh*-phrases may also come from within ADJ, but such sentences involve quite varied and subtle native speaker judgements, so we will not deal with that here.

The annotation in the rule in (22a) involves FUNCTIONAL UNCERTAINTY; at this point in the structure we do not know what GF_{wh} it refers to. We will not go into the full formal machinery of functional uncertainty here, but just sketch its workings. The rule can be satisfied by a range of f-structures, in fact an infinite number, since the GF_{wh} can be embedded within any number of COMPS or XCOMPS in principle. More specifically, it is OUTSIDE-IN FUNCTIONAL UNCERTAINTY since the path specified goes from the edge of the sentence into embedded f-structures; we saw this used also in Chapter 4. Of course we tend not to use that many embeddings when we speak because it becomes difficult for the hearer to parse, but it is not the case that it becomes completely ungrammatical at a specific point.

The functional uncertainty in the rule in (22a) is resolved because there is a "missing" GF somewhere further on in the sentence. In (23a), *which dog* will be identified as OBJ since *pat* has a PRED feature requiring both a SUBJ and an OBJ; there is no other constituent that can have this grammatical function in the sentence, and *which dog* has the right properties to fill the OBJ function, for instance in that it is a DP. In the case of (23b), on the other hand, there will not be a licit f-structure since both grammatical functions required by the PRED feature of *pat* are already satisfied. Similarly, the example in (23c) is ungrammatical because *faint* selects only for a SUBJ, and that is present in the sentence already. In (23d), *behind which dog* cannot fill the OBJ function required by 'pat' because it is a PP. In other words, in (23b) to (23d), there is no solution to the equation ($\uparrow$ FOCUS) = ($\uparrow$ {COMP|XCOMP}* GF_{wh}), and ungrammaticality is correctly predicted.

(23) a. Which dog did Ingrid pat?
b. *Which dog did Ingrid pat the golden retriever?
c. *What did Ingrid faint?
d. *Behind which dog did Ingrid pat?

The examples in (23) illustrate a more general property of discourse functions such as TOPIC and FOCUS, namely that they cannot have **just** a discourse function; they must also be integrated in the f-structure built up around a predicate; they must have some other role within the sentence. This is captured by an extension of the Coherence Condition, which we introduced in Section 2.2.

Extended Coherence Condition: all governable functions present in an f-structure must occur in the value of a local PRED feature. All functions that have a PRED value must have a θ-role. FOCUS and TOPIC must be linked to the semantic predicate argument structure of the sentence in which they occur through proper integration with the f-structure of the sentence. Proper integration is either functional equality with or anaphoric binding of a grammatical function, including ADJ.

Integration of the FOCUS by functional equality is what we have seen here, and it is achieved by means of a functional equation that includes ($\uparrow$ FOCUS) = ($\uparrow$ ... GF_{wh}) as in (22). Anaphoric binding involves a pronoun instead of a "gap". An example from Swedish is provided in (24) (from Teleman et al. 1999, 4.427).

(24) a. [Vilka elever]$_i$ var det oklart om de$_i$ skulle klara sig.
which pupil.PL be.PST it unclear if they should pass.INF
'Which students were uncertain to pass?'
b. [Vilket ord]$_i$ visste ingen hur det$_i$ skulle stavas?
which word know.PST no-one how it should spell.INF.PASS
'Which word did no-one know how to spell?'

Here *vilka elever* and *vilket ord* are associated with the subject role of *skulle klara sig* and *skulle stavas*, respectively. However, that actual subject position is filled by the pronouns *de* and *det*, and hence the connection cannot be made through a functional equation, but is instead achieved by anaphoric binding as introduced in Chapter 7. A pronoun which, like this, appears in the neutral position of the fronted element and "repeats" it is referred to as a RESUMPTIVE PRONOUN. We will see in (38) that they can also be used to "rescue" some complex *wh*-constructions in English.

There is one aspect of constituent questions in English that we still have not considered, and that is the fact that the f-structure of the fronted phrase must contain some *wh*-word. We will capture this by using a function OPER, for operator, for the *wh*-phrase and require that it has a feature WH = +, and that any *wh*-word is associated with this feature. We now need to specify how the OPER can come to have the feature. Consider the examples in (25).

(25) a. *What* did the dog eat?
b. *Which sausage* did the dog steal?
c. *From which bowl* did the dog eat?
d. *Whose sausage* did the dog eat?
e. *Whose dog's sausage* did the cat steal?

In (25a), the *wh*-phrase is a DP which consists of just a *wh*-pronoun, so the phrase as a whole clearly has the feature WH = +. In (25b), *which* is a determiner, and hence a co-head of the fronted DP. As a co-head its f-structure is shared by the DP, so the WH = + becomes part of the fronted DP. In (25c), the WH = + feature value is associated with *which bowl*, since *which* is a co-head of this DP, but here *which bowl* is the OBJ of a preposition. This means that we need to establish a path through OBJ to get to the element that has the crucial feature value WH = +. In (25d), the *wh*-word is the possessor of *sausage*, and so the path needs to go through POSS. However, in (25e), the *wh*-word is the possessor of the possessor *dog*, so the path needs to be POSS POSS. In fact, we can add further possessors, as in *the father's cousin's wife's dog*, so that the path needs to be POSS*, with the now familiar Kleene star. This means that the path to the OPER then needs to be (↑ FOCUS {OBJ | POSS*}). In (25a) and (25b), the FOCUS **is** the OPER, in (25c), it is the FOCUS OBJ, in (25d) it is FOCUS POSS and in (25e) it is FOCUS POSS POSS. We can insert the equations required to ensure that we account for the need for a *wh*-word in the fronted phrase into the rule in (18) to get (26).

(26) C-structure rule for long-distance dependencies in English (final version)

$$\text{CP} \longrightarrow \begin{array}{c} \text{XP}_{wh} \\ (\uparrow \text{FOCUS}) = \downarrow \\ (\uparrow \text{FOCUS}) = (\uparrow \{\text{COMP}|\text{XCOMP}\}^{*}\ \text{GF}_{wh}) \\ (\uparrow \text{OPER}) = (\uparrow \text{FOCUS}\ \{\text{OBJ} \mid \text{POSS}^{*}\}) \\ (\uparrow \text{OPER WH}) =_c + \end{array} \quad \begin{array}{c} \text{C}' \\ \uparrow = \downarrow \\ \\ \\ \\ \end{array}$$

Just to recap, we will go through the annotations of XP_{wh}. The first equation ensures that the XP_{wh} functions as FOCUS. The second one ensures that the FOCUS also fills some other function within the sentence. This can be any of the GF_{wh} as defined in (20b), and that function can be embedded within one or more COMPS or XCOMPS or an OBJ (the latter as specified for GF_{wh} in (22b)). The third and fourth equations ensure that there is an element with the feature value WH = + in an appropriate position within the fronted phrase. It does so by identifying a function OPER that must contain WH = + and that can either be identical to the FOCUS or it can be an OBJ or a POSS, or indeed a POSS POSS etc., inside the FOCUS.

Note the constraining equation indicated by $=_c$, a type of equation introduced in Section 3.2. This does not itself define the feature value to be WH = +, but it requires this feature value to be present in the f-structure (so it "checks" for its presence). If it was not a constraining equation, the equation could actually assign this value to any element not specified for a conflicting value.

Let's look at the c- and f-structure of the example in (25d) in some detail. The annotated tree can be found in (27). We have only included the most relevant annotations in order to keep the tree as uncluttered as possible. We have not named all the f-structures and stated the f-description, since the reader should be able to do this now. We have named the f-structure associated with the whole sentence g, since we will want to refer to this below.

(27)

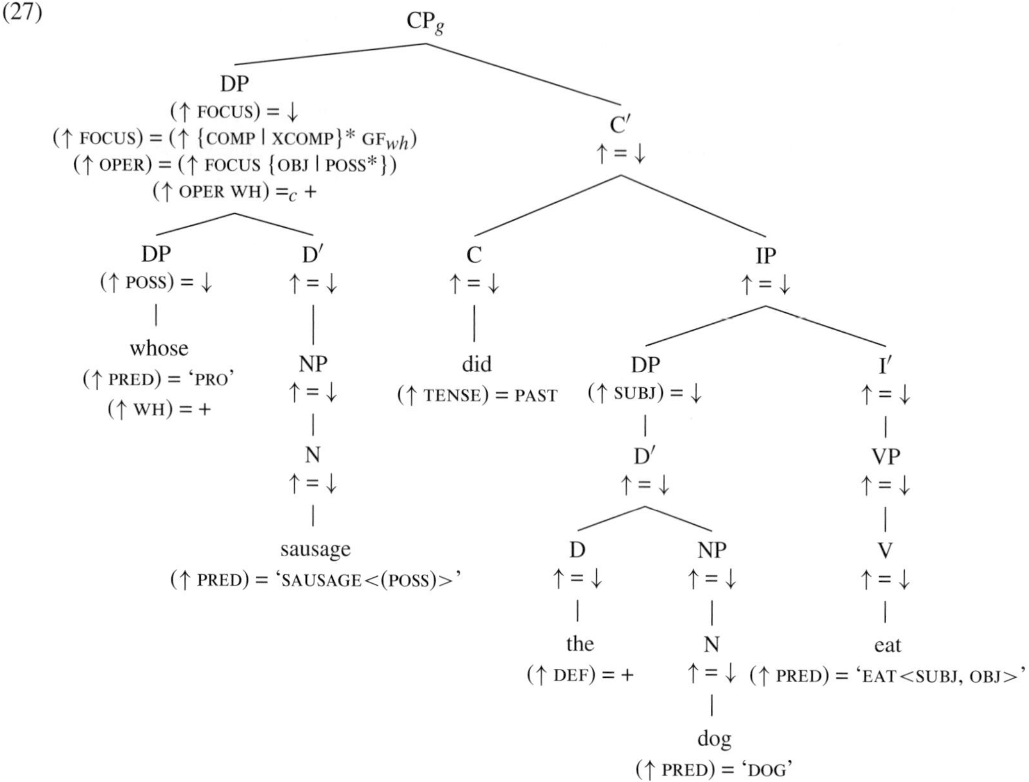

Here we have an f-description which involves some functionally uncertain equations and some constraining equations alongside the defining equations. Leaving these aside for the moment, the defining equations in (27) give us the minimal f-structure in (28).

(28)

$$
g:\left[\begin{array}{ll}
\text{FOCUS} & \left[\begin{array}{ll}\text{POSS} & \left[\begin{array}{ll}\text{PRED} & \text{`PRO'}\\ \text{WH} & +\end{array}\right]\\ \text{PRED} & \text{`SAUSAGE<(POSS)>'}\end{array}\right]\\
\text{OPER} & \\
\text{SUBJ} & \left[\begin{array}{ll}\text{PRED} & \text{`DOG'}\\ \text{DEF} & +\end{array}\right]\\
\text{TENSE} & \text{PAST}\\
\text{PRED} & \text{`EAT <SUBJ, OBJ>'}
\end{array}\right]
$$

In (28), we have included the function OPER within the f-structure associated with the sentence as a whole, but we have not given it a value since the equation (g OPER) = (g FOCUS {OBJ | POSS*}) involves functional uncertainty. The two pieces of information we have about OPER are that it must be identical to the FOCUS or the OBJ of the FOCUS or some POSS inside the FOCUS, and that whatever it is identical to must contain the feature WH = +. There is a POSS inside the FOCUS in (28), and it contains WH = +, so this offers a licit solution to the equation and we get (g OPER) = (g FOCUS POSS), indicated by the line between OPER and POSS in (29). This means that the constraining equation (g OPER WH) $=_c$ + has also been satisfied. The equation (g FOCUS) = (g {COMP | XCOMP* } GF_{wh}) remains. FOCUS cannot be identical to SUBJ because there is already a SUBJ and both the FOCUS and the SUBJ have a PRED value, so we would get a violation of Uniqueness. It could not be identical to OBL_θ, for instance, since there is no predicate in the f-structure which requires this function, and if we introduced it, there would be a violation of the Coherence Constraint. However, there is one way of solving the equation; the PRED of *eat* requires an OBJ, but there is no OBJ in (28). If we resolve the functional uncertainty as (g FOCUS) = (g OBJ), then we get the complete f-structure in (29) with the link between FOCUS and OBJ as indicated.

(29)

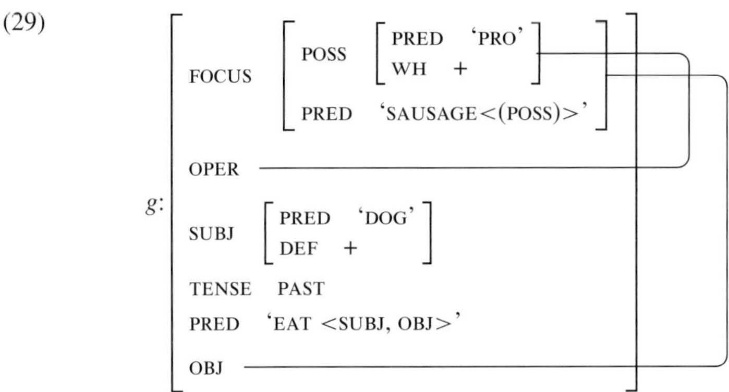

6.3 Variation in Constituent Questions

We have considered English constituent questions in some detail above. In this section we will consider a couple of languages which organise such questions in quite a different way, but our aim is just to illustrate the variation, not to provide full analyses.

For English, we defined GF_{wh} in such a way as to exclude POSS from occurring at the bottom of a path, in order to make sure that (19) was ruled out. There are, however, languages to which this restriction does not apply. Consider the Greek examples in (30).

(30) a. Tinos taise ton skilo?
whose.GEN feed.3SG.AOR DEF dog.ACC
'Whose dog did she feed?'

b. Tinos evale ta portokalia stin tsanda?
whose.GEN put.3SG.AOR DEF orange.PL.ACC in.DEF bag.ACC
'Whose oranges did she put in the bag?'

Note that both examples show pronoun incorporation, so there is no overt subject. In (30a), the fronted *wh*-word *tinos* is the possessor of 'dog', and in (30b) of 'oranges'. The questioned possessor has then been fronted from within a noun phrase, where the noun itself has been left in its canonical position. This means that in Greek POSS should not be excluded from the GF_{wh} set. There may be other constraints on Greek constituent questions that differ from those on English, but here we just wanted to show that POSS can be extracted.

An analysis using a rule like the one in (26) in Section 6.2 will be appropriate for any language where the questioned constituent occurs in a position that is reserved for such elements and not in the position normally associated with its grammatical function within the clause. However, not all languages use a dedicated position for the questioned constituent. There are languages, like Japanese, where the equivalent of the *wh*-phrase occurs in the same position as any other phrase of the same function; these are referred to as IN SITU constituent questions. This is illustrated in (31) (slightly adapted from Mycock (2007)). The questioned constituent *dare-ni* is in its canonical position in (31b), the same position as *Gorō-ni* in (31a). The final element in (31b), *ka*, is a question particle, which marks the sentence as a question, but is obligatory only in the written language.

(31) a. Mari-ga depāto-de Gorō-ni ranpu-o
Mari-NOM department store-LOC Goro-DAT lamp-ACC
eranda.
choose.PST
'Mary chose a lamp for Goro at the department store.'

b. Mari-ga depāto-de dare-ni ranpu-o
Mari-NOM department store-LOC who-DAT lamp-ACC
eranda ka?
choose.PST Q
'Who did Mary chose a lamp for at the department store?'

The analysis of Japanese constituent questions need not involve functional uncertainty since the grammatical function of the questioned constituent is indicated in the same way as it is for a non-questioned constituent; *Goro* and *dare* are marked by the same case marker *-ni*. There still needs to be a WH = + feature within the questioned constituent, and as in English that will be supplied by the question word, in this case *dare*. The questioned constituent also needs to be identified as the focus of the sentence, but in Japanese, this is not done by using a grammaticalised discourse function, so there is no f-structure FOCUS. Instead focus is purely an information-structural notion which is indicated prosodically, and hence it is identified through a mapping between p(rosodic)-structure and i(nformation)-structure. We will not deal with p-structure or i-structure in this book, but we provide relevant references at the end of the chapter.

There are also languages that do put questioned constituents in a dedicated focus position, but which permit more than one phrase to occur in this position. Hungarian is such a language as illustrated in (32) (again from Mycock (2007)). Hungarian differs from English also in not using the sentence-initial position for the focused constituent, but the position immediately preceding the finite verb. In the example in (32a) only the SUBJ precedes the verb and the OBJ and OBL_θ follow the verb, but in the constituent question, two questioned constituents are fronted to pre-verbal positions in Hungarian (in the glossing VM stands for 'verbal modifier').

(32) a. János bemutat-t-a Mari-t Anná-nak.
Janos.NOM VM.introduce-PST-DEF.3SG Mary-ACC Anna-DAT
'Janos introduced Mary to Anna.'

b. János ki-t ki-nek mutatt-ott be?
Janos.NOM who-ACC who-DAT introduce-PST.3SG VM
'Who did Janos introduce to whom?'

We can assume that the designated FOCUS position in Hungarian is in the specifier of VP position, but that more than one element can occur in this position. Since more than one question phrase can occur in this position and be focused, FOCUS has a set as its value in Hungarian constituent questions, so that the appropriate annotation refers to a set of focused constituents, and we get the rule in (33) for Hungarian. In (33), the path specified is GF*, which is another difference from English. We will not go into the data that motivates this here, but provide references at the end of the chapter. There we also provide references to an alternative analysis of the FOCUS position in Hungarian.

(33) VP $\longrightarrow$ XP* V′

	XP*	V′
VP $\longrightarrow$	$(\uparrow \text{GF*}) = \downarrow$	$\uparrow = \downarrow$
	$\downarrow \in (\uparrow \text{FOCUS})$	

More generally, Hungarian word order is more influenced by information-structural constraints than English is. It can be described as discourse-configurational, a term we will return to in Section 6.5.

6.4 Constraints on Constituent Questions

We have referred to the construction type of which constituent questions form one kind as 'unbounded' or 'long-distance' dependencies; however, it is not the case that they are completely unconstrained. We have already seen that there are constraints on the "bottom" of the path in English, so that POSS needs to be excluded. This was done by the way we defined GF_{wh} in (20b). There are also constraints on the path itself, frequently referred to as ISLANDS from which *wh*-phrases cannot escape. The full set of island constraints are complex, and we will only illustrate with a couple of examples here to show how they can be accounted for in LFG. Consider the example in (34), where, in order to make things clearer, we have used _ to indicate the position the fronted constituent would have had if it had not been fronted.

(34) a. [That Oscar bought a dog $]_{\text{SUBJ}}$ worried Ingrid.
b. *What$_i$ does [that Oscar bought $\_{}_i]_{\text{SUBJ}}$ worry Ingrid.

The example in (34b) is ungrammatical because the fronted constituent comes from within a clausal subject. This constraint on the path between the fronted constituent and its grammatical relation is accounted for in the rule in (26), since the equation (↑ FOCUS) = (↑ {COMP|XCOMP}* GF) only allows the grammatical function to be embedded inside a COMP or XCOMP, and in (34b) it comes from inside a SUBJ, so the path would be SUBJ OBJ, and this is incompatible with the equation in (26).

There are also more subtle constraints on long-distance dependencies that cannot be stated directly in terms of the path between the FOCUS and its within-clause grammatical function. For instance, in English a questioned constituent cannot be linked to a grammatical function inside an interrogative complement clause, a constraint which is often referred to as the *wh*-island constraint. This is illustrated in (35b), which is contrasted with its non-fronted equivalent (35a).

(35) a. Ingrid wondered [whether Oscar bought the dog].
b. *What did Ingrid wonder [whether Oscar bought _].

As we saw in Section 6.2, in English the path between a fronted element and its grammatical relation can go through one or more COMPs, and *whether Oscar bought* is a COMP in (35b), so the ungrammaticality of (35b) cannot be accounted for in our current formulation of the rule in (26). The crucial factor that makes (35b) ungrammatical is that COMP is a interrogative clause. This particular restriction on constituent questions in English could be captured by an OFF-PATH CONSTRAINT. We can add a constraint specifying that the path to the within-clause grammatical function cannot pass through any COMP which has the feature CLTYPE = INTER, using the feature CLTYPE which we introduced in Section 5.1. Adding this off-path constraint to the path in (26) gives us (36). In this constraint, $\rightarrow$ COMP refers to the f-structure of the attribute COMP, so the constraint says that the path cannot contain any COMPs which have an attribute CLTYPE with the value INTER. Formally, equations involving a negative constraint function the same way that constraining equations do; they are checked once the f-structure has been built. For a full account of English constituent questions and of island constraints in general, much more discussion would be required, but the example we have provided here should serve at least to illustrate how off-path constraints work.

(36) Off-path constraint for *wh*-interrogatives

$$(\uparrow \text{FOCUS}) \quad = \quad (\uparrow \{ \underset{(\rightarrow \text{CLTYPE}) \neq \text{INTER}}{\text{COMP}} \mid \text{XCOMP}\}^* \ \text{GF})$$

The path with the constraint specified for English in (36) is not a universal path. There are also languages which put stricter limits on what can be questioned. In Tagalog, for instance, only subjects can be questioned in this way, and the only grammatical function from which they can be extracted is also SUBJ, which means that whereas SUBJ clauses are islands in English, in Tagalog it is the only permitted clause type the *wh*-phrase can be extracted from. This gives the path ($\uparrow$ FOCUS) = ($\uparrow$ SUBJ$^+$) for Tagalog, where $^+$ is the Kleene plus to be read as 'one or more', just like it is in the rule for coordination that we introduced in Section 2.3.3, so that it allows for a path to a SUBJ in the clause or a SUBJ within the SUBJ of the clause etc.

Swedish shows more subtle behaviour compared to English with respect to *wh*-islands. Compare the two sentences in (37), and you see that Swedish is less constrained when it comes to *wh*-question formation (the Swedish sentence is from Engdahl (1986, 6)). We will not go into detail here; we just want show that constraints on *wh*-fronting can vary in subtle ways. We have indicated COMP boundaries and indicated with _ where the phrase would have occurred if it had not been a fronted *wh*-phrase.

(37) a. Vilken film$_i$ var det [du gärna ville veta
which film be.PST it you with pleasure want.PST know.INF
[vem$_j$ som _$_j$ hade regisserat _$_i$]]?
who that have.PST direct.SUP

b. ??Which film was it you would like to know who had directed?

Given the use of resumptive pronouns in Swedish *wh*-constructions that we saw in (24), it is interesting that a resumptive pronoun can make the question in (37b) more acceptable to some speakers of English. The relevant example is provided in (38).

(38) ?Which film was it you would like to know who had directed it?

In this section we illustrated the crucial property of the LFG account of long-distance dependencies, namely that the dependencies and the constraints on them are dealt with through f-structure. For languages that have a dedicated structural position for questioned constituents, this is captured by a phrase structure rule where the fronted phrase is annotated with an equation that identifies it as the FOCUS. Crucially the position where it would have been had it not been fronted is not filled in c-structure. The fact that the fronted constituent also fills some other function in the sentence is captured through the f-structure and the equation linking FOCUS to some other GF_{wh} from a defined list. It is not done by means of a connection between nodes in the c-structure tree. We have seen examples of languages that can front more than one constituent, in which case there must be more than one position with the appropriate information-structural properties. We have also seen that there are languages where *wh*-phrases appear in the position where the corresponding non-*wh* phrase would have occurred. There are other construction types such as topicalisation and relative clauses that we have not dealt with at all here, but references are provided at the end of the chapter.

6.5 Discourse-Configurational Languages

In the English examples we have considered here, there is one position that is information-structurally prominent, but the shape of the c-structure beyond this one position is driven by purely syntactic constraints: the SUBJ is in the specifier of IP position, the OBJ is the sister of the verb, and so on. For other languages information-structural categories play a bigger role in determining the shape of clauses; these are referred to as DISCOURSE-CONFIGURATIONAL languages and Hungarian, which we exemplified in (32), is one.

We will illustrate here with the Finnish examples in (39) (data from Karttunen and Kay (1985, 279–80), who comment that though (39f) is possible, it is rare).

(39)
a. Esa luki kirjan.
Esa.NOM.SG read.PST.3SG book.GEN.SG
'Esa read a/the book.'

b. Kirjan luki Esa.
book.GEN.SG read.PST.3SG Esa.NOM.SG

c. Esa kirjan luki.
Esa.NOM.SG book.GEN.SG read.PST.3SG

d. Kirjan Esa luki.
book.GEN.SG Esa.NOM.SG read.PST.3SG

e. Luki Esa kirjan.
read.PST.3SG Esa.NOM.SG book.GEN.SG

f. Luki kirjan Esa.
read.PST.3SG book.GEN.SG Esa.NOM.SG

All sentences in (39) capture the same basic proposition, but they differ in how the information is organised. Because of the way Finnish is organised, *kirjan* can mean either *a book* or *the book*. The difference between (39a) and (39b), which are described as neutral, relates to the topic of the sentence; (39a) is a natural answer to the question *What did Esa read?*, making *Esa* the topic of conversation, whereas the question *Who read the book?* would be more naturally answered with (39b). In each of the examples in (39c)–(39e), the initial word is focused, so that (39c) and (39d) can be represented as *It was ESA who read the book* and *It was a BOOK that Esa read*, respectively, and (39e) as *Esa DID read a book*. We can conclude that the position immediately preceding the finite verb is a TOPIC position and the one preceding that is a position indicating contrast, which we can refer to as the FOCUS position, hence Finnish clause structure includes two positions associated with grammaticalised discourse functions. We can then assume that Finnish makes use of annotated rules like those in (40), where GF stands for any grammatical function.

(40) a. $\text{CP} \longrightarrow \underset{\substack{(\uparrow \text{ FOCUS}) = \downarrow \\ (\uparrow \text{ FOCUS}) = (\uparrow \ldots \text{ GF})}}{\text{NP}} \quad \underset{\uparrow = \downarrow}{\text{C}'}$

b. $\text{IP} \longrightarrow \underset{\substack{(\uparrow \text{ TOPIC}) = \downarrow \\ (\uparrow \text{ TOPIC}) = (\uparrow \ldots \text{ GF})}}{\text{NP}} \quad \underset{\uparrow = \downarrow}{\text{I}'}$

In accordance with the Extended Coherence Condition, the grammaticalised discourse functions must be properly integrated into the sentence, in this case by functional equality with some grammatical relation GF. Since we don't want to explore what limits there are on the path between the grammaticalised discourse function and the GF in Finnish, we have just indicated that with ... in (40). We won't go into detail here, but there are reasons to assume that Finnish noun phrases are NPs, rather than DPs.

The rules in (40) give us the tree in (41) for (39d). Note that there is no VP since all elements that could have been in VP are in other positions: the finite verb is in I, and the two noun phrases are in the two discourse positions.

(41)

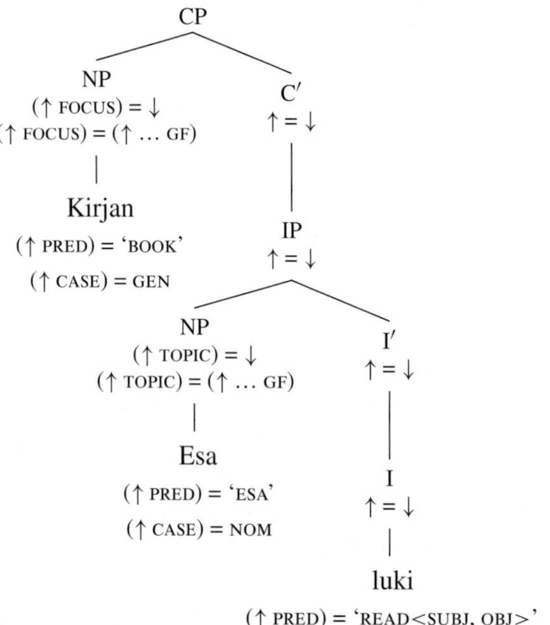

There are no annotated phrase structure rules for Finnish referring to grammatical relations like SUBJ and OBJ; these are not structurally defined, but derived from case in Finnish. The fact that *Esa* is nominative will make it the subject, and the genitive on *kirjan* will make it the object, in the way that we discussed for dependent-marking non-configurational languages in Section 4.4. We should add that the case marking of objects is a little complex in Finnish, but here the genitive clearly marks *kirjan* as the object. This gets us the f-structure in (42) for (41).

(42)

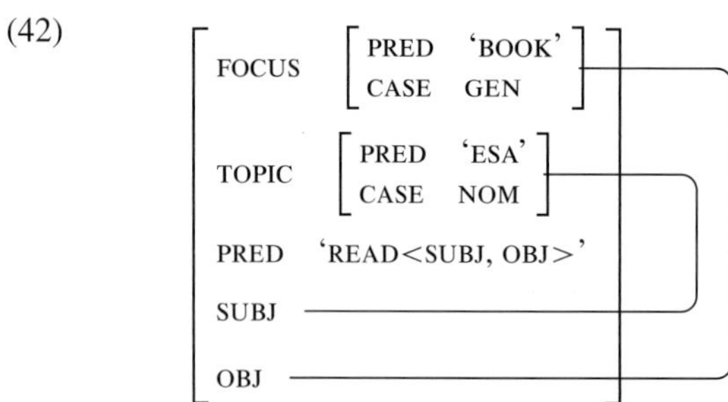

Reading

We have followed Kaplan and Zaenen (1989) in analysing long-distance dependencies in f-structure and assumed that the grammatical relation which the fronted element is linked to is not found in the c-structure. Bresnan et al. (2016) take a different approach and use an empty element in c-structure which involves inside-out functional uncertainty. Falk (2001) uses both approaches depending on whether the fronted constituent functions as the SUBJ or not. It is our view that the analysis by Kaplan and Zaenen (1989) is most in line with the principles of LFG.

One clause type that involves a long-distance dependency that we have not discussed here is the relative clause. Relative clauses show interesting cross-linguistic variation and in English they share properties with *wh*-interrogatives, but there are also some differences. We refer the reader to Dalrymple (2001, ch. 14) for an LFG analysis of relative clauses.

Though the data in (39) is from Karttunen and Kay (1985), the most relevant reference for LFG is Vilkuna (1989), who provides a study of Finnish clause structure in general and also an LFG analysis. Another example of a discourse-configurational language is Russian and a detailed LFG analysis is provided by King (1995).

Mycock (2006, 2007) has an interesting discussion of cross-linguistic variation in long-distance dependencies, and she also formalises the mapping to p-structure. Engdahl (1986) provides data on the special properties of constituent questions, especially in Swedish. For further discussion of constraints on constituent questions in Tagalog, see Kroeger (1993, 210–21). In Section 6.3, we adopted the c-structure for Hungarian proposed by Mycock. A more detailed analysis of Hungarian clause structure and 'verb modifiers' can be found in Laczkó (2014a, 2014b). Contrary to Mycock, he assumes that only one of the fronted *wh*-phrases in multiple fronting occurs in the specifier of VP, whereas the others are adjoined to VP.

More on the Swedish resumptive pronouns can be found in Zaenen et al. (1981). Sells (1984) provides an analysis of resumptive pronouns, and a more recent thorough analysis is Asudeh (2012), but his analysis involves a type of formal semantics, glue semantics, that is likely to prove a challenge to someone who has just worked through this book. An introduction to glue semantics can be found in Dalrymple (2001). A briefer and more syntactically oriented discussion of resumption can be found in Falk (2002) on Hebrew and see also Camilleri and Sadler (2016) on Maltese.

Kaplan and Zaenen (1989) provide an analysis of some island constraints with the approach to long-distance dependencies that we have outlined here. Another type of constraint on *wh*-dependencies that has been discussed frequently in the general literature on syntax is the crossover effect; LFG accounts of this can be found for instance in Bresnan (1994) and Dalrymple et al. (2001).

Exercises

6.1 For each of the sentences in (43), state what the fronted constituent is and what grammatical function it has within the sentence. Is it a grammatical function of the highest verb or is there a path through COMP(s)?

(43) a. Horses, my sister's husband dislikes.
b. When did Fred decide to buy a dog?

c. In which box did you put the baubles?
d. Which book did you say that you had borrowed?
e. Which of the three dogs in the window might Fred buy?

6.2 *Wh*-questions such as those in (44) are ambiguous. State the two readings in each case and show how this can be accounted for in LFG.

(44) a. Where did Oscar proclaim that he would build a house?
b. Why did Ingrid say that Sarah had failed the exam?

6.3 In Chapter 2 you were asked to suggest a c-structure for Swedish clauses on the basis of the data in (45). Now you should be in a position to add some annotations to your rules, at least to account for the left edge of the clause. You may not feel able to distinguish different grammaticalised discourse functions, so you can generalise over them and use GDF.

(45) a. Nils åt fyra pannkakor igår.
Nils eat.PST four pancake.PL yesterday
'Nils ate four pancakes yesterday.'
b. I förrgår åt han köttbullar
the day before yesterday.DEF eat.PST he meatball.PL
istället.
instead.
'The day before yesterday he ate meatballs instead.'
c. Ägg gillar han inte.
egg like.PRS he not
'Eggs, he doesn't like.'
d. Honom ger hon gärna alla sina pannkakor.
him give.PRS she gladly all her pancake.PL
'She happily gives **him** all her pancakes.'

6.4 Rudin (1988a, 1988b) provides data that illustrates the similarities and differences between Bulgarian and Serbo-Croatian with regards to constituent questions. She provides the data in (46) (Rudin, 1988b, 449). What does this tell us about the two languages?

(46) a. **Koj kogo** vižda? (B)
who who.ACC see.PRS.3SG
'Who sees whom?'
b. **Ko koga** vidi? (SC)
who who.ACC see.PRS.3SG
'Who sees whom?'

What does this mean for an LFG analysis, both with respect to c-structure and f-structure?

The additional data in (47) is provided, where the Bulgarian example in (47a) is described as equivalent to an English echo question such as *You saw what!?*. Though native speaker judgements on the Serbo-Croation example in (47b) vary, they are said to be more acceptable than the Bulgarian counterparts. The data is from Rudin (1988a, 7), where she used # to mark echo status. What does this tell us about fronting of the questioned constituent (the "*wh*-word") in these languages?

(47) a. #**Koj** e vidjal **kogo**? (B)
who.NOM have.3SG see.PPART who.ACC

b. (?#)**Ko** je video **koga**? (SC)
who.NOM have.3SG see.PPTCP who.ACC

Compare the data in (46) with that in (48) from Bulgarian and from Serbo-Croatian in (49) (adapted from Rudin 1988b, 450-4). Note that we now have a * for 'ungrammatical' rather # for echo-status.

(48) a. **Koj kŭde** misliš [če e otišŭl __]? (B)
who where think.PRS.2SG that have.3SG go.PPTCP
'Who do you think went where?'

b. *__Koj__ misliš [če e otišŭl _ **kŭde**]? (B)
who think.PRS.2SG that have.3SG go.PPTCP where

c. *__Kŭde__ misliš [če **koj** e otišŭl _]? (B)
where think.PRS.2SG that who have.3SG go.PPTCP

(49) a. **Ko** želite [da vam **šta** kupi _]? (SC)
who want.PRS.2PL INF you what buy.3SG
'Who do you want to buy what?'

b. **Šta** želite [da vam **ko** kupi _]? (SC)
what want.PRS.2PL INF you who buy.3SG
'What do you want who to buy?'

c. *__Ko šta__ želite [da vam kupi __]? (SC)
who what want.PRS.2PL INF you buy.3SG

d. *__Šta ko__ želite [da vam kupi __] ? (SC)
what who want.PRS.2PL INF you buy.3SG

Use LFG terminology to relate the data in (48) and (49) to that in (46) and to describe the difference between the two languages. If you can, sketch out a formal LFG analysis of the data.

7 Anaphoric Binding

7.1 Introducing Anaphoric Pronouns

In this chapter, we will look at the syntactic conditions that hold for the use of pronouns, in particular two types of pronouns: PERSONAL PRONOUNS such as *her* and *them* and REFLEXIVE PRONOUNS such as *herself* and *themselves*. In very broad terms, pronouns in general will often be used to refer to the same thing as another noun phrase in the clause or the wider sentential or discourse context. When this is the case the pronoun and the other noun phrase are COREFERENTIAL, and the pronoun is used ANAPHORICALLY. In this chapter, we will see that there are particular constraints on what pronouns can be coreferential with, and these are referred to as constraints on BINDING. In this chapter we will consider some of the syntactic constraints on binding. Let's start with a simple example. Consider the following two sentences.

(1) a. Lydia$_i$ introduced her$_j$ to everyone in the room.
b. Lydia$_i$ introduced herself$_i$ to everyone in the room.

These are both grammatical, but there is a crucial difference in interpretation. In (1a) the person who Lydia introduces to the assembled multitudes is some other person, while in (1b) it is Lydia herself. The personal pronoun *her* in (1a) cannot be interpreted as referring to Lydia; *her* cannot be coreferential with *Lydia*. The reflexive *herself* in (1b), on the other hand, has to be coreferential with *Lydia*. As we saw in Section 5.3, coreferentiality is indicated with indices in the form of subscript letters; in (1b), the subscript i indicates that *Lydia* and *herself* are coreferential, whereas in (1a), we assume that $i \neq j$, so that the pronoun and the noun phrase are not coreferential. When a pronoun is coreferential with another noun phrase, we refer to that noun phrase as the ANTECEDENT and we call a pronoun that has an antecedent an ANAPHOR.

We will start by looking at the environments in which reflexive forms such as *herself* can appear. The first thing to note is that an example such as (2) is ungrammatical. This is because the only potential antecedent of the reflexive *himself* is *Lydia*, but this is not a possible antecedent since it is GEND = FEM and the anaphor is GEND = MASC, hence it must be the case that $i \neq j$. The anaphor and the antecedent need to agree with respect to features such as GEND, NUM and PERS.

(2) *Lydia$_i$ hurt *himself*$_j$.

A reflexive argument pronoun must have an appropriate antecedent somewhere in the sentence. The examples in (3) are all grammatical and tell us something about where that antecedent can be.

(3) a. Lydia$_i$ hurt herself$_i$.
b. Oscar$_i$ pulled the cover over himself$_i$.
c. Nobody told Eve$_i$ about herself$_i$.

In (3a) the anaphor *herself* is the OBJ in the f-structure of the clause and the antecedent is the SUBJ. In (3b) the antecedent is again the SUBJ but the anaphor is a little more deeply embedded. The prepositional phrase *over himself* is the OBL$_\theta$ argument of the clause as a whole. It consists of a preposition *over* which has the PRED feature 'OVER <OBJ>' and hence takes an OBJ as its complement (the analysis of prepositions was introduced in Section 3.3). This means that the anaphor *himself* is the OBJ within an OBL$_\theta$, and hence we can refer to it as OBL$_\theta$ OBJ. The anaphor is the OBL$_\theta$ OBJ also in (3c), but here the antecedent is the OBJ.

The f-structures in (4)–(6) correspond to these sentences, with the f-structure of the antecedent labelled *a* and the f-structure of the anaphor labelled *p*. As these f-structures show, we use a PRONTYPE feature to distinguish reflexive pronouns from other types of pronoun. Since we are discussing coreference between pronouns and their antecedents in this chapter, we will often indicate this informally in our f-structures by attaching indices to nominal and pronominal PRED values. We will sometimes include some INDEX feature to illustrate why an antecedent may or may not be acceptable, but in order not to make the f-structures too complex, we will not include all agreement features.

(4)
$$\left[\begin{array}{ll} \text{PRED} & \text{`HURT<SUBJ, OBJ>'} \\ \text{TENSE} & \text{PAST} \\ \text{SUBJ} & a{:}\left[\begin{array}{ll}\text{PRED} & \text{`LYDIA}_i\text{'} \\ \text{INDEX} & \left[\text{GEND} \quad \text{FEM}\right]\end{array}\right] \\ \text{OBJ} & p{:}\left[\begin{array}{ll}\text{PRED} & \text{`PRO}_i\text{'}\\ \text{INDEX} & \left[\text{GEND} \quad \text{FEM}\right] \\ \text{PRONTYPE} & \text{REFL}\end{array}\right]\end{array}\right]$$

(5)
$$\left[\begin{array}{ll} \text{PRED} & \text{`PULL<SUBJ, OBJ, OBL}_\theta\text{>'} \\ \text{TENSE} & \text{PAST} \\ \text{SUBJ} & a{:}\left[\begin{array}{ll}\text{PRED} & \text{`OSCAR}_i\text{'} \\ \text{INDEX} & \left[\text{GEND} \quad \text{MASC}\right]\end{array}\right] \\ \text{OBL}_\theta & \left[\begin{array}{ll}\text{PRED} & \text{`OVER <OBJ>'} \\ \text{OBJ} & p{:}\left[\begin{array}{ll}\text{PRED} & \text{`PRO}_i\text{'}\\ \text{INDEX} & \left[\text{GEND} \quad \text{MASC}\right] \\ \text{PRONTYPE} & \text{REFL}\end{array}\right]\end{array}\right] \\ \text{OBJ} & \left[\begin{array}{ll}\text{PRED} & \text{`COVER'} \\ \text{DEF} & +\end{array}\right]\end{array}\right]$$

(6)

$$\left[\begin{array}{ll}
\text{PRED} & \text{`TELL<SUBJ, OBJ, OBL}_\theta\text{>'}\\
\text{TENSE} & \text{PAST}\\
\text{SUBJ} & \left[\begin{array}{ll}\text{PRED} & \text{`NOBODY'}\end{array}\right]\\
\text{OBL}_\theta & \left[\begin{array}{ll}
\text{PRED} & \text{`ABOUT <OBJ>'}\\
\text{OBJ} & p{:}\left[\begin{array}{ll}
\text{PRED} & \text{`PRO}_i\text{'}\\
\text{INDEX} & \left[\begin{array}{ll}\text{GEND} & \text{FEM}\end{array}\right]\\
\text{PRONTYPE} & \text{REFL}
\end{array}\right]
\end{array}\right]\\
\text{OBJ} & a{:}\left[\begin{array}{ll}
\text{PRED} & \text{`EVE}_i\text{'}\\
\text{INDEX} & \left[\begin{array}{ll}\text{GEND} & \text{FEM}\end{array}\right]
\end{array}\right]
\end{array}\right]$$

On the other hand, the ungrammaticality of (7), in which the intended antecedent and the anaphor are not in the same clause, suggests that the antecedent cannot be too far away. Since there is no other potential antecedent in (7) (remember that the anaphor and antecedent cannot clash in terms of GEND, NUM and PERS features, so *John* is not a possible antecedent), the sentence is ungrammatical (the coindexation signals the intended coreference).

(7) *Lydia$_i$ told me that John hurt herself$_i$.

(8)

$$*\left[\begin{array}{ll}
\text{PRED} & \text{`TELL<SUBJ, OBJ, COMP>'}\\
\text{TENSE} & \text{PAST}\\
\text{SUBJ} & a{:}\left[\begin{array}{ll}
\text{PRED} & \text{`LYDIA}_i\text{'}\\
\text{INDEX} & \left[\begin{array}{ll}\text{GEND} & \text{FEM}\end{array}\right]
\end{array}\right]\\
\text{COMP} & \left[\begin{array}{ll}
\text{TENSE} & \text{PAST}\\
\text{SUBJ} & \left[\begin{array}{ll}
\text{PRED} & \text{`JOHN'}\\
\text{INDEX} & \left[\begin{array}{ll}\text{GEND} & \text{MASC}\end{array}\right]
\end{array}\right]\\
\text{PRED} & \text{`HURT <SUBJ, OBJ>'}\\
\text{OBJ} & p{:}\left[\begin{array}{ll}
\text{PRED} & \text{`PRO}_i\text{'}\\
\text{INDEX} & \left[\begin{array}{ll}\text{GEND} & \text{FEM}\end{array}\right]\\
\text{PRONTYPE} & \text{REFL}
\end{array}\right]
\end{array}\right]\\
\text{OBJ} & \left[\begin{array}{ll}\text{PRED} & \text{`PRO'}\end{array}\right]
\end{array}\right]$$

For English, the syntactic DOMAIN within which a reflexive anaphor such as *himself*, *herself* or *myself* must find an antecedent is what we call the MINIMAL COMPLETE NUCLEUS (MINCOMPN). The term NUCLEUS refers to the f-structure containing a PRED and its arguments. The term COMPLETE NUCLEUS refers to an f-structure containing a PRED and its arguments, where those arguments include a SUBJ. The MINIMAL COMPLETE NUCLEUS is the smallest f-structure that contains the reflexive and a SUBJ function. This is not the only domain relevant to binding, as we will see in Section 7.2.

Before we consider the role these notions play when it comes to analysing the relation between anaphors and their antecedents, let's look at a few examples to illustrate the differences. The verb *hurt* has two arguments, and one of these arguments is a SUBJ. This means that the f-structure for a sentence such as *Lydia hurt herself* – provided in (4) – is a nucleus because it contains both the arguments of *hurt*. It is also a complete nucleus because it includes a SUBJ. Now consider the sentence in (9a). The f-structure for the sentence is provided as *g* in (9b).

(9) a. Anna$_i$ said that Lydia$_j$ hurt herself$_{*i/j}$.

b.

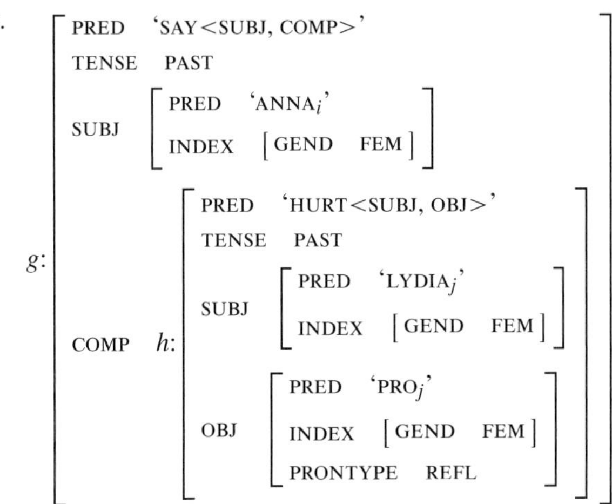

The f-structure *h* is a minimal complete nucleus for the reflexive since it contains all the arguments of *hurt* and a SUBJ. Hence the reflexive must find its antecedent within *h*. The larger f-structure, *g* would also be a complete nucleus containing *herself* since it contains all the arguments of *hurt* and a SUBJ. However, it is not the **minimal** complete nucleus, since there is a smaller f-structure, namely *h*, which also contains all the arguments and a SUBJ. Hence *Anna* is not a possible antecedent for the reflexive.

Returning now to (3b), we assume the f-structure in (10) for the prepositional phrase *over himself.*

(10)

$$\begin{bmatrix} \text{PRED} & \text{`OVER<OBJ>'} \\ \text{OBJ} & \begin{bmatrix} \text{PRED} & \text{`PRO}_i\text{'} \\ \text{PRONTYPE} & \text{REFL} \end{bmatrix} \end{bmatrix}$$

This f-structure is a nucleus since it has all the arguments required by the PRED feature of *over*, but it is not a complete nucleus since there is no SUBJ. The nearest SUBJ in (3b) is *Oscar*, and hence the f-structure for the whole sentence, which was shown in (5), is the smallest complete nucleus for the reflexive.

With respect to defining a complete nucleus, POSS functions in a similar way to SUBJ, so that an f-structure that contains a POSS is also a complete nucleus. Compare the two examples in (11).

(11) a. Oscar$_i$ constantly boasts about himself$_i$.

b. Oscar$_i$'s constant boasting about himself$_i$

The example in (11a) is a sentence in which *Oscar* is the SUBJ and is the antecedent of the reflexive within the OBL_θ *about himself*. (11b), on the other hand, is a noun phrase in which *Oscar* is a POSS, but we see that it can be the antecedent of the reflexive much like the SUBJ in (11a). We could then rephrase the definition of COMPLETE NUCLEUS to say that it is an f-structure containing a PRED and its arguments where these include a SUBJ **or** POSS argument.

Now that we have identified the notion MINCOMPN, we can return to the condition that holds between a reflexive pronoun in English and its antecedent:

(12) An English reflexive must find an antecedent within the Minimal Complete Nucleus containing the reflexive pronoun.

So for the anaphoric pronoun *herself* in (8), the MINCOMPN is the f-structure of the COMP, so *Lydia* is too far away, outside the domain within which the reflexive must find its antecedent. This is why (7) is ungrammatical. Of course, the SUBJ of the COMP in (8) would be a possible antecedent if only the PERS, NUM and GEND features matched. Since the antecedent *John* is GEND = MASC, the reflexive cannot have a different GEND value, as it does in (7). However, with a masculine reflexive, the example is grammatical, as (13) shows.

(13) Lydia told me that John_i hurt himself_i.

7.2 Binding Domains

We saw in the last section that English reflexive pronouns such as *myself, yourself, herself* and so on, must find an antecedent – that is, they must be BOUND – within the Minimal Complete Nucleus. We can now ask whether this is the only BINDING DOMAIN relevant to reflexive and personal pronouns. The answer to this question is that it is not. In taking a quick look at English personal pronouns such as *me, you, her, him* we will come across another binding domain which is important for capturing the distribution of these elements.

The first thing to notice about personal pronouns is that they differ from reflexive pronouns in a crucial respect – they do not **have** to have an antecedent in the sentence. So examples like (14) are, of course, perfectly grammatical, although the pronouns *me* and *her* do not have any syntactic antecedents in the sentence.

(14) a. Kim's answer sent *me* into a rage.
b. Oscar asked *her* to leave the room.

When a pronoun does not have a syntactic antecedent, we say that it is not bound, or that it is FREE. In the examples in (14), then, the pronouns *me* and *her* are free, or DISJOINT in reference from other NPs in the sentence.

In order to work out what binding domain is relevant for pronouns, we'll now look at the examples in (15) and consider what the possible interpretations are for the personal pronoun *her*. As shown by the indices, in (15a), where we assume that $i \neq j$, we can only interpret *her* as disjoint from Eve, while in (15b) *her* can be coreferential with or disjoint from the SUBJ Eve.

(15) a. Eve$_i$ sent her$_{*i/j}$ a postcard from Italy.
b. Eve$_i$ put the book down beside her$_{i/j}$.

The examples in (15) show us that an OBJ personal pronoun cannot be bound to a SUBJ in its own clause but that it can be bound to the SUBJ if it is OBJ of an OBL$_\theta$. As we see in (16) a pronoun can also have a syntactic antecedent which is further away, outside its own clause: *him* can be interpreted as referring to *John*, or as disjoint, in which case it is interpreted as referring to some other male person.

(16) John$_i$ claimed that Ellen tried to outwit him$_{i/j}$.

The key point about English pronouns is that they have to be free within a local domain. This local domain is the nucleus which contains them – remember that a nucleus is the f-structure which contains a PRED and its arguments. This domain is usually referred to as the COARGUMENT DOMAIN (COARGD). In (15a), the OBJ *her* is an argument of *sent*, hence it must be disjoint from all other arguments of that verb, including the SUBJ. In (15b), the OBJ *her* is an argument of *beside*, and is only required to be disjoint from any other arguments of that preposition. Since *beside* has the PRED value 'BESIDE <OBJ>', there are no other arguments, hence *her* is free in its coargument domain. The constraint on personal pronouns is captured in (17).

(17) An English personal pronoun cannot have an antecedent within the nucleus that contains it: it must be free in the Coargument Domain.

Now consider an example like (18).

(18) Lydia$_i$ saw her$_{i/j}$ friend in town.

Because the pronoun is only required to be disjoint in the COARGD, there are two possible interpretations in (18), as shown by the indices. One possibility is that the pronoun is interpreted as referring to *Lydia*, because the pronoun is an argument of *friend* – specifically, it is its POSS – and *friend* does not have any other arguments, which means that *Lydia* is outside the coargument domain of the pronoun, and hence *her* is free in its COARGD. The alternative interpretation is that it has no antecedent in the sentence, but refers to some other female individual, which would, of course, still make it free in its COARGD.

We have seen that the binding domain for reflexive anaphors in English is not the same as the domain which is relevant for personal pronouns in English. Since reflexive anaphors in English must be bound within the MINCOMPN and pronouns must be free in the COARGD, they are not always in complementary distribution. The examples in (19) illustrate a case of this sort: either a reflexive *himself* or a personal pronoun *him* can be used to refer to Oscar. The relevant f-structures are given in (20) and (21).

(19) a. Oscar$_i$ pulled the cover over himself$_i$.
b. Oscar$_i$ pulled the cover over him$_{i/j}$.

(20)

(21)

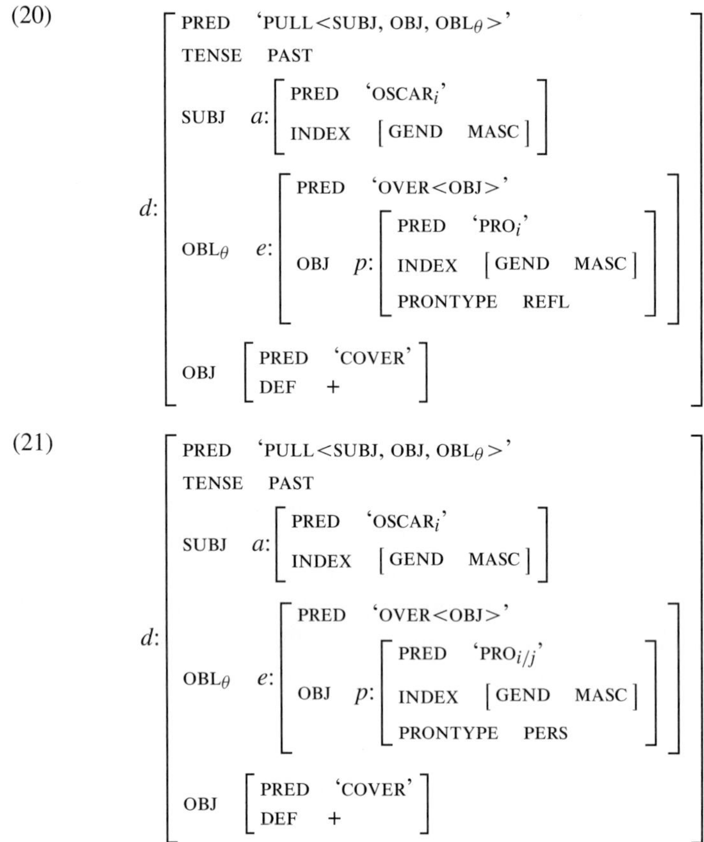

In (20) and (21) there is only one SUBJ, and that is the SUBJ of the sentence as a whole. Hence the MINCOMPN of either *himself* or *him* is the whole f-structure, labelled as *d*. The two pronouns occur as OBJ of the preposition *over*, which only takes one argument, and hence the COARGD of the pronouns is the f-structure labelled *e*. In (20), the reflexive is bound within the MINCOMPN and in (21), the personal pronoun is free within its COARGD, hence both the reflexive and the personal pronoun satisfy their binding conditions, and both examples in (19) are grammatical.

Consider now a further pair of examples, shown in (22).

(22) a. *Lydia$_i$ ignored [Kevin's remarks about herself$_i$].
b. Lydia$_i$ ignored [Kevin's remarks about her$_{i/j}$].

Here the personal pronoun and the reflexive pronoun are in complementary distribution. We can see why this is by looking at the f-structure for these examples. The f-structure in (23) represents the sentence in (22a), with a reflexive pronoun. A reflexive pronoun in English must be bound – that is, it must find an antecedent – within the MINCOMPN that contains it. In (23) the MINCOMPN is the f-structure *d* because the POSS function within NPs corresponds to the SUBJ function in clauses. Because the reflexive does not have an acceptable antecedent within the phrase *Kevin's remarks about herself*, the sentence in (22a) is ungrammatical because of a conflict of GEND values. By contrast, the sentence in (22b) with *her* construed as referring to *Lydia* is perfectly grammatical. The associated f-structure is found in (24), and here we see that the personal pronoun *her* is disjoint in reference from anything within its COARGD domain, which is the f-structure labelled *c*; *about* only has one argument and that is the pronoun itself, hence there is no coargument.

(23)

$$\begin{bmatrix} \text{PRED} & \text{`IGNORE<SUBJ, OBJ>'} \\ \text{TENSE} & \text{PAST} \\ \text{SUBJ} & a{:}\begin{bmatrix} \text{PRED} & \text{`LYDIA}_i\text{'} \\ \text{INDEX} & \begin{bmatrix} \text{GEND} & \text{FEM} \end{bmatrix} \end{bmatrix} \\ \text{OBJ} & d{:}\begin{bmatrix} \text{PRED} & \text{`REMARK <POSS>'} \\ \text{ADJ} & \left\{ c{:}\begin{bmatrix} \text{PRED} & \text{`ABOUT<OBJ>'} \\ \text{OBJ} & p{:}\begin{bmatrix} \text{PRED} & \text{`PRO}_i\text{'} \\ \text{INDEX} & \begin{bmatrix} \text{GEND} & \text{FEM} \end{bmatrix} \\ \text{PRONTYPE} & \text{REFL} \end{bmatrix} \end{bmatrix} \right\} \\ \text{POSS} & \begin{bmatrix} \text{PRED} & \text{`KEVIN'} \\ \text{INDEX} & \begin{bmatrix} \text{GEND} & \text{MASC} \end{bmatrix} \end{bmatrix} \end{bmatrix} \end{bmatrix}$$

(24)

$$\begin{bmatrix} \text{PRED} & \text{`IGNORE<SUBJ, OBJ>'} \\ \text{TENSE} & \text{PAST} \\ \text{SUBJ} & a{:}\begin{bmatrix} \text{PRED} & \text{`LYDIA}_i\text{'} \\ \text{INDEX} & \begin{bmatrix} \text{GEND} & \text{FEM} \end{bmatrix} \end{bmatrix} \\ \text{OBJ} & d{:}\begin{bmatrix} \text{PRED} & \text{`REMARK <POSS>'} \\ \text{ADJ} & \left\{ c{:}\begin{bmatrix} \text{PRED} & \text{`ABOUT<OBJ>'} \\ \text{OBJ} & p{:}\begin{bmatrix} \text{PRED} & \text{`PRO}_{i/j}\text{'} \\ \text{INDEX} & \begin{bmatrix} \text{GEND} & \text{FEM} \end{bmatrix} \\ \text{PRONTYPE} & \text{PERS} \end{bmatrix} \end{bmatrix} \right\} \\ \text{POSS} & \begin{bmatrix} \text{PRED} & \text{`KEVIN'} \\ \text{INDEX} & \begin{bmatrix} \text{GEND} & \text{MASC} \end{bmatrix} \end{bmatrix} \end{bmatrix} \end{bmatrix}$$

So far we have characterised English reflexives and personal pronouns by introducing a positive ('must be bound') and a negative ('must not be bound') constraint on domains, and by using two different domains, the MINCOMPN and the COARGD. We will now look at one more aspect of binding in English, and consider why an example like (25a) is ungrammatical, while (25b) is fine.

(25)
a. *Leila$_i$'s promotion surprised herself$_i$.
b. Leila$_i$ surprised herself$_i$ by accepting the job.

In each of these examples, the putative antecedent *Leila* is within the MinCompN which contains the reflexive pronoun, so that is not the issue. The problem with (25a) is that the antecedent *Leila* is too deeply embedded in that domain. You can see this by looking at the f-structure for example (25a) in (26) and in particular the relative position of *Leila* and *herself*. The path from the f-structure of the whole clause (f) to the reflexive anaphor is OBJ while the path to the antecedent is the **longer** path SUBJ POSS. The reason why sentences such as (25a) are ungrammatical is that it is generally the case that the antecedent of an anaphor must not be more deeply embedded in the f-structure than the anaphor itself.

(26)

$$
f:\left[\begin{array}{ll}
\text{PRED} & \text{`SURPRISE}<\text{SUBJ, OBJ}>\text{'}\\
\text{TENSE} & \text{PAST}\\
\text{OBJ} & p:\left[\begin{array}{ll}\text{PRED} & \text{`PRO}_i\text{'}\\ \text{PRONTYPE} & \text{REFL}\end{array}\right]\\
\text{SUBJ} & b:\left[\begin{array}{ll}\text{PRED} & \text{`PROMOTION}<\text{POSS}>\text{'}\\ \text{POSS} & a:\left[\begin{array}{ll}\text{PRED} & \text{`LEILA}_i\text{'}\end{array}\right]\end{array}\right]
\end{array}\right]
$$

To capture this constraint, we will define a notion of f-command as in (27).

(27) F-structure *a* f-commands f-structure *b* if and only if *a* does not contain *b* and every f-structure that contains *a* contains *b*.

Having defined f-command we can now state an additional condition:

(28) An antecedent must f-command its anaphor.

Let's look at (26) (for (25a)) in this light: the antecedent *Leila* must f-command the anaphor *herself*. This means that the f-structure for *Leila*, that is *a* in (26), must not contain the f-structure for *herself*, which is *p* in (26). This is fine; *a* does not contain *p*. However, (27) also requires that every f-structure that contains *a* in (26) must also contain *p*, and that is not the case: *b* contains *a*, but not *p*. This means that *Leila* does not f-command *herself*, which accounts for why (25a) is ungrammatical. In (25b), on the other hand, the f-structure is similar to that in (4), where the antecedent is the SUBJ of the sentence and the reflexive is the OBJ. This means that the f-structure that contains the antecedent, that is, the one for the sentence as a whole, also contains the reflexive, and the f-structure for the SUBJ does of course not contain the f-structure for the anaphor. In this case, the antecedent *Leila* does f-command the anaphor *herself*.

So reflexive anaphors in English must be bound within the MinCompN, and the antecedent is also required to f-command the anaphor. When we look at how binding conditions are formalised in Section 7.4, we will see that the f-command condition actually follows directly from the way we specify the domain condition itself, but for the moment, we can simply assume that it is a separate condition.

7.3 More on Domains and Antecedents

Although we have looked only at English so far, the theory of anaphoric binding developed in LFG is intended to be applicable to languages in general. The approach to anaphora in LFG owes much to the insight that there are two dimensions along which anaphoric binding may vary cross-linguistically: the SIZE of the domain and the GRAMMATICAL STATUS of the antecedent. This is captured in LFG by the choice of the domain and the choice of the antecedent being lexically determined, that is, a property of individual lexical items.

In looking at English we have introduced two relevant domains, the MINCOMPN and the COARGD. Cross-linguistically, two further domains are important, the MINIMAL FINITE DOMAIN (MINFIND) and the ROOT DOMAIN (ROOTD).

(29) The Minimal Finite Domain is the smallest f-structure containing a TENSE feature.

(30) The Root Domain is the complete f-structure of the utterance.

Beyond gender, number and person agreement, English has no particular conditions on the properties of the antecedent itself, but if we look at other languages, we see that the grammatical status of the antecedent, and in particular whether the antecedent is a SUBJ or a non-subject, is important to the choice of anaphor. We can see this in Swedish, a language which has anaphors which require their antecedents to have the grammatical function SUBJ.

We will start our discussion by looking at the Swedish *sin*, a reflexive form of the possessive pronoun, used when the antecedent is third person. Swedish has two genders, neuter and common. The reflexive possessive agrees with the noun it combines with; it is *sin* when it combines with a singular common gender noun, *sitt* with a singular neuter noun and *sina* with any plural noun. In (31), we provide sentences similar to the English ones in (3a) and (3b), but with the anaphor being a possessive pronoun. Here we see that the reflexive possessive *sin* has to be used, rather than a personal possessive (*hans/hennes*). We will also see that the distribution of Swedish reflexives is different from that of the English reflexives in two ways: there are specific constraints on the antecedent, and the domain within which they must be bound is different.

(31) a. Björn$_i$ slog sitt$_i$ / *hans$_i$ rekord.
Björn beat.PST POSS.REFL.N he.POSS record(N)
'Björn beat his (own) record.'

b. Anna$_i$ drog skynket över sin$_i$ / *hennes$_i$
Anna pull.PST cover.DEF over POSS.REFL.COM she.POSS
snarkande hund.
snoring dog(COM)
'Anna pulled the cover over her snoring dog.'

Consider first the antecedent constraint on Swedish anaphors like *sin*, namely the requirement that the antecedent must be a subject. In (32a), both *Johan* and *Björn* are potential antecedents as far as features go, as they are both third person, but only the SUBJ *Johan* is a licit antecedent as the coindexing shows (many of the examples that follow involve subtle judgements and some speakers may disagree). If the personal possessive *hans* is used in the same environment, then the antecedent is either *Björn* or the pronoun is interpreted as referring to some individual other than either *Björn* or *Johan*, as in (32b).

(32) a. Johan$_i$ gav Björn$_j$ sin$_{i/*j}$ bok.
Johan give.PST Björn POSS.REFL book
'Johan gave Björn his (=Johan's) book.'

b. Johan$_i$ gav Björn$_j$ hans$_{*i/j/k}$ bok.
Johan give.PST Björn POSS.M book
'Johan gave Björn his (=Björn's/someone else's) book.'

Consider now (33a). As expected given what we have seen so far, *sitt* cannot be coreferential with *Johan*, since this is an OBJ. Instead the non-reflexive possessive *hans* has to be used. Also in line with our expectations based on what we have said so far is the fact that the reflexive possessive can have the SUBJ as its antecedent in (33b). If we make *Johan* the SUBJ by converting the sentence to a passive, as in (33c), then *Johan* is a suitable antecedent for the reflexive possessive.

(33) a. De fotograferade Johan$_i$ i hans$_i$ / *sitt$_i$ hus.
they photograph.PST Johan in POSS.M POSS.REFL house
'They photographed Johan in his (own) house.'

b. De$_i$ fotograferade Johan i sitt$_i$ hus.
they photograph.PST Johan in POSS.REFL house
'They photographed Johan in their house.'

c. Johan$_i$ fotograferades i sitt$_i$ hus.
Johan photograph.PST.PASS in POSS.REFL house
'Johan was photographed in his house.'

Now to compare Swedish with English, consider the two sentences in (34), containing the (non-possessive) reflexives *himself* and *sig* respectively.

(34) a. Oscar$_i$ congratulated himself$_i$ on having chosen the right moment.

b. *Oscar$_i$ gratulerade sig$_i$ till att ha valt rätt
Oscar congratulate.PST REFL to INF have.INF choose.SUP right
tidpunkt.
moment
'Oscar congratulated himself on having chosen the right moment.'

Just like the reflexive possessives *sin, sitt* and *sina*, the reflexive *sig* requires its antecedent to be a subject. *Oscar* in (34b) **is** a SUBJ, so in principle a good antecedent for the reflexive *sig*, but still the sentence is not grammatical. This shows that the domain within which *sig* is bound must be different from that of *himself*, which is grammatical in (34a). In (34b), *Oscar* and *sig* are coarguments of the verb *gratulera*, and since it is ungrammatical we can assume that *sig* must not be bound in its CoargD. This would also explain the apparent similarity to (31), where *sitt* and *sin* are arguments of their respective nouns, so not coarguments of *Björn* and *Anna*, respectively. To illustrate, we provide the f-structure for (31a) in (35).

(35)

$$\left[\begin{array}{ll} \text{PRED} & \text{`BEAT}\langle\text{SUBJ, OBJ}\rangle\text{'} \\ \text{TENSE} & \text{PAST} \\ \text{SUBJ} & a{:}\left[\begin{array}{ll}\text{PRED} & \text{`BJÖRN}_i\text{'}\end{array}\right] \\ \text{OBJ} & d{:}\left[\begin{array}{ll} \text{PRED} & \text{`RECORD}\ \langle\text{POSS}\rangle\text{'} \\ \text{POSS} & p{:}\left[\begin{array}{ll}\text{PRED} & \text{PRO}_i \\ \text{PRONTYPE} & \text{REFL}\end{array}\right]\end{array}\right] \end{array}\right]$$

In (35), the reflexive fills the POSS function of 'record', which has no other argument, hence the reflexive's CoargD is the f-structure indicated with *d*. Since the antecedent *a* is outside the CoargD, *sitt* is free in its CoargD, and the version of (31a) with *sitt* is correctly predicted to be grammatical.

Consider now the examples in (36), where the reflexive is a possessor within the OBJ within a finite COMP.

(36)
a. *Björn$_i$ trodde [att jag$_j$ gillade [sina$_{*i/*j}$ hundar]].
Björn believe.PST C 1SG like.PST POSS.REFL.PL dog.PL

b. Björn$_i$ trodde [att Johan$_j$ gillade [sina$_{*i/j}$ hundar]].
Björn believe.PST C Johan like.PST POSS.REFL.PL dog.PL
'Björn believed that Johan liked his (own) dogs.'

In both examples in (36), *sina* is a POSS argument of the noun *hundar*, so none of the potential antecedents is a coargument of *sina*, so the cause of the ungrammaticality cannot be a violation of the requirement that *sina* is disjoint from its coarguments: this requirement is satisfied. The example in (36a) is ungrammatical no matter what the antecedent of *sina* is taken to be. The first person pronoun *jag* cannot be an antecedent because *sina* requires a third person antecedent. *Björn* is a SUBJ and is third person, so is a potential antecedent, yet the interpretation in which *sina* refers to *Björn* is also not possible. The subordinate clause *att jag gillade sina hundar* is a finite clause, so we could hypothesise that the problem is that *Björn* is "too far away", that *sina* must be bound by a subject within its minimal finite domain, its MinFinD, defined in (29). In (36b), we see that if we replace the subordinate SUBJ with *Johan*, which is third person and hence has the right features, then the sentence is grammatical with *Johan* as an antecedent. *Björn* is of course still not a good antecedent.

From this, we can characterise the binding constraints of *sig* and *sin/sitt/sina* as in (37).

(37) The antecedent of *sig* and *sin/sitt/sina* must be a SUBJ within the Minimal Finite Domain, and they must be free within their Coargument Domain.

Because it cannot be bound by a coargument, *sig* is sometimes referred to as an OBVIATIVE reflexive pronoun. For situations where the antecedent is a coargument, an alternative form *sig själv* must be used, so that the grammatical alternative to (34b) is (38).

(38) Oscar$_i$ gratulerade sig själv$_i$ till att ha valt
Oscar congratulate.PST REFL.SELF to INF have.INF choose.SUP
rätt tidpunkt.
right moment
'Oscar congratulated himself on having chosen the right moment.'

Let's now consider a couple of more complex examples. The Swedish verb *påstå* ('claim') behaves in ways similar to the English *expect*, which we looked at in Section 5.2.2, in that the noun phrase that follows can be shown to be an OBJ of the matrix verb, but not an argument of it; it is a non-thematic OBJ. The lexical entry in (39) captures the behaviour of *påstå* with a functional control equation.

(39) *påstår* V (↑ PRED) = 'CLAIM <SUBJ, XCOMP> OBJ'
(↑ OBJ) = (↑ XCOMP SUBJ)

Now consider the example in (40).

(40) Anna$_i$ påstår sig$_i$ vara en bra målvakt.
Anna claim.PRS REFL be.INF a good goalkeeper
'Anna claims to be a good goalkeeper.'

Anna is a SUBJ and occurs in the smallest finite domain of *sig*, but it may appear to violate the restriction that *sig* must not be a coargument of its antecedent. However, even though *sig* is an OBJ of the matrix verb in this example, it is a non-thematic OBJ – as indicated by its position outside the angled brackets in the PRED value of *påstå* – and so it is not an **argument** of this verb. This in turn means that the antecedent *Anna* is not a coargument, *sig* is only an argument of the lower verb, and hence the constraints we defined for *sig* in (37) correctly predict that (40) is grammatical with the indicated coreference.

The Swedish verb *be* ('ask') differs from *påstå* in that the noun phrase that follows the matrix verb is both an OBJ and an argument of the verb *be*. This means that it shares properties with *persuade*, as described in Section 5.2.2, and has the lexical entry in (41) for the past tense of the verb.

(41) *bad* V (↑ PRED) = 'ASK <SUBJ, OBJ, XCOMP>'
(↑ OBJ) = (↑ XCOMP SUBJ)

Now consider the potential binding of *sig* in (42).

(42) Psykiatern$_i$ bad patienten$_j$ att hjälpa sig$_{i/*j}$
psychiatrist.DEF ask.PST patient.DEF INF help.INF REFL
bli bättre.
become.INF better
'The psychiatrist asked the patient to help him (the psychiatrist) get better.'

In order to see what is going on in (42), it is helpful to look at the f-structure in (43). In order to keep the f-structure a little simpler, we have left *bli bättre* out. The control equation in the lexical entry for *bad* in (41) makes *patienten* both the OBJ of the matrix clause and the SUBJ of the embedded clause. This means that both *psykiatern* and *patienten* satisfy the requirement that the antecedent of *sig* is a SUBJ. However, *sig* cannot be bound by *patienten* because they are coarguments (as *patienten* is the subject of *hjälpa*). Thus the only possible antecedent for *sig* in (42) is *psykiatern*. It should be pointed out that in this environment instead of *sig* a personal pronoun *honom* 'he.OBJ' can also be used to refer to *psykiatern*.

(43)

$$\left[\begin{array}{ll} \text{PRED} & \text{`ASK}<\text{SUBJ, OBJ, XCOMP}>\text{'} \\ \text{TENSE} & \text{PAST} \\ \text{OBJ} & \left[\begin{array}{ll} \text{PRED} & \text{`PATIENT'} \\ \text{DEF} & + \end{array}\right]_{1} \\ \text{SUBJ} & \left[\begin{array}{ll} \text{PRED} & \text{`PSYCHIATRIST'} \\ \text{DEF} & + \end{array}\right] \\ \text{XCOMP} & \left[\begin{array}{ll} \text{PRED} & \text{`HELP}<\text{SUBJ, OBJ}>\text{'} \\ \text{SUBJ} & [\;]_{1} \\ \text{OBJ} & \left[\begin{array}{ll} \text{PRED} & \text{`PRO'} \\ \text{PRONTYPE} & \text{REFL} \end{array}\right] \end{array}\right] \end{array}\right]$$

In order to achieve coreference between the reflexive and *patienten*, we must use the form *sig själv*, as in (44), since this form does not exclude a coargument antecedent.

(44) Psykiatern$_i$ bad patienten$_j$ att hjälpa sig själv$_{*i/j}$
psychiatrist.DEF ask.PST patient.DEF INF help.INF REFL.SELF
bli bättre.
become.INF better
'The psychiatrist asked the patient to help himself get better.'

7.4 Formalising Binding Constraints

We will now show how we can express in a more formal manner the binding conditions which we have discussed. We have said that cross-linguistically, four different domains are relevant to the binding conditions. An anaphor can be required to be bound or free within these domains.

(45)
a. Coargument Domain (COARGD)
b. Minimal Complete Nucleus (MINCOMPN)
c. Mininal Finite Domain (MINFIND)
d. Root Domain (ROOTD)

We saw that English reflexive anaphors are subject to the MINCOMPN domain requirement, meaning that the reflexive pronoun must find an antecedent within that domain. To understand how we can formally capture this domain requirement, we will start with the schematic f-structure in (46) as an example, in which we have a reflexive anaphor (such as *herself* or *himself*) as the OBJ within an OBL_θ in a complement clause, where the f-structure of the reflexive anaphor is labelled *p*. We are not thinking of a specific example, but are just interested in what the possibilities are in principle.

(46)

$$g:\begin{bmatrix} \text{PRED} & \ldots \\ \text{SUBJ} & [\ldots] \\ \text{COMP} & h:\begin{bmatrix} \text{SUBJ} & [\ldots] \\ \text{PRED} & \ldots \\ \text{OBJ} & [\ldots] \\ \text{OBL}_\theta & \begin{bmatrix} \text{OBJ} & p:\begin{bmatrix} \text{PRED} & \text{`PRO'} \\ \text{PRONTYPE} & \text{REFL} \end{bmatrix} \end{bmatrix} \end{bmatrix} \\ \text{OBJ} & [\ldots] \end{bmatrix}$$

The question is, what are the possible antecedents for this reflexive pronoun? The MINCOMPN for the anaphor *p* is the f-structure *h* – this is the smallest f-structure that contains the reflexive and a SUBJ – so the SUBJ and the OBJ in the f-structure *h* are possible antecedents. On the other hand, the SUBJ and the OBJ functions in the root f-structure, labelled *g*, are not possible antecedents, because they lie outside the **smallest** complete nucleus, which is *h*. To specify the domain within which an antecedent must be found we are going to use an inside-out functional uncertainty, something which was introduced in the discussion of constructive case in Chapter 4. So where ↑ refers to the f-structure of the anaphor, we specify the possible antecedents for the reflexive pronoun as in (47). These are possible antecedents because they are within the MINCOMPN. We introduce the informal labels *sh* and *oh* (for SUBJ of *h* and OBJ of *h*) in order to allow us to refer to these functions in a simple way below.

(47) a. $((\text{OBL}_\theta\ \text{OBJ}\ \uparrow)\ \text{SUBJ})\ (=sh)$

b. $((\text{OBL}_\theta\ \text{OBJ}\ \uparrow)\ \text{OBJ})\ (=oh)$

Remember the way an inside-out functional application works: (47a) describes the f-structure in (48), where *f* stands for ↑.

(48)

$$\begin{bmatrix} \text{SUBJ} & [\ldots] \\ \text{OBL}_\theta & \begin{bmatrix} \text{OBJ} & f[\ldots] \end{bmatrix} \end{bmatrix}$$

The following are **not** possible antecedents, because they are too far away; they are outside the smallest domain which contains the anaphor and a SUBJ.

(49) a. ((COMP OBL_θ OBJ $\uparrow$) SUBJ) (=*sg*)
b. ((COMP OBL_θ OBJ $\uparrow$) OBJ) (=*og*)

We can state the MINCOMPN domain requirement as shown in (50), where $\uparrow$ refers to the f-structure of the anaphor, GF stands for any grammatical function and the Kleene star as usual means zero or more instances. This involves putting a constraint somewhere on the path, a so-called OFF-PATH constraint, a notion which was introduced in Section 6.4. In (50) $\neg(\rightarrow$ SUBJ) puts a constraint on the path from the anaphor to the MINCOMPN. Informally, it tells us that the path out from the anaphor to the f-structure containing the antecedent **cannot** go through any grammatical function whose f-structure contains a SUBJ (the symbol $\neg$ stands for 'not').

(50) $\Big(\underset{\neg(\rightarrow \text{SUBJ})}{\text{GF}^*} \quad \text{GF} \uparrow \Big)$

It is worth taking a moment to see how (50) defines the domain within which the antecedent must be found. Consider first the embedded SUBJ and OBJ f-structures, *sh* and *oh*, which are possible antecedents and are contained within the f-structure *h* in (46). The path out from *p* to *h* is (OBL_θ OBJ $\uparrow$) where $\uparrow$ is the f-structure *p*. This means that for this example, GF in (50) is equivalent to OBJ, and GF* is set to OBL_θ. The off-path constraint $\neg(\rightarrow$ SUBJ) specifies that none of the attributes corresponding to GF* may contain a SUBJ attribute. So in this example, the off-path constraint states that the f-structure of the OBL_θ may not contain a SUBJ. This constraint is satisfied, so either the SUBJ or OBJ inside *h* in (46) may serve as antecedent. Now consider the root SUBJ and OBJ f-structures *sg* and *og*. Now the path out is (COMP OBL_θ OBJ $\uparrow$), again with $\uparrow$ referring to *p*, with GF in (50) being equivalent to OBJ in (49), as it was in (47), but GF* now being equivalent to both COMP and OBL_θ in (49). In this case, the off-path constraint requires that neither the COMP nor the OBL_θ contains a SUBJ. **This** constraint is not satisfied, because the f-structure of the COMP contains a SUBJ attribute, and so the SUBJ and OBJ in the root f-structure *g* are not possible antecedents because they are outside the binding domain.

So the statement in (50) captures the domain requirement for English reflexives and other anaphors that must find an antecedent within the closest complete nucleus. Now it remains to specify the possible antecedents within the domain. We do this by using the abbreviation ANTE-GF to stand for the grammatical function of the antecedent. The expression in (51) picks out possible antecedents within the minimal complete nucleus.

(51) $\Big(\Big(\underset{\neg(\rightarrow \text{SUBJ})}{\text{GF}^*} \quad \text{GF} \uparrow \Big) \text{ ANTE-GF} \Big)$

We turn now to the issue of how to state the relationship between the anaphor and the antecedent. We observed above that it is essentially semantic, which is why we represent it informally by means of coindexation on the words in the string. In LFG we can express an approach to the binding constraints which captures the semantic nature of antecedent–anaphor relations. The basic idea is that the semantic relationship between the antecedent and the anaphor is captured in the mapping to the semantics, using a projection from the f-structure which is known as the σ projection, which maps from f-structures to their corresponding semantic structures. On this approach, the lexical entry for a reflexive pronoun in English such as *herself* would introduce the binding equation in (52). This specifies that the semantic structure of the antecedent, which must be found within the minimal complete nucleus, appears as the value of the ANTECEDENT attribute in the semantic structure of the anaphor. Discussing this approach would lead us into highly complex areas, and take us well beyond purely syntactic concerns, so we just provide the binding equation in (52) to give a flavour of the approach.

(52) *herself* D

$$(\uparrow_{\sigma}\ \text{ANTECEDENT}) = ((\underset{\neg(\rightarrow\ \text{SUBJ})}{\text{GF}^{*}}\quad \text{GF}\uparrow)\ \text{ANTE-GF})_{\sigma}$$

In much of the syntactic literature, the syntactic INDEX features (which were introduced in Section 4.6) are used as an informal proxy for the semantic relationships between antecedents and anaphors, and this is what we will do here. We state the binding condition for English *herself* using the INDEX feature in (53). This says that the INDEX features of the antecedent and the INDEX features of the anaphor are identical. We can understand this as simply a convenient shorthand or proxy for an account of the semantic relationship between these elements. (54) shows a more complete version of the f-structure for the sentence in (3a) above (*Lydia$_i$ hurt herself$_i$*), where we informally identify the coindexation by adding a dotted line linking the INDEX features, which stands for this semantic relationship. In the simple example in (3a), GF in (53) would be OBJ, GF* would be zero and ANTE-GF would be SUBJ.

(53) *herself* D

$$(\uparrow\ \text{INDEX}) = ((\underset{\neg(\rightarrow\ \text{SUBJ})}{\text{GF}^{*}}\quad \text{GF}\uparrow)\ \text{ANTE-GF INDEX})$$

(54)

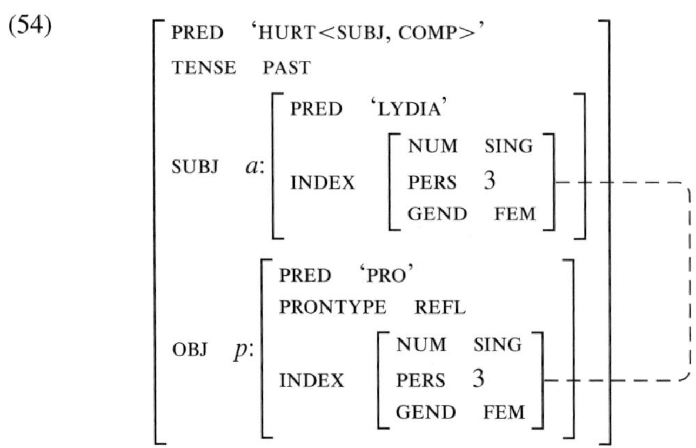

The other domains which are relevant to binding can be characterised in a similar way, again using inside-out functional uncertainty. The statements in (55) and (57) characterise the CoargD and the MinFinD, respectively. In the case of CoargD, each GF in the series of attributes which constitutes the path GF* is subject to the constraint that it cannot include a PRED attribute. We can see the effect of this by looking at (56) in relation to (55), where ↑ is the f-structure of the anaphor, OBJ corresponds to the attribute at the bottom of the path (GF* [GF] ↑) and COMP corresponds to the GF* part of the path ([GF*] GF ↑). The constraint requires that the GF* part of the path does not contain a PRED value – it does not place any constraint on the [GF ↑] part. If we consider the domain labelled *n*, we see that this f-structure **does** contain a PRED; therefore, *n* is not a possible domain for binding an anaphor subject to this constraint. By contrast the smaller domain (labelled *c*) corresponds to the path out OBJ ↑ and is not subject to any constraint. The anaphor can be bound within this domain, which is the domain of its coarguments.

(55) Coargument Domain: $\left(\underset{\neg(\rightarrow \text{PRED})}{\text{GF}^*}\quad \text{GF}\uparrow\right)$

(56)

$$n:\begin{bmatrix} \text{PRED} & \ldots \\ \text{SUBJ} & [\ldots] \\ \text{COMP} & c:\begin{bmatrix} \text{SUBJ} & [\ldots] \\ \text{PRED} & \ldots \\ \text{OBJ} & p:\begin{bmatrix} \text{PRED} & \text{`PRO'} \\ \text{PRONTYPE} & \text{REFL} \end{bmatrix} \end{bmatrix} \end{bmatrix}$$

In precisely the same way, in the case of the MinFinD, the path GF* cannot contain a TENSE attribute; if the path went through a GF with TENSE, it would have left the **minimal** finite domain.

(57) Minimal Finite Domain : $\left(\underset{\neg(\rightarrow \text{TENSE})}{\text{GF}^*}\quad \text{GF}\uparrow\right)$

The Root Domain can be simply characterised as in (58).

(58) Root Domain: (GF* GF ↑)

The constraint on personal pronouns in English is that they **cannot** find an antecedent within the CoargD, so we state this by means of a negative constraint, shown in (59). This captures what is said in words in (17): the pronoun *him* cannot be coindexed with anything it is a coargument of.

(59) *him* D

$(\uparrow \text{INDEX}) \neq \left(\left(\underset{\neg(\rightarrow \text{PRED})}{\text{GF}^*}\quad \text{GF}\uparrow\right) \text{ANTE-GF INDEX}\right)$

Earlier we saw that anaphoric elements may also place conditions on the grammatical function of their antecedents, and in particular that they may be subject-oriented, that is, they may require their antecedent to be a SUBJ. In fact, they may also constrain their antecedent **not** to be a SUBJ, but we have not provided data from such languages here. The positive SUBJ requirement, which we encountered with the Swedish *sig* and *sin* elements, is captured by placing a requirement on the ANTE-GF attribute. For example, the statement in (60) would be appropriate for a subject-oriented anaphor which must be bound within the MINFIND. (60) states that the INDEX of the anaphor is identical to that of a SUBJ within the smallest f-structure with the TENSE attribute.

(60) *sig* D

$$(\uparrow \text{INDEX}) = ((\underset{\neg(\rightarrow \text{TENSE})}{\text{GF}^*} \quad \text{GF} \uparrow) \text{ SUBJ INDEX })$$

So far in this section we have sketched out how both positive and negative constraints on the domain and the antecedent can be stated using inside-out functional uncertainty. In our earlier discussion of examples such as (25a) (repeated here as (61)) we saw that a further structural condition generally holds of the relationship between the antecedent and the anaphor. This f-command condition can be informally stated as in (62).

(61) *Leila's promotion surprised herself.

(62) The antecedent of an anaphor must f-command it.

We can now see that we do not need to state this as a separate requirement on binding, because it follows directly from the way in which we have specified the domain conditions. A relationship of f-command between the antecedent and the anaphor follows from the fact that the path upwards to the antecedent is always **at least as long** as the path to the anaphor, since the binding conditions all have the form shown schematically in (63).

(63) ((GF* ANAPH-GF ↑) ANTE-GF)

We can show that this is the case by considering two instances. If the GF* is "zero", we have the structure shown schematically in (64). In this case, ANTE-GF and ANAPH-GF mutually f-command each other, so the antecedent **does** f-command the antecedent. Now consider the case where GF* is not "zero", shown schematically in (65). Here too the ANTE-GF f-commands the ANAPH-GF, which is more deeply embedded in the f-structure.

(64)

$$\begin{bmatrix} \text{PRED} & \ldots \\ \text{ANTE-GF} & \begin{bmatrix} \ldots \end{bmatrix} \\ \text{ANAPH-GF} & \begin{bmatrix} \text{PRED} & \text{`PRO'} \end{bmatrix} \end{bmatrix}$$

(65)

$$\begin{bmatrix} \text{PRED} & \ldots \\ \text{ANTE-GF} & \begin{bmatrix} \ldots \end{bmatrix} \\ \text{GF} & \begin{bmatrix} \text{ANAPH-GF} & \begin{bmatrix} \text{PRED} & \text{`PRO'} \end{bmatrix} \end{bmatrix} \end{bmatrix}$$

Now we can see why (61) is ungrammatical: the anaphor is higher up in the structure than the supposed antecedent: the ANAPH-GF is OBJ but the path to the antecedent is SUBJ POSS (cf. (66)).

(66)

$$\begin{bmatrix} \text{PRED} & \text{`SURPRISE<SUBJ, OBJ>'} \\ \boxed{\text{OBJ}} & \begin{bmatrix} \text{PRED} & \text{`PRO}_j\text{'} \end{bmatrix} \\ \text{SUBJ} & \begin{bmatrix} \text{PRED} & \text{`PROMOTION<POSS>'} \\ \boxed{\text{POSS}} & \begin{bmatrix} \text{PRED} & \text{`LEILA}_i\text{'} \end{bmatrix} \end{bmatrix} \end{bmatrix}$$

7.5 Morphological Reflexives

We saw in Section 4.2.3 that pronominal arguments can be expressed morphologically, rather than as separate syntactic words; so too can reflexive arguments. An example is the Chicheŵa verbal prefix *-dzi-*, exemplified in (67) from Sells et al. (1987, 187). The verb here is transitive, and *-dzi-* functions as an incorporated OBJ.

(67) alenje a-na-**dzí**-lúm-a.
hunters SM-PST-self-bite-IND
'The hunters bit themselves.'

(68)

$$\begin{bmatrix} \text{PRED} & \text{`BITE<SUBJ, OBJ>'} \\ \text{TENSE} & \text{PAST} \\ \text{SUBJ} & a\text{:} \begin{bmatrix} \text{PRED} & \text{`HUNTER'} \\ \text{INDEX} & \begin{bmatrix} \text{NUM} & \text{PL} \\ \text{PERS} & 3 \end{bmatrix} \end{bmatrix} \\ \text{OBJ} & p\text{:} \begin{bmatrix} \text{PRED} & \text{`PRO'} \\ \text{PRONTYPE} & \text{REFL} \end{bmatrix} \end{bmatrix}$$

The Australian language Warlpiri also has a morphologically bound reflexive object. In (69) you see that the bound element *-nyanu* is glossed as REFL. Warlpiri has an ergative–accusative case marking system, a notion which was introduced in Section 2.3.4. This means that if the verb was intransitive the subject would be in the absolutive case, but in (69) (from Hale (1983, 43)) it is in the ergative case, indicating that the sentence contains a transitive predicate. So even though the reflexive is bound to the TENSE marker *ka*, rather than the verb *nya*, it functions as the reflexive OBJ.

(69) Ngarrka-ngku ka-**nyanu** nya-nyi.
man-ERG PRES-REFL see-NPST
'The man sees himself.'

We have some further evidence that the bound reflexive element *-nyanu* really is an incorporated pronominal corresponding to an OBJ in the f-structure. As we saw in Section 5.5, Warlpiri has a set of complementising elements which specify control properties for a complement clause: the suffix *-kurra* (glossed C for *complementising marker*) occurs in cases of object control. When a controlled complement clause is added to (69), we see the complementising suffix *-kurra*, as shown in (70) from Simpson (1983, 185), confirming that the reflexive element corresponds to an OBJ at f-structure.

(70) Kurdu-ngku ka-nyanu nya-nyi karri-nya-kurra.
child-ERG PRS-REFL see-NPST stand-INF-C
'The child sees her/himself standing.'

The theory of anaphoric binding which we have presented in this chapter can apply without alteration to languages such as these in which reflexive pronouns (and other pronominals) are expressed morphologically, because at the level of f-structure the Chichewa sentence in (67) and the English sentence *The hunters bit themselves* are structurally similar. On the basis of the data we have seen in this section, we might conclude that the Chichewa *-dzi-* and the Warlpiri *-nyanu* are subject to the MINCOMPN condition, similar to English reflexive pronouns:

(71) $$\left(\underset{\neg(\rightarrow \text{SUBJ})}{\text{GF}^*} \quad \text{GF} \uparrow \right)$$

Reading

The analysis of anaphora in LFG owes much to the work of Faltz (1985) (originally written in 1977). The identification of the two dimensions along which anaphoric binding may vary cross-linguistically – the size of the domain and the grammatical status of the antecedent – is due to him. An early study of variation in reflexivisation from an LFG perspective is Sells et al. (1987). We have based our discussion of anaphoric binding most closely on the ideas presented in Dalrymple (1993) and Dalrymple (2001). The approach to capturing the binding constraints in the mapping to the semantics is developed in Dalrymple (1993). Other presentations of the syntax of anaphoric binding are found in Bresnan (2001c), Bresnan et al. (2016) and Falk (2001). These sources develop a slightly different approach to anaphoric binding in which the notion of OUTRANKING plays an important role. Syntactic rank is the idea that coarguments can be ranked according to prominence. The relevant rankings can be found in Bresnan et al. (2016, 229–30).

We have outlined an approach to anaphoric binding which captures the syntactic constraints on anaphora in terms of f-structure. However this does not mean we exclude the possibility that the relationship between referentially dependent elements (such as reflexives and pronouns) and their antecedents also makes reference to other dimensions of linguistic structure. Two other aspects which are relevant to anaphoric relations in some languages are thematic prominence and linear order. For instance, Arka and Wechsler (1996) show that both prominence at the level of argument structure and the distinction between terms and non-terms are relevant to binding in Balinese. The role of thematic constraints on binding in Albanian is discussed by Sells (1988); Dalrymple and Zaenen (1991) and Dalrymple (1993) deal with thematic constraints for English and Norwegian.

Linear order can also play a role for binding. This is the case in Malayalam, and relevant data and analysis is provided by Mohanan (1983), and the data is also discussed by Dalrymple (2001) and Bresnan et al. (2016). The role of linear precedence and Japanese anaphors is discussed in Kameyama (1985).

In discussing binding we have concentrated solely on pronominal elements such as personal pronouns and reflexives. We have not said anything here about the behaviour of other nominals (such as *the book* and *Kevin*), which generally cannot have a coindexed antecedent. Extensive discussion of this complex matter can be found in Bresnan et al. (2016, 239–46).

Another area which we have not touched on at all here is the notion of a LOGOPHORIC PRONOUN. Some languages have special pronominal forms which are used to track the person whose perspective is represented in indirect discourse. Clements (1975) showed that the West African language Ewe has logophoric pronouns distinct from both personal and reflexive pronouns. Logophoric pronouns have also been described for a number of other West African languages including Wan and Abe (both from the Ivory Coast), Gokana, Japanese, Chinese and Icelandic. Bresnan et al. (2016) provide an extensive discussion of the notion of logophoricity and of logophoric pronouns in Ewe and Icelandic (drawing on Maling (1984)), and Strahan (2009) also discusses logophoricity and long-distance anaphors in Icelandic and Faroese.

Further details on binding in Scandinavian languages can be found in Kiparsky (2002); Lødrup (1999a, 2007, 2008); Maling (1986).

Sells et al. (1987) and Bresnan and Mchombo (1987) provide more data and discussion of bound reflexives in Chicheŵa, and see Simpson (1983) for further data and analysis of Warlpiri.

Discussion of aspects of binding in a range of languages can be found in the LFG literature, for example: Hungarian (Rákosi, 2009, 2010), Modern Greek (Lapata, 1998), Korean (Sung, 1996), Warlpiri (Snijders, 2014) (drawing on early work by Simpson (1991)), Sinhala, an Indo-Aryan language of Sri Lanka (Henadeerage, 1998), Yag̨ Dii, a language of Cameroon (Dalrymple, 2015b). Jaeger (2004) discusses the distribution of pronominals and anaphors in so-called picture NPs in English.

Exercises

7.1 Give the f-structures for the sentences in (72) and explain how the binding theory presented in this chapter accounts for the observed pattern of grammaticality.

(72) a. John$_i$ tried to believe in himself$_i$.
b. John$_i$ expected Mary$_j$ to believe in him$_{i/k}$/*himself$_i$/herself$_j$.

7.2 We noted in Section 7.2 that the conditions on binding which are based on f-structure may be combined with additional thematic 'ranking' or 'superiority' conditions based on θ-roles, which we have not discussed here. Consider the examples in (75) and the f-description given in (74), and explain in words how reference to the Thematic Hierarchy introduced in Section 8.2 of Chapter 8 and given in (73), might be relevant to these examples.

(73) Agent > Benef > Recip/Exper > Instr > Theme/Patient/Stimu > Loc

(74) (↑ PRED) = 'TALK <SUBJ, OBL$_{Rec}$, OBL$_{Theme}$ >'

(75) a. Lydia talked to Oscar about himself.
b. *Lydia talked about Oscar to himself.

7.3 We saw in the text that the Swedish anaphors *sig* and *sin* are required to be disjoint from any coarguments but bound to a subject. Look at the following example with the reflexive possessive *sin* and explain (in words) why it is grammatical on both readings indicated by the coindexation, on the assumption that *förbjuda* 'forbid' is an object control verb, with the PRED value shown in (77). Provide the f-structure for the example.

(76) Oscar$_i$ förbjöd Fredrik$_j$ att sälja sin$_{i/j}$ bil.
Oscar forbid.PST Frederik to sell REFL car
'Oscar forbade Frederik from selling his car.'

(77) *förbjuda* V (↑ PRED) = 'FORBID<SUBJ, OBJ, XCOMP>'
(↑ OBJ) = (↑ XCOMP SUBJ)

Now look at the following example from Kiparsky (2002) and explain why it is ungrammatical on both readings indicated by the coindexation, on the assumption that *lova* 'promise' is a subject control verb. The PRED value for *lova* 'promise' is shown in (79). Provide the f-structure for the example.

(78) Generalen$_i$ lovade översten$_j$ att undersöka sig$_{*i,*j}$
general.DEF promise.PST colonel.DEF to examine REFL
'The general promised the colonel to examine himself.'

(79) *lova* V (↑ PRED) = 'PROMISE<SUBJ, OBJ, XCOMP>'
(↑ SUBJ) = (↑ XCOMP SUBJ)

7.4 Consider the grammaticality judgements given in the following examples.

(80) a. Kevin$_i$ found a picture of him$_{i/j}$.
b. Kevin$_i$ found a picture of himself$_i$.

(81) a. Kevin$_i$ saw Lydia's picture of him$_{i/j}$.
b. Kevin$_i$ saw Lydia's picture of himself$_i$.

Suppose as in the text that the pronoun must be disjoint in the CoargD and the reflexive must be bound in the MinCompN. Give the f-structures and explain how the sentences in (80) follow on this view. You can treat *of* as a grammatical (PRED-less) preposition and assume that the PRED value of *picture* is 'PICTURE <OBL$_{of}$>'.

Now look at (81). In these sentences *Lydia's* corresponds to a POSS function at f-structure. Assume that the PRED value of *picture* in such examples is 'PICTURE <POSS, OBL$_{of}$>'. Give the f-structures. Does the pattern of grammaticality shown in (81) suggest that the POSS function 'counts' as a SUBJ in relation to the MinCompN domain requirement or not? Judgements for 'picture' NPs such as these are notoriously tricky and subject to variability. You might find it interesting to put together a selection of examples and gather judgements from native speakers.

8 A-structure and Lexical Mapping Theory

8.1 Introduction

As discussed in Chapter 2, a-structure is the level in LFG that encodes syntactically relevant information about the arguments of predicates so that they can be mapped to grammatical functions in f-structure. A-structure is an important part of the interface between the semantics and the syntax since it plays a key role in determining the grammatical functions of the semantic arguments of the predicate. The a-structure of a predicate (usually, but not necessarily, a verb) typically encodes the number of arguments that the predicate takes, a ranking of these arguments in terms of prominence on a hierarchy of θ-roles and a classification for arguments which determines their mapping to grammatical functions in the f-structure according to general correspondence principles. In this chapter we will see how this works in LFG.

We saw in Chapter 1 that there are good reasons for separating thematic roles from grammatical functions, since there is not necessarily a one-to-one relationship between them. The same grammatical function can correspond to different θ-roles depending on the predicate, as shown in (1) for SUBJ.

(1) a. [Oscar]$_{Agent}$ tickled Sarah.
b. [Oscar]$_{Recipient}$ received the present from his sister.
c. [The hammer]$_{Instrument}$ drove the nail into the wood.
d. [On the beach]$_{Location}$ is a great place to be.
e. [Boris]$_{Stimulus}$ was loved by most of his flatmates.

The same is true cross-linguistically, where we can find predicates with similar semantics, but with different associations between their arguments' thematic roles and grammatical functions. Consider the example in (2) from Murrinh-patha (northern Australia), and its English translation. In each language the same semantics is expressed, but it is done in a different way. In English, the Experiencer role is encoded as the subject (here *I*). In the Murrinhpatha version, however, the literal translation is something like *It rests me*, with a third person singular subject – encoded here by *bangam-* – and the Experiencer encoded as the object – here encoded as an incorporated object *-ngi-*. Thus, while the semantics is the same, the languages differ in terms of whether the Experiencer is expressed as the subject in English or the object in Murrinhpatha.

(2) bangam-ngi-yuk
3SG.SUBJ.NFUT-1SG.OBJ-rest
'I am resting.' (Literal translation: 'It rests me')

We also find grammatical processes which affect the mapping of arguments to grammatical functions, while the θ-roles associated with the predicate remain the same. A typical example of such a grammatical process is passive formation, as shown in (3). In both of these examples the predicate *paint* selects for an Agent (*the painter*) and a Patient (*the wall*), but in the active sentence in (3a) these are mapped to subject and object respectively, while in the passive version in (3b) the Patient is mapped to the subject and the Agent to an optional adjunct (or possibly an OBL_θ; we will return to this choice shortly).

(3) a. Sarah painted the wall.
b. The wall was painted (by Sarah).

Facts such as these demonstrate that we need to distinguish the semantic arguments of a predicate from the grammatical functions they perform. We do this by assuming a distinction between a-structure (where the semantic arguments are encoded) and f-structure (where grammatical functions are encoded). We also know that there are systematic correspondences between these structures. For example, Agents map to SUBJ or ADJ, rather than OBJ. Thus, we also want to be able to capture these systematic relationships between a-structure roles and f-structure grammatical functions with general correspondence principles, rather than having to define this mapping for each predicate individually. To do this, LFG assumes a mapping theory called LEXICAL MAPPING THEORY (LMT), which governs the way in which arguments at a-structure are mapped to grammatical functions at f-structure. We discuss LMT in Section 8.4, but we will first deal with some preliminaries.

8.2 θ-roles and the Thematic Hierarchy

In Chapter 2, we said that there is no complete agreement among researchers on how to categorise thematic roles, or θ-roles, as we will call them. We did, however, identify a list of such roles that most linguists would be quite happy to agree with.

Agent causer or initiator of action
Experiencer animate entity which experiences a sensation or emotion or perceives a stimulus
Patient entity which is affected by action
Theme entity which undergoes a change of state, location or possession or whose location is specified
Stimulus object of perception, cognition or emotion (this is often lumped together with Theme)
Location spatial reference point of an event or an entity

Recipient entity which receives something
Benefactive entity that benefits from an action or an event
Instrument inanimate entity used by some participant to perform an action

Recipient and Benefactive may sound too similar to be worth distinguishing, but they are worth keeping apart. Consider the examples in (4) for instance.

(4) a. Fred gave **Sarah** a book.
b. Fred wrote **Sarah** a poem.

The example in (4a) entails that Sarah received the book, that is, she is the Recipient. In (4b), on the other hand, Fred wrote the poem for Sarah's benefit, but it is not certain that he gave it to her. This can be shown by the fact that whereas (5a) makes no sense, (5b) does.

(5) a. #Fred gave **Sarah** a book, but he never handed it over to her.
b. Fred wrote **Sarah** a poem, but he never handed it over to her.

There is cross-linguistic evidence that argument structure, and in particular the mapping from arguments to grammatical functions, relies on a semantically driven hierarchy of θ-roles, with Agent at the top. Since linguists disagree on exactly what the correct set of θ-roles is, it will not surprise you that there is also some disagreement as to the exact details of the hierarchy, but these differences need not concern us here. We assume the THEMATIC HIERARCHY below.

THEMATIC HIERARCHY
Agent > Benef > Recip/Exper > Instr > Theme/Patient/Stimulus > Loc

One of the intuitions behind the hierarchy is that the lower down on the hierarchy a θ-role is, the more integrated it is with the semantics of the individual verb. In English, this can be seen in idioms. It turns out that idioms that are built around a verb that has more than one argument can involve θ-roles at the lower end of the hierarchy, leaving a higher θ-role to be filled in. It rarely involves a higher θ-role, leaving a lower one to be filled in. Take verbs that have an Agent and a Theme/Patient; we get idioms involving the verb and the Theme/Patient, but very few involving only the verb and the Agent. Examples of Verb+Theme/Patient idioms can be found in Table 8.1. A similar point holds for verbs that take an Agent, a Theme and a Location, where it is the Location that is most easily integrated into an idiom, as the examples in Table 8.2 show.

Whereas we have idioms like *X bites the dust*, we do not have *tired children bite X*, we have *leave X in the lurch*, but not *leave angry dogs in X*.

If you want to know more about the motivation for the Thematic Hierarchy, there are references at the end of the chapter. The Thematic Hierarchy will be crucial to Lexical Mapping Theory, which provides a mapping between a-structure and f-structure, as we will see in Section 8.4.

Table 8.1 *Idioms with Verb+Theme/Patient*

rock the boat	kick the bucket	bite the dust
hit the road	take the biscuit	lift a finger
settle a score	steal the show	smell a rat
hold the fort	save the day	hit the spot
draw the line	drop a bombshell	burn the midnight oil

Table 8.2 *Idioms with Verb+Location*

leave x in the lurch	haul x over the coals
lay x on the line	wrap x around one's little finger
put x on the map	keep x under one's hat

8.3 Correspondences between θ-roles and Grammatical Functions

We said above that the argument structure of a predicate consists of a list of its arguments, ordered according to the Thematic Hierarchy, and a classification which determines the mapping from these arguments to grammatical functions, via Lexical Mapping Theory (LMT). The a-structure of a basic transitive predicate such as *tickle* is given in (6). The θ-roles are listed from left to right, according to their relative position on the Thematic Hierarchy. The [–o] and [–r] features are the intrinsic classification, and will be explained shortly. The lines linking the arguments to the grammatical functions represent the application of LMT, as we will see below.

(6)

```
tickle  <  Agent   Patient  >
           [–o]    [–r]
            |       |
           SUBJ    OBJ
```

Underlying LMT is the observation that even though there is no one-to-one relation between θ-roles and grammatical relations, it is the case that there are general patterns and principles of mapping between θ-roles and grammatical functions within languages, and cross-linguistically. For example, in English and many other languages of the world, if a predicate requires an Agent argument and a Patient argument, then normally the Agent will be subject and the Patient will be object in the canonical mapping (for an active verb – we will see how mapping works for passive verbs in Section 8.6). In fact, certain θ-roles can only occur as certain grammatical functions and certain grammatical functions can only be filled by specific θ-roles. Below are some of these correspondences.

Patients can be either OBJ or SUBJ.

(7) a. Oscar tickled **Fred**. *Patient* OBJ

b. **Fred** was tickled by Oscar. *Patient* SUBJ

c. *Oscar tickled of/to **Fred**. attempt to make *Patient* OBL_θ

Themes/Stimuli are also mapped to either OBJ or SUBJ.

(8) a. Oscar loved **Fred**. *Stimulus* OBJ
b. **Fred** was loved by Oscar. *Stimulus* SUBJ
c. *Oscar loved of/to **Fred**. *Stimulus* cannot be OBL_θ

An Instrument can be SUBJ or ADJ, as in (9a) and (9b), but not OBJ as in (9c).

(9) a. **The knife** killed Fred. *Instrument* SUBJ
b. Oscar killed Fred with **the knife**. *Instrument* ADJ
c. *Oscar killed the knife Fred. *Instrument* cannot be OBJ

OBJ_θ is a very restricted grammatical function. Not all languages have it, and those that do restrict it to a very small number of θ-roles; in English it is only Theme.

(10) Fred gave Oscar **the knife**. *Theme* OBJ_θ

Considering the connection from the point of view of functions now, SUBJ and OBJ are not restricted as to which θ-roles can fill them. As the examples in (11) show, the phrase which functions as SUBJ, for instance, can have at least the following θ-roles:

(11)		
	a. **Oscar** tickled Fred.	*Agent*
	b. **Fred** was tickled by Oscar.	*Patient*
	c. **Oscar** loved Fred.	*Experiencer*
	d. **Fred** was loved by Oscar.	*Stimulus*
	e. **The car** had been moved by Oscar.	*Theme*
	f. **The knife** killed Fred.	*Instrument*
	g. **Behind the sofa** is a good place to hide.	*Location*

The OBJ function is not quite as unrestricted as SUBJ; however, OBJ is less restricted than OBL_θ and OBJ_θ. These functions are restricted to certain θ-roles. OBL_θ arguments are explicitly marked for a particular θ-role, e.g. *with* marks an Instrument, OBL_{Instr}, *to* can mark OBL_{Rec} etc., and OBJ_θ can only be a Theme.

8.4 Lexical Mapping Theory

These generalisations show us that grammatical functions such as SUBJ and OBJ can be grouped into natural classes in terms of their association with θ-roles. That is, some grammatical functions are unrestricted in terms of the θ-roles they can realise, while others are more restricted. And some θ-roles seem to be incompatible with the object functions OBJ and OBJ_θ, while others are not.

To capture these natural classes, we can introduce two features [± r(estricted)], and [± o(bjective)] and use these to cross-classify the grammatical functions. The feature [± r] indicates whether or not a function is restricted as to which θ-roles can fill it. SUBJ and OBJ are [–r] and all other functions are [+r]. The feature [± o]

Table 8.3 *Features and grammatical functions*

	[–o]	[+o]
[–r]	SUBJ	OBJ
[+r]	OBL$_\theta$	OBJ$_\theta$

is straightforward: the functions OBJ and OBJ$_\theta$ are [+o] and the other functions are [–o]. We will only deal with these four functions in this section. The two binary features [± r] and [± o] give us the feature combinations in Table 8.3. The fact that SUBJ and OBJ are [–r] is what allows these grammatical functions to be filled by expletive arguments, which have no θ-role at all, such as the pronoun *it* in *It is raining today* or *there* in *Sam believes there to be a problem*. We introduced expletive arguments in Chapter 5, and we will discuss them in more detail in Section 8.5.

Taking the minus values to be unmarked, this cross-classification defines a Markedness Hierarchy of grammatical functions, such that SUBJ is the least marked, since both its feature values are minus, and OBJ$_\theta$ is the most marked, since neither of its feature values is minus. Empirical support for this classification includes the fact that we can assume that all languages have subjects (least marked), but only some languages have the particular construction types that involve OBJ$_\theta$ (most marked). The MARKEDNESS HIERARCHY OF GRAMMATICAL FUNCTIONS is shown in (12). We will return to it when we define the mapping rules below.

(12) MARKEDNESS HIERARCHY OF GRAMMATICAL FUNCTIONS:
SUBJ > OBJ, OBL$_\theta$ > OBJ$_\theta$

These features now group our grammatical functions into classes: SUBJ and OBJ are both [–r] for example, while SUBJ and OBL$_\theta$ are both [–o]. We can use these features to capture the relation between classes of θ-roles and grammatical functions by associating these features with θ-roles in the argument structure of predicates in order to constrain the grammatical functions to which they are mapped by LMT. This is called INTRINSIC CLASSIFICATION, whereby certain θ-roles are intrinsically associated with particular feature values.

(13) **Intrinsic classification of a-structure roles:**

patientlike roles:	θ [–r]
secondary patientlike roles:	θ [+o]
other θ-roles:	θ [–o]

Roles like Theme, Patient and Stimulus behave in a similar way in this respect and can be grouped together as PATIENTLIKE – these roles are intrinsically linked to [–r]. This means that these roles are unrestricted; as we have seen, they can appear as both SUBJ and OBJ. In some languages we need to account for two patientlike roles in ditransitive constructions. In this case, the secondary patientlike role is mapped to [+o]. We will return to secondary patientlike roles and how their mapping works in our discussion of English dative-shift constructions in Section 8.6. Finally, Agents and all other θ-roles (e.g. Experiencer, Location, Instrument, etc.) are intrinsically classified with [–o]. This ensures that an Agent is realised as a non-objective function, that is, as SUBJ or as ADJ (or possibly OBL_θ in the passive, but this is an option which we will not discuss), and does not occur as an OBJ or an OBJ_θ. This is exactly the generalisation we stated about Agents in Section 8.3.

So, with an a-structure like the one for *tickle*, which takes an Agent and a Patient, we get the intrinsic classification in (14).

(14)	*tickle*	<	Agent	Patient	>
			[–o]	[–r]	

Mapping principles then map these argument structures to grammatical functions at f-structure according to the following simple mapping principles. $\hat{\theta}$ refers to the most prominent θ-role in the predicate's argument structure, that is, the one that is highest on the Thematic Hierarchy. In other words, this is the left-most θ-role in an argument structure.

(15) **Mapping principles:**

a. $\hat{\theta}$ is mapped onto SUBJ
   [–o]

b. otherwise θ is mapped onto SUBJ
   [–r]

c. other roles are mapped onto the lowest (i.e. most marked) compatible function on the Markedness Hierarchy (12)

There are also two general conditions on the mapping:

Function–Argument Bi-uniqueness Each a-structure role corresponds to a unique f-structure function and each f-structure function corresponds to a unique a-structure role.

The Subject Condition Every verb must have a SUBJ.

The Function–Argument Bi-uniqueness Condition ensures that no grammatical relation carries more than one θ-role and that every θ-role is assigned to just one unique grammatical relation; for instance, the SUBJ cannot be both Agent and Patient, and the Agent cannot be associated with both SUBJ and OBL_θ.

So, if we now continue to map our example in (14), we get (16).

(16)					
	tickle	<	Agent	Patient	>
	Intrinsic classification:		[–o]	[–r]	
			|	|	
	Mapping:		SUBJ	OBJ	

The Agent is [–o] intrinsically and initial in the a-structure, hence is mapped to SUBJ according to (15a). The remaining θ-role, Patient, already has [–r] intrinsically. According to (15c) this role will be mapped to the lowest compatible role on the Markedness Hierarchy of grammatical functions (12): since the only grammatical functions compatible with [–r] are SUBJ and OBJ, the Patient will be mapped to the OBJ since it is lower than SUBJ on the Markedness Hierarchy. Note that in this particular case, mapping to SUBJ would also be ruled out by Function-Argument Bi-uniqueness since the Agent has already been mapped to SUBJ.

Let's now consider the verb *put*. LMT would work as in (17).

(17)	*put*	<	Agent	Theme	Location	>
	Intrinsic classification:		[–o]	[–r]	[–o]	
			|	|	|	
	Mapping:		SUBJ	OBJ	OBL_θ	

The intrinsic classification given in (13) assigns [–o] to the Agent and the Location and [–r] to the Theme. The mapping links the Agent, as the initial [–o] θ-role, to the SUBJ. As with *tickle*, the Theme is compatible with both SUBJ and OBJ (since both are [–r]), so it maps to OBJ, which is the lowest of the two on the Markedness Hierarchy of GFs. The Location is [–o] and hence compatible with both SUBJ and OBL_θ, but maps to OBL_θ, since this is lower than SUBJ on the hierarchy. The θ-variable in OBL_θ will be instantiated to the particular θ-role (here, Location) via the choice of preposition in a language like English and hence will be OBL_{Loc}. This is done through the PCASE feature, as we saw in Chapter 3, which instantiates the subtype of OBL_θ to OBL_{Loc} or OBL_{Rec}, and so forth. In languages which use case rather than prepositions, this is done by the case marker itself via constructive case, as we saw in Chapter 4. That is, the case marker will encode the particular subtype of OBL_θ that it realises, carrying an f-description such as (OBL_{Loc} ↑), for example.

Now let's look at verbs with just one argument. You might at first sight think that there would not be a lot of interesting work to be done with LMT and verbs with one argument. However, there is evidence that there are actually two different types of constructions with intransitive verbs. This evidence is based for instance on the RESULTATIVE construction. Consider the three sentences in (18).

(18) a. The boys scrubbed the floor clean.
b. The boys scrubbed the floor naked.
c. #The boys scrubbed the floor tired.

In (18a), *clean* refers to the floor, not the boys. Furthermore, the floor being clean is a result of the scrubbing. This is therefore a resultative construction, as we discussed in Chapter 5. In a sentence with a subject and an object, a resultative can only predicate on the object. In (18b), the adjective *naked* does refer to the subject, but it is not resultative since it is not as if the scrubbing has made the boys naked. Rather, these constructions are referred to as DEPICTIVE constructions. In

(18c), we have tried to get a subject resultative with an adjective that could in principle be the result for the boys of the scrubbing. However, (18c) can either mean that the floor became tired, which does not make sense, or that the boys were already tired when they started. It can not be understood as 'the tiredness was the result of the scrubbing'.

Given what we have just said, we would not expect there to be resultatives with verbs with just one argument, i.e. with just a subject. In other words, we don't expect intransitive resultatives. This may appear to be true if you consider sentences such as that in (19a). As can be expected, it does work if we add an object, even if it is just a reflexive pronoun referring to the same entity as the subject, as in (19b).

(19) a. *He drank silly.
b. He drank himself silly.

There is, however, a different kind of intransitive verb which does function with resultatives. Two examples are provided in (20).

(20) a. The water froze solid.
b. The kettle boiled dry.

Here, the water is solid as a result of the freezing and the kettle is dry as a result of the boiling. Hence they are both resultative constructions, even if there is no object. The kind of intransitive that allows the resultative is called UNACCUSATIVE. These are intransitive verbs that have Patients/Themes as their subjects, and it is often the case that these sort of subjects pattern with objects in various respects, as we see here. LMT allows us to capture their similarities with objects, while still appropriately mapping them to SUBJ, as we shall now see. To do so, we will go back to resultative constructions with two arguments first. Looking at (18), *the boys* is an Agent and *the floor* is a Patient. In terms of the features we have used here, we would get the intrinsic features in (21).

(21)	*scrub*	<	Agent	Patient	>
	Intrinsic classification:		[–o]	[–r]	

Remember that the resultative only works with the second argument here, that is the one that has the feature [–r] intrinsically. We could then tentatively conclude that we can get a resultative reading when an adjective is predicated of an argument with the intrinsic feature [–r].

Consider now the verb *drink* in (19). In this use, this is an intransitive verb with a single Agent argument; such verbs are sometimes called UNERGATIVE. This verb has the intrinsic features in (22).

(22)	*drink*	<	Agent	>
	Intrinsic classification:		[–o]	

Given that *drink* does not allow the resultative reading as in (19a), on the basis of this evidence, we could maintain the generalisation that a resultative only works with the argument that is intrinsically [–r]. This is further supported by the fact that *drink* allows the resultative once we add a 'fake' or 'dummy' object such as *himself* in (19b). This is a type of ATHEMATIC argument which doesn't have a θ-role, and is therefore [–r] by definition (we return to the discussion of athematic arguments in Section 8.5). Thus, by adding this [–r] argument into the argument structure for *drink*, the resultative is licensed.

The verbs in (20) both have a single argument which is a Theme. This gives the intrinsic features in (23).

(23)	*freeze/boil*	<	Theme	>
	Intrinsic classification:		[–r]	

The generalisation can therefore be expressed as follows: a predicate involving a resultative meaning can be added when it is predicated of an argument intrinsically linked to [–r]. Given that [–r] arguments can map to either SUBJ or OBJ in LMT, we capture the fact that unaccusative subjects pattern with transitive objects in this way without having to assume they share the same grammatical function at f-structure. We also capture the fact that unergative intransitive verbs cannot enter into the resultative construction unless their argument structure is augmented to include a 'dummy' [–r] argument, as in (19b). We discussed the f-structure analysis of resultative constructions in Chapter 5.

Of course LMT predicts that the one argument in intransitive verbs will end up as the subject, whatever its θ-role, since (15a) will map the Agent ([–o]) argument to SUBJ as in (24) and (15b) will map the Theme ([–r]) argument to SUBJ, as in (25).

(24)	*drink*	<	Agent	>
	Intrinsic classification:		[–o]	
			|	
	Mapping:		SUBJ	

(25)	*freeze/boil*	<	Theme	>
	Intrinsic classification:		[–r]	
			|	
	Mapping		SUBJ	

8.5 Mapping Athematic Arguments

As we discussed in Chapter 5, it is possible for verbs to select for arguments that have no semantic content. There we referred to them as expletives, but in this context, we can refer to them as athematic arguments since they have no θ-role. In English, these are usually expressed with *it* or *there*, as in the examples in (26). Another type of athematic argument in English is the dummy reflexive pronoun in sentences such as *He drank himself silly*, discussed in (19) above.

(26)
a. It rained yesterday.
b. It seems to me to be hotter today.
c. There is a problem with this analysis.
d. I believe there to be many advantages to this approach.

As these athematic arguments have no semantic content and therefore no θ-role, they are intrinsically classified as [–r] since the [± r] feature concerns whether or not a function is restricted as to which θ-roles can fill it. Clearly an athematic argument cannot be restricted to particular θ-roles since, by definition, it is not filled by any θ-role; it is therefore intrinsically [–r]. The mapping of athematic roles to grammatical functions then follows from the mapping rules presented in Section 8.4, as we shall now see.

First, consider a verb such as *rain* in (26a). Its a-structure and mapping is shown in (27). This verb subcategorises for no thematic arguments, just a single athematic element. As you know from Chapter 5, athematic arguments are written outside the angled brackets of the argument structure.

(27)

rain	__	< >
Intrinsic classification:	[–r]	
Mapping	SUBJ	

The athematic argument is intrinsically classified as [–r] which, by virtue of (15b), ensures that it is mapped to SUBJ.

Now let's consider a more complex argument structure, such as that for *seem* in (26b). For present purposes, we will assume that the clausal argument *to be hotter today* has the θ-role of PROPOSITION (a role additional to those listed in Section 8.2). We discussed the c- and f-structure properties of clausal arguments in Chapter 5, but note that now we are writing the athematic element before the argument structure, for reasons that will become clear shortly.

(28)

seem	__	<	Experiencer	Proposition	>
Intrinsic classification:	[–r]		[–o]	[–o]	
Mapping	SUBJ		OBL_θ	OBL_θ	

Our mapping rules in (15) state that a [–o] will be mapped to SUBJ but only when it is initial in the a-structure (15a). We now see why it is worded this way, and why it's important to put the athematic element before the argument structure in this case, since it ensures that the [–o] argument is *not* mapped to SUBJ in this case, but rather the athematic argument is. Since the [–o] argument is not initial in the a-structure, the [–r] athematic argument is mapped to SUBJ by virtue of (15b). The two [–o] arguments are then mapped to OBL_θ according to (15c). In fact, as we saw in Chapter 5, the propositional argument will ultimately have the grammatical function of XCOMP. The basic LMT that we present here does not explicitly incorporate the mapping to XCOMP and COMP, so for illustrative purposes here we treat them as a special subtype of OBL_θ, an account which would need to be augmented to give a fully general treatment.

Finally, athematic arguments can be realised as objects as well, as we saw in (19b), repeated here.

(29) He drank himself silly.

In this case, the athematic argument is positioned in the final position of the argument structure, which allows the Agent argument to be mapped to SUBJ according to (15a). The athematic argument is then mapped to OBJ by (15c) in the now familiar way.

(30)					
	drink	<	Agent	>	—
	Intrinsic classification:		[–o]		[–r]
	Mapping		SUBJ		OBJ

In the next section we will see how LMT can be used to account for function-changing operations, such as passive and dative shift.

8.6 Function-Changing Operations

A passive sentence involves suppressing the highest argument; either it is deleted completely, or it occurs within a *by*-phrase. In LMT, this is captured as the highest θ-role not being available for mapping. As we have seen, the suppressed argument does not have to be an Agent; it can also be an Experiencer, as in the alternation *Oscar likes Fred* and *Fred is liked (by Oscar)*. If we assume a passive form of *tickle*, we get the mapping in (31).

(31)					
	tickle	<	Agent	Patient	>
	Intrinsic classification:		[–o]	[–r]	
	Passive:		Ø		
	Mapping:			SUBJ	

The suppression of the highest argument is marked by Ø here. The Patient is intrinsically linked to [–r], and since the highest argument in the a-structure is unavailable for linking, the Patient is mapped to SUBJ by (15b) as with unaccusative verbs (and by virtue of the Subject Condition, which requires there to be a subject). Note that under this analysis, the *by*-phrase has to be an ADJ, rather than an OBL_θ, because it cannot map to any of the core functions defined in terms of [± r] and [± o]. At the end of the chapter, you can find references to work on other valence-changing processes, such as locative inversion and causatives.

Another type of function-changing operation found in English is known as DATIVE-SHIFT, and is illustrated in (32).

(32) a. Sam baked a cake for Fred.
b. Sam baked Fred a cake.

These two sentences have the same broad meaning, but the mapping from arguments to grammatical functions is different in each one: in the first example, *a cake* is mapped to OBJ, and *Fred* is an OBL_{Ben}. When we make a passive version of this sentence, it is *a cake* which is mapped to SUBJ, as in (33b); it is not possible to map *Fred* to SUBJ in this case as shown in (33c).

(33) a. Sam baked a cake for Fred.
b. A cake was baked for Fred (by Sam).
c. *Fred was baked a cake for (by Sam).

However, in (34), *Fred* is in the object position immediately after the verb, and is the argument that maps to SUBJ when passive is applied, as shown in (34b). In this case, it is not possible to map *a cake* to SUBJ so we have exactly the opposite facts to what we saw in (33).

(34) a. Sam baked Fred a cake.
b. Fred was baked a cake (by Sam).
c. *A cake was baked Fred (by Sam).

As shown in (34c), when Fred is in the object position immediately following the verb, it is not possible for *a cake* to become SUBJ of the passive verb. In this case, *Fred* must be the passive subject for the sentence to be grammatical as in (34b). As we have seen above, our mapping rules capture the active/passive alternation by virtue of the fact that [–r] arguments can be mapped to either SUBJ or OBJ. In a passive verb, as in (31), the Agent role is suppressed, and so the [–r] Patient/Theme is mapped to SUBJ. Thus, the Theme argument *a cake* in (33b) must be intrinsically classified [–r] in order that it be mapped to SUBJ, and the Benefactive *Fred* in (34b) must be so classified as well, even though it is not a Patient/Theme. The rules and principles outlined in Section 8.4 above can capture this alternation, if we assume that the dative-shift operation allows Benefactive roles to be treated as patientlike and therefore receive [–r] intrinsically according to (13).

To see how this works, consider first the argument structure for the regular ditransitive in (32a).

(35)

	bake	<	Agent	Benefactive	Theme	>
	Intrinsic classification:		[–o]	[–o]	[–r]	
			|	|	|	
	Mapping:		SUBJ	OBL_θ	OBJ	

Agent and Benefactive are both intrinsically classified as [–o], and the Theme as [–r]. According to the mapping principles in (15), Agent is mapped to SUBJ (15a), and the other two roles map to the lowest compatible functions on the Markedness Hierarchy, namely OBL_θ and OBJ, respectively.

Now consider the argument structure for (32b).

(36)

	bake-for	<	Agent	Benefactive	Theme	>
	Intrinsic classification:		[–o]	[–r]	[+o]	
			|	|	|	
	Mapping:		SUBJ	OBJ	OBJ_θ	

In this case, due to the dative-shift operation the Benefactive has become patientlike, and is thus intrinsically classified as [–r]. The Theme, in this case, is now a secondary patientlike argument, and so gets the intrinsic classification [+o]. The mapping principles then map the Benefactive to OBJ, and the Theme to OBJ_θ, since it is the lowest function compatible with [+o] on the Markedness Hierarchy of GFs. We therefore account for the fact that it is the Benefactive role that maps to passive subject in this case, as in (34b).

	bake-for	<	Agent	Benefactive	Theme	>
	Intrinsic classification:		[–o]	[–r]	[+o]	
(37)	Passive:		Ø	|	|	
				|	|	
	Mapping:			SUBJ	OBJ_θ	

Since the Agent is suppressed and cannot be linked to a grammatical function, the Benefactive [–r] argument is mapped to SUBJ by (15b), and the Theme is again mapped to OBJ_θ, as it is the lowest grammatical function on the Markedness Hierarchy compatible with [+o].

Reading

In this chapter we have used the version of Lexical Mapping Theory presented by Bresnan (2001c); Bresnan et al. (2016). Those who are interested in further details can read the discussion in Chapter 14 of Bresnan et al. (2016). Other versions of LMT are presented by Dalrymple (2001, 195–215) and Falk (2001), and if you are interested you can read either of these for comparison. Bresnan and Kanerva (1989) and Bresnan and Moshi (1990) were crucial in developing Lexical Mapping Theory, though there are earlier versions of similar ideas. Dalrymple (2001, 205) mentions some cross-linguistic variation in the linking between a-structure and f-structure. One of these is discussed by Lødrup (1999b), who claims that Agents can be OBJ in Norwegian, but this is argued against by Börjars and Vincent (2005). As we mention above, the grammatical functions of COMP and XCOMP are not incorporated into basic LMT; here we follow the suggestion of Zaenen and Engdahl (1994) by treating them as mapping to OBL_θ.

A detailed extension and refinement of Lexical Mapping Theory has been undertaken in recent years by Anna Kibort, see Kibort (2004, 2007, 2008, 2014) as examples of this work. There has also been much work examining ditransitives cross-linguistically and the language-specific realisations of grammatical functions such as OBJ_θ in these contexts, including Toivonen (2013); Sadler and Camilleri (2013); Camilleri et al. (2014). Other work on argument structure in LFG has been undertaken by Ackerman and Moore (2001) and Alsina (see, for example, Alsina (1996) and later work). Although the approaches of many of these authors differ in certain respects from what we have presented here, you should now be equipped to read and understand them for yourself.

For convenience in this chapter, we have represented the arguments in a-structure with θ-role labels such as Agent and Patient. However, there is a lot more to be said about the content and representation of argument structure within LFG, and researchers differ in the semantic content that they assume to be present at this level of structure. See Dalrymple (2001, 197–200) for an overview of two major approaches to the content and representation of argument structure within LFG – Jackendovian and Dowtyian; and Butt (2006, ch. 5) for a critical account of Jackendoff's and Dowty's linking theories and the way they have been combined with LMT. Kibort (2007) presents arguments for separating θ-roles from argument structure; Falk (2001) does this in a separate level of representation he calls θ-structure.

Several types of justification for the Thematic Hierarchy have been given in the literature. The idiom data we have used here are adapted from O'Grady (1998, 295). Some linguists refer to pragmatics to justify the hierarchy. For example, functional linguists such as Givón (1984) have proposed that the hierarchy reflects the degree of topicality of arguments, with the highest being most topical. More often, the justification for the hierarchy has been semantic. Scholars such as Larson (1988) believe that the hierarchy is a reflection of the order of composition of arguments with the verb. The argument lowest in the hierarchy combines with the verb first, whereas the argument highest in the hierarchy combines last. Subject/object asymmetries in English idioms are often used as evidence for this interpretation of the hierarchy. Mithun (1984) finds that facts relating to noun incorporation can be used as evidence in favour of the hierarchy.

Sadler and Spencer (1998) discuss the relationship between morphology and argument structure, and in particular the different types of morphological operations that can affect argument structure. The analysis of function-changing operations such as causatives and applicatives in LFG has been discussed by Alsina (1996); Alsina and Mchombo (1990, 1993); Seiss and Nordlinger (2010); locative inversion has been the subject of work by Bresnan (1994) and Bresnan and Kanerva (1989).

We have not discussed in this chapter languages with ergative syntax or Philippine-style voice systems, which may have a more complex mapping from argument structure to grammatical functions. Manning (1996) discusses syntactic ergativity within the LFG framework. LFG-related work on different types of voice systems include Arka (2003) on Balinese, Kroeger (1993) on Tagalog and the papers in Musgrave and Austin (2008).

Exercises

8.1 For each of the following sentences, show how the grammatical functions of the arguments are derived from the a-structure of the verb by LMT.

(38) a. The child ran quickly.
b. The plant died.
c. The fox chased the mouse.

d. I gave a present to the teacher.
e. We put some books on the table.
f. I gave the teacher a present.
g. It snowed.
h. It seems to me to be a problem.
i. The thief was caught.
j. The teacher was given a present.
k. The child laughed herself hoarse.

8.2 Explain the ungrammaticality of each of the following using LMT (note that some native speakers may disagree with some of these judgements).

(39) a. *The fox chased on the monkey.
b. *A present was given the teacher.
c. *The monkey slept it.
d. *He ran tired.
e. *The water rained.

8.3 Consider the following examples from Wambaya and determine the argument structures of the verbs *nyagajbi*, *ardbi*, *bardbi*, *wugbardi* and *manku*. Provide the a-structures for each verb, and show how each argument is mapped to the correct grammatical function by LMT.

(40) a. Nyagajbi ngi
be.tired AUX.1SG.SUBJ.PRS
'I'm tired.'

b. Ardbi irri alanyi-nka
call.out AUX.3PL.SUBJ.PRS child-DAT
'They call out to the child.'

c. Juwa ga bardbi gajigajirra
man.NOM AUX.3SG.PST run fast
'The man ran fast.'

d. Wugbardi ngiya manganyma
cook AUX.3SG.F.SUBJ.PST bread.ACC
'She cooked some bread.'

e. Alanyi-nka ngiya wugbardi manganyma
child-DAT AUX.3SG.F.SUBJ.PST cook bread.ACC
'She cooked some bread for the child.'

f. Nyamirniji nga manku
2SG.ACC AUX.1SG.SUBJ.PST hear
'I heard you.'

8.4 The verb *enter* as it occurs in (41) seems to have a Location as its second argument. What are the grammatical relations we should associate with the two arguments of *enter* in (41)? Using LMT as presented in this chapter, show why taking the argument structure of (41) to be <Agent, Location> fails to predict the observed mapping in (41).

(41) Oscar entered the room.

In order to account for (41), we need to recognise that specific predicates can allow idiosyncratic intrinsic classifications to be assigned to their arguments. What intrinsic classification would we (exceptionally) have to assign to the Locative argument of *enter* in order to account for (41)? Show how assuming this idiosyncratic intrinsic classification accounts for the observed mapping using LMT.

9 Further Topics

In this chapter, we introduce a number of areas in which LFG has been used, but which we have not had the space to deal with in this book. Our aim is not to explain how LFG works in these areas, or provide details of analyses. The aim is just to provide an outline of the work done with references to the literature. The references we provide will by necessity be a (small) selection of what is available, but should be enough to allow a reader interested in a particular area to follow up.

9.1 The Architecture

Asudeh (2006, 369) provides a full picture of the parallel correspondence architecture including all the dimensions we referred to in Section 1.2: a-structure, c-structure, f-structure, i-structure, m-structure, p-structure and s-structure; and the mappings between them. However, though there is general agreement on how the three dimensions we have dealt with in more detail in this book connect – a-structure, f-structure and c-structure – there are different views on the relation between the other dimensions within the architecture. Mycock (2007, 198) provides a partial representation of the architecture that differs in some respects from that of Asudeh (2006), and a more recent proposal can be found in Dalrymple and Nikolaeva (2011, esp. 90–3).

With respect to the position of m-structure in the overall architecture, Butt et al. (1996) argue that it is mapped from c-structure, whereas Frank and Zaenen (2002) (first presented in 1998) argue that it is mapped from f-structure. Dalrymple (2015a) provides an outline of the role of morphology within LFG, and a number of relevant articles can be found in Sadler and Spencer (2004) (including reprints of Butt et al. (1996) and Frank and Zaenen (2002)).

There are a number of different formalisations of both i-structure and p-structure. Bresnan and Mchombo (1987) show that information-structural concepts such as TOPIC and FOCUS can be syntactically encoded in some languages, like the Bantu language Chicheŵa, and hence that they are best represented in f-structure. These are the grammaticalised discourse functions we have referred to throughout this book. King (1995) shows that such an analysis is motivated also for Russian clausal word order. Choi (1999) analyses scrambling, that is, a degree of flexibility in word order, in Korean and German and shows that a number of factors influence the order of elements in c-structure: a-structure, f-structure, i-structure and s-structure (she also includes prosodic and morphological factors, but does not posit separate dimensions for these). King (1997) provides actual representations of i-structure using a restricted set of features. Butt and King (2000) take this work further and develop the categories introduced by Choi (1999) in an explicit proposal of a separate i-structure. Butt and King (1998) posit a p-structure representation that takes the shape of an attribute–value matrix. They illustrate the mapping between p-structure and c-structure, for instance by considering mismatches between the two. They also consider the relation between p-structure and discourse-structure, which is their version of i-structure. O'Connor (2006), who uses d-structure where others use i-structure, develops a more subtle approach to p-structure concentrating on the role of intonation. An approach to p-structure built around the syllable has been developed by Bögel (2015), who is mainly concerned with its interaction with c-structure. Mycock (2006, 2007) uses the interaction between p-structure and i-structure to provide a typological survey of constituent questions. This approach to the interaction has been extended in Mycock and Lowe (2013).

Choi (1999) is one of a number of researchers who have worked on LFG within an Optimality Theory (OT) setting. Optimality Theory (Prince and Smolensky, 2004) is a linguistic model which defines grammars as arising through language-particular optimisations of ranked universal constraints (for a general introduction to OT in syntax, see Legendre (2001)). OT-LFG uses LFG to generate the candidate space for this optimisation and OT to account for how the competition between the constraints is resolved. For more work in OT-LFG, see Bresnan (2000, 2001a, 2001b); Kuhn (2003); Sells (2001a, 2001b).

9.2 Semantics

In this book we have focused very largely on the core areas of LFG as a syntactic framework for synchronic morphosyntactic description and analysis. However a considerable body of work in LFG addresses issues concerning other dimensions of linguistic structure, and the mapping between the syntactic representations and these other dimensions. The major focus of most LFG work in the area of semantics has been on the mapping or connection between syntax and semantic interpretation (rather than on the nature of the meaning representations themselves). In LFG it is f-structures rather than c-structures which are the basis for semantic analysis (Chapter 2 of Fenstad et al. (1987) provides early discussion of this point, and the advantages of using f-structures rather than c-structures as input to semantic interpretation). As we have seen, because f-structures are based on grammatical functions such as SUBJ and OBJ, they are rather similar across languages which differ very considerably in their c-structures. This in turn means that the rules for semantic composition, that is, the process of putting together the meaning of the whole sentence from the meanings of the parts, are also very similar across languages.

In the main, LFG makes use of an approach often called GLUE SEMANTICS to connect syntax to the semantic resources from which a meaning is derived. We cannot do any more here than give the basic flavour of the approach, but a relatively accessible introduction is provided in Dalrymple (2001, ch. 9). In this approach, a particular logical language, LINEAR LOGIC, serves as a 'glue language' in specifying how the meanings of the parts are assembled to produce the meaning of the whole. The particular advantage of linear logic is that it is RESOURCE SENSITIVE in the sense that when premises are used they are consumed, which means that they cannot be used again. By using expressions in linear logic to provide instructions as to how the meanings of the parts are to be combined, we can ensure that semantic interpretation is complete, using all and only the meanings associated with the parts. The "instructions for combination" are expressed alongside the meanings of the parts in MEANING CONSTRUCTORS. The examples in (1) and (2) are meaning constructors for the intransitive verb *leave* in (1) and the NP *Jo* in (2), using simple predicate logic expressions to express meanings (these meaning constructors are given in the lexical entries for these words).

(1) $\lambda\ x.leave(x) : (\uparrow \text{SUBJ})_\sigma \multimap \uparrow_\sigma$

(2) $Jo : \uparrow_\sigma$

Meaning constructors have a left-hand side and a right-hand side, separated by a colon. The left-hand side gives the meaning representation and the right-hand side states how meanings are to be combined. In this example the meaning of *leave* is taken to be a function which will take a single argument, and the meaning of *Jo* is taken to be a simple constant referring to the individual *Jo*. The meaning of the sentence *Jo leaves* or *Jo left* (abstracting away from the contribution of tense) will be *leave(Jo)*. The meaning constructor for *Jo* simply pairs the meaning *Jo* with the semantic structure projected from the f-structure corresponding to *Jo* — it says that *Jo* is the semantic resource for the f-structure associated with *Jo*. These meaning constructors use the σ function, which maps from f-structures to semantic structures.

The right-hand side of the meaning constructor for *leave* contains the instruction for combination – it can be read as saying that it will consume a premise corresponding to the semantic resource of the SUBJ (this is $(\uparrow \text{SUBJ})_\sigma$) and produce the semantic resource for the sentence as a whole ($\uparrow_\sigma$). On the meaning side, this will correspond to applying the function $\lambda\ x.leave(x)$ to the argument *Jo*, yielding the meaning representation for the sentence *Jo leaves* which is *leave(Jo)*.

The foundational paper for the glue semantics approach is Dalrymple et al. (1993). Dalrymple (1999) is a collection of early work, but the approach is notationally very different, which presents something of a challenge. The collection Dalrymple et al. (1995) contains a brief and accessible history of early work and some early important papers. Many papers using the glue semantics approach are too technical in nature to be mentioned here, or discuss phenomena which we have not discussed at all here. As well as providing a basic introduction to the approach, Dalrymple (2001) provides analyses of the semantics of a number of core syntactic phenomena. A number of papers address issues concerning the mapping between argument structure and f-structure, including Asudeh and Giorgolo (2012), Giorgolo and Asudeh (2012), Asudeh et al. (2013) and Findlay (2016). Semantic aspects of control are discussed in Asudeh (2005) and Haug (2013). Asudeh (2012) is a book-length discussion of pronominal resumption from a resource sensitive perspective.

9.3 Computational Work

From the outset, LFG was designed as a formally responsible linguistic theory, which means that LFG grammars can be computationally interpreted. Work on implemented grammars has been an important part of LFG from the beginning, both on a small scale, as researchers use the Xerox Linguistic Environment (XLE) grammar development platform to test out their analyses of particular constructions in a language, and on a much larger scale, notably within the long-running large-scale grammar development project PARGRAM. This long-running project started as a collaborative effort developing implemented grammars for English, French and German, using the XLE parser and grammar development platform developed at XEROX-PARC. Over the years, other grammars of various sizes for a typologically diverse set of languages have been developed including Georgian, Hungarian, Indonesian, Japanese, Malagasy, Norwegian, Polish, Tigrinya, Turkish, Urdu, Welsh and Wolof.

An important leading idea in this project is the use of f-structure as a level of abstraction which allows for cross-linguistic parallelism, so that where possible the analyses are very similar across languages. For example, the c-structures of *wh*-interrogatives in German and Urdu differ considerably. In German the *wh*-constituent is in initial position, preceding the finite verb, while in Urdu the finite verb is normally in final position and the *wh*-constituent can appear in a number of different positions in the clause. This is shown in the German and Urdu examples in (3) and (4) respectively, from Butt et al. (2002). The f-structure analyses for the Urdu and German examples will be very similar, despite these differences in c-structure (in (4) we follow the glossing in the original).

(3) Was hat John Maria gegeben?
what have.PRS.3SG John Maria give.PPTCP
'What did John give to Mary?'

(4) a. jon=nee marii=koo kyaa diiyaa?
John=ERG Mary=DAT what give.PERF.M.SG
'What did John give to Mary?'

b. jon=nee kyaa marii=koo diiyaa?
John=ERG what Mary=DAT give.PERF.M.SG
'What did John give to Mary?'

c. jon=nee marii=koo diiyaa kyaa?
John=ERG Mary=DAT gave what
'What did John give to Mary?'

An interesting aspect of this project is that because it is oriented towards real-life applications of computationally interpreted grammars, it has developed potential analyses for a number of phenomena which are not often discussed in the theoretical literature, but which are found in abundance in real text. Butt et al. (1999) provide a very accessible guide to grammar engineering using the XLE. Although there have been many developments since this was written, it is still a very useful resource, and gives a good flavour of what is involved in developing implemented grammars. Butt et al. (2002) also provide an introduction to the PARGRAM project.

A number of doctoral theses and associated papers are substantially concerned with the development of implemented LFG grammars, morphologies and grammar fragments including Dipper (2003) (German), Chatsiou (2010) (Greek) Sulger (2017) (Hindi/Urdu), Seiss (2013) (Murrinhpatha), Patejuk (2015) (Polish) and Dione (2014) (Wolof), as well as many others. In addition, a considerable number of papers providing implemented analyses of phenomena beyond the core syntactic constructions for a range of languages have come out of this work, and many have appeared in the annual proceedings of the LFG conference (see the end of this chapter for more information about these proceedings). Dalrymple et al. (2004) introduce the use of templates, which provide a convenient notation for bundling up information, making the statement of lexical descriptions much more compact.

The collection Butt et al. (2006) contains a number of papers focused on practical matters of natural language processing using the XLE LFG grammar development platform. For example, Burton (2006) discusses using the (very substantial) English XLE grammar in an intelligent tutoring system, building a digital tutor for a course to teach network administration. Van Genabith (2006) gives an overview of treebank-based acquisition of multilingual LFG grammars, building on earlier work including van Genabith et al. (1999); Sadler et al. (2000a); Sadler et al. (2000b); Frank et al. (2003), and much subsequent work.

The starting point for finding out about obtaining and using the XLE is http://ling.uni-konstanz.de/pages/xle/ which also provides access to tutorials and other useful resources.

9.4 Linguistic Change

LFG was developed from the start with typological variation in mind and hence, as we hope to have shown throughout this book, it provides a formalism that does justice to typologically diverse languages and allows us to analyse them on their own terms. Linguistic diversity is not just geographic, but also diachronic; languages vary across space, and they vary across time. Using

LFG to analyse earlier stages of a language is then not much different from using it to analyse synchronic variation. More importantly, a number of aspects of LFG make it suited to analysing linguistic change, that is, how different historical stages of a language are connected. Vincent (2001) provides a general discussion of the contribution LFG can make to the study of morphosyntactic change, and the other papers in Butt and King (2001) illustrate specific analyses of a range of diachronic data. Börjars and Vincent (2017) highlight some aspects of LFG that make it particularly suited to diachronic analysis.

Linguistic change is frequently described as 'gradual', but this is actually taken to mean that change progresses in small steps. Furthermore, a small change, say, in category or constituent structure may not be immediately accompanied by a change in function, indeed, may never be accompanied by a change in function, and the other way around. LFG's expectation of non-one-to-one mapping between c-structure and f-structure makes the historical stages that result from such uni-dimensional change expected rather than problematic, as it is in some other models. Börjars and Vincent (2019) illustrate this with the development of the WILL verb across a number of Germanic languages. The change from lexical to more functional verbs is a commonly cited example of grammaticalisation, and one that can be accounted for within LFG. Camilleri and Sadler (2017) explore the grammaticalisation of posture verbs, and Butt and Lahiri (2013) contrast the development of auxiliaries from lexical verbs with that of light verbs.

Aspects of the changes involved in grammaticalisation can be captured as loss of features. Bresnan and Mchombo (1987) analyse the development of agreement marking in terms of a loss of the PRED feature, and Coppock and Wechsler (2010) consider similar processes in terms of loss of person and number features.

LFG's flexible approach to c-structure, allowing both endocentric and exocentric categories, makes it an excellent model for analysis of languages where word order changes from being determined to a large extent by information-structural considerations to being limited by syntactic rules. This can be captured as the development of an articulated c-structure involving functional categories (Vincent 1999; Börjars et al. 2016). Lowe (2015) uses LEXICAL SHARING, an expansion of c-structure, to account for the apparent gradualness of changes to the English possessive.

LFG accounts of the changes to case systems, and the consequences for the organisation of grammar in the history of English are explored in terms of mapping between f-structure and a-structure in Allen (1995). Kibort and Maling (2015) use Mapping Theory to account for recent changes in Icelandic.

If there is anything specific you are interested in, you can get a good idea of work that has been done within LFG by browsing the online proceedings of the annual LFG conference. These can be found at http://cslipublications.stanford.edu/LFG/. General information about LFG can be found at http://ling.uni-konstanz.de/pages/home/lfg.

References

Abney, Steven. 1987. *The English noun phrase in its sentential aspect*. Ph.D. thesis, Massachusetts Institute of Technology.

Ackerman, Farrell, and Moore, John. 2001. *Proto-properties and grammatical encoding*. Stanford, CA: CSLI Publications.

Allen, Cynthia. 1995. *Case marking and reanalysis: grammatical relations from Old to Early Modern English*. Oxford: Clarendon Press.

Alsina, Alex. 1996. *The role of argument structure in grammar: evidence from Romance*. Stanford, CA: CSLI Publications.

Alsina, Alex, and Arsenijević, Boban. 2012. Hierarchies and competing generalizations in Serbo-Croatian hybrid agreement. Pages 6–22 of: Butt, Miriam, and King, Tracy Holloway (eds.), *Proceedings of the LFG12 conference*. Stanford, CA: CSLI Publications. cslipublications.stanford.edu/LFG/.

Alsina, Alex, and Mchombo, Sam. 1990. The syntax of applicatives in Chicheŵa: problems for a theta theoretic asymmetry. *Natural Language and Linguistic Theory*, **8**, 493–506.

1993. Object asymmetries and the Chicheŵa applicative construction. Pages 17–45 of: Mchombo, Sam A. (ed.), *Theoretical aspects of Bantu grammar*. Stanford, CA: CSLI Publications.

Alsina, Alex, Mohanan, K. P., and Mohanan, Tara. 2005. How to get rid of the COMP. In: Butt, Miriam, and King, Tracy Holloway (eds.), *Proceedings of the LFG05 conference*. Stanford, CA: CSLI Publications. cslipublications.stanford.edu/LFG/.

Andrews, Avery D. 1982. The representation of case in modern Icelandic. Pages 427–503 of: Bresnan, Joan (ed.), *The mental representation of grammatical relations*. Cambridge, MA: MIT Press.

1990a. Case structures and control in modern Icelandic. Pages 165–85 of: Maling, Joan, and Zaenen, Annie (eds.), *Modern Icelandic syntax*. San Diego, CA: Academic Press.

1990b. Unification and morphological blocking. *Natural Language and Linguistic Theory*, **8**(4), 507–58.

Arka, I. Wayan. 2003. *Balinese morphosyntax: a lexical functional approach*. Canberra: Pacific Linguistics.

Arka, I. Wayan, and Wechsler, Stephen. 1996. Argument structure and linear order in Balinese binding. In: Butt, Miriam, and King, Tracy Holloway (eds.), *Proceedings of the LFG96 conference*. Stanford, CA: CSLI Publications. cslipublications.stanford.edu/LFG/.

Asudeh, Ash. 2005. Control and semantic resource sensitivity. *Journal of Linguistics*, **41**(3), 465–511.

2006. Direct compositionality and the architecture of LFG. Pages 363–87 of: Butt, Miriam, Dalrymple, Mary, and King, Tracy Holloway (eds.), *Intelligent linguistic architectures: variations on themes by Ronald M. Kaplan*. Stanford, CA: CSLI Publications.

2012. *The logic of pronominal resumption*. Oxford: Oxford University Press.

Asudeh, Ash, Dalrymple, Mary, and Toivonen, Ida. 2013. Constructions with lexical integrity. *Journal of Language Modelling*, **1**(1), 1–54.

Asudeh, Ash, and Giorgolo, Gianluca. 2012. Flexible composition for optional and derived arguments. Pages 64–84 of: Butt, Miriam, and King, Tracy Holloway (eds.), *Proceedings of the LFG2012 conference*. Stanford, CA: CSLI Publications: cslipublications.stanford.edu/LFG/.

Austin, Peter K. 2001. Word order in a free word order language: the case of Jiwarli. Pages 305–23 of: Simpson, Jane, Nash, David, Laughren, Mary, Austin, Peter, and Alpher, Barry (eds.), *Forty years on: Ken Hale and Australian languages*. Canberra: Pacific Linguistics.

Austin, Peter, and Bresnan, Joan. 1996. Non-configurationality in Australian aboriginal languages. *Natural Language and Linguistic Theory*, **14**, 215–68.

Bögel, Tina. 2015. *The syntax–prosody interface in Lexical Functional Grammar*. Ph.D. thesis, Universität Konstanz.

Börjars, Kersti, and Burridge, Kate. 2019. *Introducing English grammar* (3d edn). London: Hodder Education.

Börjars, Kersti, Harries, Pauline, and Vincent, Nigel. 2016. Growing syntax: the development of a DP in Northern Germanic. *Language*, **91**, e1–37.

Börjars, Kersti, Payne, John, and Chisarik, Erika. 1999. On the justification for functional categories in LFG. In: Butt, Miriam, and King, Tracy Holloway (eds.), *Proceedings of the LFG99 conference*. Stanford, CA: CSLI Publications. cslipublications.stanford.edu/LFG/.

Börjars, Kersti, and Vincent, Nigel. 2005. Position vs function in Scandinavian presentational constructions. In: Butt, Miriam, and King, Tracy Holloway (eds.), *Proceedings of the LFG05 conference*. Stanford, CA: CSLI Publications. cslipublications.stanford.edu/LFG/.

2008. Objects and OBJ. Pages 150–68 of: Butt, Miriam, and King, Tracy Holloway (eds.), *Proceedings of the LFG08 conference*. Stanford, CA: CSLI Publications. cslipublications.stanford.edu/LFG/.

2017. Lexical-Functional Grammar. Pages 642–63 of: Ledgeway, Adam, and Roberts, Ian (eds.), *The Cambridge handbook of historical syntax*. Cambridge: Cambridge University Press.

2019. Modelling step change: the history of WILL-verbs in Germanic. Pages 283–314 of: Yáñez-Bouza, Nuria, Hollmann, Willem, Moore, Emma, and van Bergen, Linda (eds.), *Categories, constructions and change in English syntax*. Cambridge: Cambridge University Press.

Bostoen, Koen, and Mundeke, Leon. 2012. Subject marking, object–verb order and focus in Mbuun (Bantu, B87). *Southern African Linguistics and Applied Language Studies*, **30**(2), 139–54.

Bresnan, Joan. 1978. A realistic transformational grammar. Pages 1–59 of: Halle, Morris, Bresnan, Joan, and Miller, George A (eds.), *Linguistic theory and psychological reality*. Cambridge, MA: MIT Press.

1982a. Control and complementation. Pages 282–390 of: Bresnan, Joan (ed.), *The mental representation of grammatical relations*. Cambridge, MA: MIT Press.

1982b. Control and complementation. *Linguistic Inquiry*, **13**(3), 343–92.

(ed.). 1982c. *The mental representation of grammatical relations*. Cambridge, MA: MIT Press.

1994. Locative inversion and the architecture of universal grammar. *Language*, **70**, 72–131.

1998. Morphology competes with syntax: explaining typological variation in weak crossover effects. Pages 59–92 of: Barbosa, Pilar, Fox, Danny, Hagstrom, Paul, McGinnis, Martha, and Pesetsky, David (eds.), *Is the best good enough? Proceedings from the workshop on optimality in syntax*. Cambridge, MA: MIT Press.

2000. Optimal syntax. Pages 334–85 of: Dekkers, Joost, van der Leeuw, Frank, and van de Weijer, Jereon (eds.), *Optimality theory: phonology, syntax and acquisition*. Oxford: Oxford University Press.

2001a. The emergence of the unmarked pronoun. Pages 113–42 of: Legendre, Géraldine, Vikner, Sten, and Grimshaw, Jane (eds.), *Optimality-theoretic syntax*. Cambridge, MA: MIT Press.

2001b. Explaining morphosyntactic competition. Pages 11–44 of: Baltin, Mark, and Collins, Chris (eds.), *Handbook of contemporary syntactic theory*. Oxford: Blackwell.

2001c. *Lexical-functional syntax*. Oxford: Blackwell.

Bresnan, Joan, Asudeh, Ash, Toivonen, Ida, and Wechsler, Stephen. 2016. *Lexical-Functional Syntax*. (2nd edn) Oxford: Blackwell.

Bresnan, Joan, and Kanerva, Jonni M. 1989. Locative inversion in Chicheŵa: a case study in the factorization of grammar. *Linguistic Inquiry*, **20**, 1–50.

Bresnan, Joan, and Mchombo, Sam A. 1987. Topic, pronoun, and agreement in Chicheŵa. *Language*, **63**(4), 741–82.

Bresnan, Joan, and Moshi, Lioba. 1990. Object asymmetries in comparative Bantu syntax. *Linguistic Inquiry*, **21**, 147–86.

Burton, Richard R. 2006. Using XLE in an intelligent tutoring system. Pages 75–90 of: Butt, Miriam, Dalrymple, Mary, and King, Tracy Holloway (eds.), *Intelligent linguistic architectures: variations on themes by Ronald M. Kaplan*. Stanford, CA: CSLI Publications.

Butt, Miriam. 2006. *Theories of case*. Cambridge: Cambridge University Press.

Butt, Miriam, Dyvik, Helge, King, Tracy Holloway, Masuichi, Hiroshi, and Rohrer, Christian. 2002. The Parallel Grammar Project. Pages 1–7 of: *Proceedings of COLING-2002 workshop on grammar engineering and evaluation*.

Butt, Miriam, Dalrymple, Mary, and King, Tracy Holloway (eds.). 2006. *Intelligent linguistic architectures: variations on themes by Ronald M. Kaplan*. Stanford, CA: CSLI Publications.

Butt, Miriam, and King, Tracy Holloway. 1998. Interfacing phonology with LFG. In: Butt, Miriam, and King, Tracy Holloway (eds.), *Proceedings of the LFG98 conference*. Stanford, CA: CSLI Publications. cslipublications.stanford.edu/LFG/.

2000. Null elements in discourse structure. In: Subbarao, K.V. (ed.), *Papers from the NULLS seminar*. Delhi: Motilal Banarasidas.

(eds.). 2001. *Time over matter. Diachronic perspectives on morphosyntax*. Stanford, CA: CSLI Publications.

Butt, Miriam, King, Tracy Holloway, Niño, María-Eugenia, and Segond, Fédérique. 1999. *A grammar writer's cookbook*. Stanford, CA: CSLI Publications.

Butt, Miriam, and Lahiri, Aditi. 2013. Diachronic pertinacity of light verbs. *Lingua*, **135**, 7–29.

Butt, Miriam, Niño, María-Eugenia, and Segond, Frédérique. 1996. Multilingual processing of auxiliaries in LFG. Pages 111–22 of: Gibbon, Dafydd (ed.), *Natural language processing and speech technology: results of the 3d KONVENS conference*. [Reprinted in Sadler, L. and Spencer, A. 2004. *Projecting morphology*. Stanford, CA: CSLI Publications. 11–22.]. Berlin: Mouton de Gruyter.

Camilleri, Maris, ElSadek, Shaimaa, and Sadler, Louisa. 2014. A cross dialectal view of the Arabic dative alternation. *Acta Hungarica Linguistica*, **61**(1), 3–44.

Camilleri, Maris, and Sadler, Louisa. 2016. Relativisation in Maltese. *Transactions of the Philological Society*, **114**(1), 117–45.

2017. Posture verbs and aspect: a view from vernacular Arabic. Pages 167–87 of: Butt, Miriam, and King, Tracy Holloway (eds.), *Proceedings of the LFG17 conference*. Stanford, CA: CSLI Publications. cslipublications.stanford.edu/LFG/.

Chatsiou, Aikaterina. 2010. *An LFG approach to modern Greek relative clauses*. Ph.D. thesis, University of Essex.

Choi, Hye-Won. 1999. *Optimizing structure in context: scrambling and information structure*. Stanford, CA: CSLI Publications.

Clements, George N. 1975. The logophoric pronoun in Ewe: its role in discourse. *Journal of West African Languages*, **10**, 141–77.

Coppock, Elizabeth, and Wechsler, Stephen. 2010. Less-travelled paths from pronoun to agreement: the case of the Uralic objective conjugations. Pages 165–85 of: Butt, Miriam, and King, Tracy Holloway (eds.), *Proceedings of the LFG10 conference*. Stanford, CA: CSLI Publications. cslipublications.stanford.edu/LFG/.

Corbett, Greville G. 1983. Resolution rules: agreement in person, number, and gender. Pages 175–206 of: Gazdar, Gerald, Klein, Ewan, and Pullum, Geoffrey K. (eds.), *Order, concord, and constituency*. Dordrecht: Foris.

Dalrymple, Mary. 1993. *The syntax of anaphoric binding*. Stanford, CA: CSLI Publications.

(ed.). 1999. *Semantics and syntax in Lexical-Functional Grammar: the resource logic approach*. Cambridge, MA: MIT Press.

2001. *Lexical-Functional Grammar*. New York: Academic Press.

2015a. Morphology in the LFG architecture. Pages 43–62 of: Butt, Miriam, and King, Tracy Holloway (eds.), *Proceedings of the LFG15 conference*. Stanford, CA: CSLI Publications. cslipublications.stanford.edu/LFG/.

2015b. Obligatory nonlocal binding: an exclusively long distance anaphor in Yag Dii. *Natural Language & Linguistic Theory*, **33**(4), 1089–120.

Dalrymple, Mary, Dyvik, Helge, and King, Tracy Holloway. 2004. Copular complements: closed or open? Pages 173–93 of: Butt, Miriam, and King, Tracy Holloway (eds.), *Proceedings of the LFG04 conference*. Stanford, CA: CSLI Publications. cslipublications.stanford.edu/LFG/.

Dalrymple, Mary, and Kaplan, Ronald M. 2000. Feature indeterminacy and feature resolution. *Language*, **76**(4), 759–98.

Dalrymple, Mary, Kaplan, Ronald M., Maxwell, John T., and Zaenen, Annie (eds.). 1995. *Formal issues in Lexical-Functional Grammar*. Stanford, CA: CSLI Publications.

Dalrymple, Mary, Kaplan, Ronald M., and King, Tracy Holloway. 2001. Weak crossover and the absence of traces. In: Butt, Miriam, and King, Tracy Holloway (eds.), *Proceedings of the LFG01 conference*. Stanford, CA: CSLI Publications. cslipublications.stanford.edu/LFG/.

Dalrymple, Mary, Kaplan, Ronald M., and King, Tracy Holloway. 2004. Linguistic generalizations over descriptions. Pages 199–208 of: Butt, Miriam, and King, Tracy Holloway (eds.), *Proceedings of the LFG04 conference*. Stanford, CA: CSLI Publications. cslipublications.stanford.edu/LFG/.

2015. Economy of expression as a principle of syntax. *Journal of Language Modelling*, **3**(2), 377–412.

Dalrymple, Mary, Lamping, John, and Saraswat, Vijay A. 1993. LFG semantics via constraints. Pages 97–105 of: *Proceedings of the 6th meeting of the EACL*.

Dalrymple, Mary, and Lødrup, Helge. 2000. The grammatical functions of complement clauses. In: Butt, Miriam, and King, Tracy Holloway (eds.), *Proceedings of the LFG00 conference*. Stanford, CA: CSLI Publications. cslipublications.stanford.edu/LFG/.

Dalrymple, Mary, and Nikolaeva, Irina. 2011. *Objects and information structure*. Cambridge: Cambridge University Press.

Dalrymple, Mary, and Zaenen, Annie. 1991. Modeling anaphoric superiority. In: *Proceedings of the international conference on current issues in computational linguistics*.

Dench, Alan Charles. 1995. *Martuthunira: a language of the Pilbara region of Western Australia*. Canberra: Pacific Linguistics.

Dione, Cheikh Bamba. 2014. LFG parse disambiguation for Wolof. *Journal of Language Modelling*, **2**(1), 105–65.

Dipper, Stefanie. 2003. *Implementing and documenting large-scale grammars – German LFG*. Ph.D. thesis, IMS, University of Stuttgart.

Dowty, David. 1991. Thematic proto-roles and argument selection. *Language*, **67**, 547–619.

Engdahl, Elisabet. 1986. *Constituent questions. The syntax and semantics of questions with special reference to Swedish*. Dordrecht: Reidel.

Falk, Yehuda. 2001. *Lexical-Functional Grammar*. Stanford, CA: CSLI Publications.

2002. Resumptive pronouns in LFG. Pages 154–73 of: Butt, Miriam, and King, Tracy Holloway (eds.), *Proceedings of the LFG02 conference*. Stanford, CA: CSLI Publications. cslipublications.stanford.edu/LFG/.

2004. The Hebrew present tense copula as a mixed category. In: Butt, Miriam, and King, Tracy Holloway (eds.), *Proceedings of LFG04*. Stanford, CA: CSLI Publications. cslipublications.stanford.edu/LFG/.

Faltz, Leonard M. 1985. *Reflexivization: a study in universal syntax*. New York: Garland Press.

Fenstad, Jens-Erik, Halvorsen, Per-Kristian, Langholm, Tore, and van Benthem, Johan. 1987. *Situations, language, and logic*. Dordrecht: Reidel.

Findlay, Jamie. 2016. Mapping theory without argument structure. *Journal of Language Modelling*, **4**(2), 293–338.

Frank, Anette, Sadler, Louisa, van Genabith, Josef, and Way, Andy. 2003. From treebank resources to LFG f-structures. Pages 367–89 of: Abeillé, Anne (ed.), *Treebanks: building and using parsed corpora*. Dordrecht: Kluwer.

Frank, Anette, and Zaenen, Annie. 2002. Tense in LFG: syntax and morphology. Pages 17–51 of: Kamp, Hans, and Reyle, Uwe (eds.), *How we say WHEN it happens: contributions to the theory of temporal reference in natural language*. Tübingen: Max Niemeyer Verlag.

Giorgolo, Gianluca, and Asudeh, Ash. 2012. Missing resources in a resource-sensitive semantics. Pages 219–39 of: Butt, Miriam, and King, Tracy Holloway (eds.), *Proceedings of the LFG2012 conference*. Stanford, CA: CSLI Publications. cslipublications.stanford.edu/LFG/.

Givón, Talmy. 1976. Topic, pronoun, and grammatical agreement. Pages 149–88 of: Li, Charles N. (ed.), *Subject and topic*. University of California: Academic Press.

1984. *Syntax: a functional-typological introduction*. Amsterdam: John Benjamins.

Hale, Ken. 1983. Warlpiri and the grammar of non-configurational languages. *Natural Language and Linguistic Theory*, **1**, 5–47.

Haug, Dag. 2013. Partial control and anaphoric control in LFG. Pages 274–94 of: Butt, Miriam, and King, Tracy Holloway (eds.), *Proceedings of LFG13 conference*. Stanford, CA: CSLI Publications. cslipublications.stanford.edu/LFG/.

Henadeerage, Kumara. 1998. Anaphoric binding in colloquial Sinhala. In: Butt, Miriam, and King, Tracy Holloway (eds.), *Proceedings of the LFG98 Conference*. Stanford, CA: CSLI Publications. cslipublications.stanford.edu/LFG/.

Hudson, Richard A. 1987. Zwicky on heads. *Journal of Linguistics*, **23**, 109–32.

Jackendoff, Ray. 1990. *Semantic structures*. Cambridge, MA: MIT Press.

Jaeger, Florian. 2004. Binding in picture NPs revisited: evidence for a semantic principle of extended argument-hood. Pages 268–88 of: Butt, Miriam, and King, Tracy Holloway (eds.), *Proceedings of the LFG04 conference*. Stanford, CA: CSLI Publications. cslipublications.stanford.edu/LFG/.

Jøhndal, Marius L. 2012. *Non-finiteness in Latin*. Ph.D. thesis, University of Cambridge.

Kameyama, Megumi. 1985. *Zero anaphora: the case of Japanese*. Ph.D. thesis, Stanford University.

Kaplan, Ronald M, and Zaenen, Annie. 1989. Long-distance dependencies, constituent structure, and functional uncertainty. Pages 17–42 of: Baltin, Mark R., and Kroch, Anthony S. (eds.), *Alternative conceptions of phrase structure*. Chicago: University of Chicago Press.

2003. West-Germanic verb clusters in LFG. Pages 127–50 of: Seuren, Pieter, and Kempen, Gerard (eds.), *Verb constructions in German and Dutch*. Amsterdam: John Benjamins.

Karttunen, Lauri, and Kay, Martin. 1985. Parsing in a free word order language. Pages 279–319 of: Dowty, David R., Karttunen, Lauri, and Zwicky, Arnold (eds.), *Natural language parsing. Psychological, computational, and theoretical perspectives*. Cambridge: Cambridge University Press.

Kibort, Anna. 2004. *Passive and passive-like constructions in English and Polish*. Ph.D. thesis, University of Cambridge.

2007. Extending the applicability of lexical mapping theory. Pages 250–70 of: Butt, Miriam, and King, Tracy Holloway (eds.), *Proceedings of the LFG07 conference*. Stanford, CA: CSLI Publications. cslipublications.stanford.edu/LFG/.

2008. On the syntax of ditransitive constructions. Pages 312–32 of: Butt, Miriam, and King, Tracy Holloway (eds.), *Proceedings of the LFG08 conference*. Stanford, CA: CSLI Publications. cslipublications.stanford.edu/LFG/.

2014. Mapping out a construction inventory with (lexical) mapping theory. Pages 262–82 of: Butt, Miriam, and King, Tracy Holloway (eds.), *Proceedings of the LFG14 conference*. Stanford, CA: CSLI Publications. cslipublications.stanford.edu/LFG/.

Kibort, Anna, and Maling, Joan. 2015. Modelling the syntactic ambiguity of the active vs. passive impersonal in LFG. Pages 145–65 of: Butt, Miriam, and King, Tracy Holloway (eds.), *Proceedings of the LFG15 conference*. Stanford, CA: CSLI Publications. cslipublications.stanford.edu/LFG/.

King, Tracy Holloway. 1997. Focus domains and information and information-structure. In: Butt, Miriam, and King, Tracy Holloway (eds.), *Proceedings of the LFG97 conference*. Stanford, CA: CSLI Publications. cslipublications.stanford.edu/LFG/.

1995. *Configuring topic and focus in Russian*. Stanford, CA: CSLI Publications.

King, Tracy Holloway, and Dalrymple, Mary. 2004. Determiner agreement and noun conjunction. *Journal of Linguistics*, **40**(1), 69–104.

Kiparsky, Paul. 2002. Disjoint reference and the typology of pronouns. Pages 179–226 of: Kaufmann, Ingrid, and Stiebels, Barbara (eds.), *More than words*. Studia Grammatica, no. 53. Berlin: Akademie Verlag.

Klokeid, Terry. 1976. *Topics in Lardil grammar*. Ph.D. thesis, MIT.

Kroeger, Paul R. 1993. *Phrase structure and grammatical relations in Tagalog*. Stanford, CA: CSLI Publications.

2005. *Analyzing grammar. An introduction*. Cambridge: Cambridge University Press.

Kuhn, Jonas. 2003. *Optimality-theoretic syntax: a declarative approach*. Stanford, CA: CSLI Publications.

Laczkó, Tibor. 2014a. Essentials of an LFG analysis of Hungarian finite sentences. Pages 325–45 of: Butt, Miriam, and King, Tracy Holloway (eds.), *Proceedings of the LFG14 conference*. Stanford, CA: CSLI Publications. cslipublications.stanford.edu/LFG/.

2014b. An LFG analysis of verbal modifiers in Hungarian. Pages 346–66 of: Butt, Miriam, and King, Tracy Holloway (eds.), *Proceedings of the LFG14 conference*. Stanford, CA: CSLI Publications. cslipublications.stanford.edu/LFG/.

Lapata, Maria. 1998. Anaphoric binding in modern Greek. In: Butt, Miriam, and King, Tracy Holloway (eds.), *Proceedings of the LFG98 conference*. Stanford, CA: CSLI Publications. cslipublications.stanford.edu/LFG/.

Larson, Richard K. 1988. On the double object construction. *Linguistic Inquiry*, **19**, 335–91.

Legendre, Géraldine. 2001. An introduction to Optimality Theory in syntax. Pages 1–27 of: Legendre, Géraldine, Grimshaw, Jane, and Vikner, Sten (eds.), *Optimality-theoretic syntax*. Cambridge, MA: MIT Press.

Lødrup, Helge. 1999a. Inalienables in Norwegian and binding theory. *Linguistics*, **37**, 365–88.

1999b. Linking optimality in the Norwegian presentational construction. *Nordic Journal of Linguistics*, **22**, 205–30.

2007. A new account of simple and complex reflexives in Norwegian. *Journal of Comparative Germanic Linguistics*, **10**(3), 183–201.

2008. Local binding without coargumenthood: Norwegian noun phrases. Pages 333–51 of: Butt, Miriam, and King, Tracy Holloway (eds.), *Proceedings of the LFG08 Conference*. Stanford, CA: CSLI Publications. cslipublications.stanford.edu/LFG/.

Lowe, John. 2015. Degrees of degrammaticalization: a lexical sharing approach to the English possessive. Pages 208–28 of: Butt, Miriam, and King, Tracy Holloway (eds.), *Proceedings of the LFG15 conference*. Stanford, CA: CSLI Publications. cslipublications.stanford.edu/LFG/.

Maling, Joan. 1984. Non-clause-bounded reflexives in modern Icelandic. *Linguistics and Philosophy*, **7**(3), 211–41.

1986. Clause-bounded reflexives in modern Icelandic. Pages 53–63 of: Hellan, Lars, and Koch Christiansen, Kirsti (eds.), *Topics in Scandinavian syntax*. Dordrecht: Reidel.

Manning, Christopher D. 1996. *Ergativity: argument structure and grammatical relations*. Stanford, CA: CSLI Publications.

Mithun, Marianne. 1984. The evolution of noun incorporation. *Language*, **60**, 847–89.

Mittendorf, Ingo, and Sadler, Louisa. 2005. Nouns, numerals and number in Welsh NPs. Pages 294–312 of: Butt, Miriam, and King, Tracy Holloway (eds.), *Proceedings of the LFG05 conference*. Stanford, CA: CSLI Publications. cslipublications.stanford.edu/LFG/.

Mohanan, K.P. 1983. Functional and anaphoric control. *Linguistic Inquiry*, **14**, 641–74.

Musgrave, Simon, and Austin, Peter K. (eds.). 2008. *Voice and grammatical relations in Austronesian*. Stanford, CA: CSLI Publications.

Mycock, Louise. 2006. *A typology of constituent questions: a Lexical-Functional Grammar analysis of 'wh'-questions*. Ph.D. thesis, University of Manchester.

2007. Constituent question formation and focus: a new typological perspective. *Transactions of the Philological Society*, **105**, 192–251.

Mycock, Louise, and Lowe, John. 2013. The prosodic encoding of discourse functions. Pages 440–60 of: Butt, Miriam, and King, Tracy Holloway (eds.), *Proceedings of the LFG13 conference*. Stanford, CA: CSLI Publications. cslipublications.stanford.edu/LFG/.

Nichols, Johanna. 1986. Head-marking and dependent-marking grammar. *Language*, **62**(1), 56–119.

Nordlinger, Rachel. 1998. *Constructive case: evidence from Australian languages*. Stanford, CA: CSLI Publications.

Nordlinger, Rachel, and Bresnan, Joan. 2011. Lexical-Functional Grammar: interactions between morphology and syntax. Pages 112–40 of: Borsley, Robert D., and Börjars, Kersti (eds.), *Non-transformational syntax: formal and explicit models of grammar*. Oxford: Wiley-Blackwell.

Nordlinger, Rachel, and Sadler, Louisa. 2004a. Nominal tense in crosslinguistic perspective. *Language*, **80**(4), 776–806.

2004b. Tense beyond the verb: encoding clausal tense/aspect/mood on nominal dependents. *Natural Language and Linguistic Theory*, **22**, 597–641.

2019. Morphology in LFG and HPSG. Pages 212–243 of: Audring, Jenny, and Masini, Francesca (eds.), *The Oxford handbook of morphological theory*. Oxford: Oxford University Press.

O'Connor, Robert. 2006. *Information structure in Lexical-Functional Grammar: the discourse–prosody correspondence*. Ph.D. thesis, University of Manchester.

O'Grady, William. 1998. The syntax of idioms. *Natural Language and Linguistic Theory*, **16**, 279–312.

Parker, Steve. 1999. On the behavior of definite articles in Chamicuro. *Language*, **75**(3), 552–62.

Patejuk, Agnieszka. 2015. *Unlike coordination in Polish: an LFG account*. Ph.D. thesis, University of Warsaw.

Payne, John, and Börjars, Kersti. 2015. Features and selection in LFG: the English VP. Pages 289–303 of: Butt, Miriam, and King, Tracy Holloway (eds.), *Proceedings of the LFG15 conference*. Stanford, CA: CSLI Publications. cslipublications.stanford.edu/LFG/.

Payne, John, Pullum, Geoffrey K., Scholz, Barbara C., and Berlage, Eva. 2013. Anaphoric one and its implications. *Language*, **89**(4), 794–829.

Payne, Thomas E. 2010. *Understanding English grammar. A linguistic introduction*. Cambridge: Cambridge University Press.

Prince, Alan, and Smolensky, Paul. 2004. *Optimality Theory: Constraint interaction in generative grammar*. Oxford: Blackwell.

Radford, Andrew, Atkinson, Martin, Britain, David, Clahsen, Harald, and Spencer, Andrew. 2009. *Linguistics. An introduction* (2nd edn). Cambridge: Cambridge University Press.

Rákosi, György. 2009. Beyond identity: the case of a complex Hungarian reflexive. Pages 459–79 of: Butt, Miriam, and King, Tracy Holloway (eds.), *Proceedings of the LFG09 conference*. Stanford, CA: CSLI Publications. cslipublications.stanford.edu/LFG/.

2010. On snakes and locative binding in Hungarian. Pages 395–415 of: Butt, Miriam, and King, Tracy Holloway (eds.), *Proceedings of the LFG10 conference*. Stanford, CA: CSLI Publications. cslipublications.stanford.edu/LFG/.

Rudin, Catherine. 1988a. Multiple questions in South Slavic, West Slavic, and Romanian. *Slavic and East European Journal*, **32**, 1–24.

1988b. On multiple questions and multiple *wh*-fronting. *Natural Language and Linguistic Theory*, **6**, 455–501.

Sadler, Louisa. 1998. English auxiliaries as tense inflections. *Essex Research Reports in Linguistics*, **24**, 1–16.

2016. Agreement in Archi: an LFG perspective. Pages 150–83 of: Bond, Oliver, Corbett, Greville C., Chumakina, Marina, and Brown, Dunstan (eds.), *Archi: complexities of agreement in cross-theoretical perspective*. Oxford: Oxford University Press.

Sadler, Louisa, and Camilleri, Maris. 2013. Ditransitive predicates and dative arguments in Maltese. *Lingua*, **134**, 36–61.

Sadler, Louisa, and Spencer, Andrew. 1998. Argument structure and morphology. Pages 206–36 of: Spencer, Andrew, and Zwicky, Arnold (eds.), *The handbook of morphology*. Oxford: Blackwell.

(eds.). 2004. *Projecting morphology*. Stanford, CA: CSLI Publications.

Sadler, Louisa, van Genabith, Josef, and Way, Andy. 2000a. Automatic f-structure annotation from the AP Treebank. Pages 226–43 of: Butt, Miriam, and King, Tracy Holloway (eds.), *Proceedings of the LFG00 conference*. cslipublications.stanford.edu/LFG/.

2000b. Automatic f-structure annotation of treebank trees. Pages 139–60 of: Butt, Miriam, and King, Tracy Holloway (eds.), *Proceedings of the LFG00 conference*. cslipublications.stanford.edu/LFG/.

Seiss, Melanie. 2013. *Murrinh-Patha complex verbs: syntactic theory and computational implementation*. Ph.D. thesis, University of Konstanz.

Seiss, Melanie, and Nordlinger, Rachel. 2010. Applicativizing complex predicates: a case study from Murrinh-Patha. Pages 416–36 of: Butt, Miriam, and King, Tracy Holloway (eds.), *Proceedings of the LFG10 conference*. Stanford, CA: CSLI Publications. cslipublications.stanford.edu/LFG/.

Sells, Peter. 1984. *Syntax and semantics of resumptive pronouns*. Ph.D. thesis, University of Massachusetts at Amherst.

1988. Thematic and grammatical hierarchies: Albanian reflexivization. Pages 293–303 of: Borer, Hagit (ed.), *Proceedings of the Seventh West Coast conference on formal linguistics*. Stanford, CA: Stanford Linguistics Association.

(ed.) 2001a. *Formal and empirical issues in optimality-theoretic syntax*. Stanford, CA: CSLI Publications.

2001b. *Structure, alignment and optimality in Swedish*. Stanford, CA: CSLI Publications.

Sells, Peter, Zaenen, Annie, and Zec, Draga. 1987. Reflexivization variation: relations between syntax, semantics, and lexical structure. Pages 169–238 of: Iida, Masayo, Wechsler, Stephen, and Zec, Draga (eds.), *Working papers in grammatical theory and discourse structure*. Chicago, IL: University of Chicago Press.

Simpson, Jane. 1983. *Aspects of Warlpiri morphology and syntax*. Ph.D. thesis, MIT.

1991. *Warlpiri morpho-syntax. A lexicalist approach*. Dordrecht: Kluwer.

Simpson, Jane, and Bresnan, Joan. 1983. Control and obviation in Warlpiri. *Natural Language & Linguistic Theory*, **1**, 49–64.

Snijders, Liselotte. 2014. Non-reflexive binding in Warlpiri. Pages 524–44 of: Butt, Miriam, and King, Tracy Holloway (eds.), *Proceedings of the LFG14 conference*. Stanford, CA: CSLI Publications. cslipublications.stanford.edu/LFG/.

Spencer, Andrew. 1991. *Morphological theory*. Oxford: Blackwell.

Strahan, Tania. 2009. Outside-in binding of reflexives in insular Scandinavian. Pages 541–61 of: Butt, Miriam, and King, Tracy Holloway (eds.), *Proceedings of the LFG09 conference*. Stanford, CA: CSLI Publications. cslipublications.stanford.edu/LFG/.

Sulger, Sebastian. 2017. *Modeling nominal predications in Hindi/Urdu*. Ph.D. thesis, University of Konstanz.

Sung, Won-Kyung. 1996. *Etude des pronoms coréens*. Ph.D. thesis, Université Paris 7.

Teleman, Ulf, Hellberg, Staffan, and Andersson, Erik. 1999. *Svenska akademiens grammatik, Vol 1–4*. Stockholm: Svenska Akademien.

Toivonen, Ida. 2000. The morphosyntax of Finnish possessives. *Natural Language and Linguistic Theory*, **18**(3), 579–609.

2003. *Non-projecting words: a case study of Swedish particles*. Dordrecht: Kluwer.

2013. English benefactive NPs. Pages 503–23 of: Butt, Miriam, and King, Tracy Holloway (eds.), *Proceedings of the LFG13 conference*. Stanford, CA: CSLI Publications. cslipublications.stanford.edu/LFG/.

van Genabith, Josef. 2006. Rapid treebank-based acquisition of multilingual LFG resources. Pages 111–36 of: Butt, Miriam, Dalrymple, Mary, and King, Tracy Holloway (eds.), *Intelligent linguistic architectures: variations on themes by Ronald M. Kaplan*. Stanford, CA: CSLI Publications.

van Genabith, Josef, Way, Andy, and Sadler, Louisa. 1999. Semi-automatic generation of F-structures from tree banks. In: Butt, Miriam, and King, Tracy Holloway (eds.), *Proceedings of LFG99*. Stanford, CA: CSLI Publications. cslipublications.stanford.edu/LFG/.

Vilkuna, Maria. 1989. *Free word order in Finnish: its syntax and discourse function*. Helsinki: Suomen Kirjallisuuden Seura.

Vincent, Nigel. 1999. The evolution of c-structure: prepositions and PPs from Indo-European to Romance. *Linguistics*, **37**(6), 1111–53.

2001. LFG as a model of syntactic change. Pages 1–42 of: Butt, Miriam, and King, Tracy Holloway (eds.), *Time over matter. Diachronic perspectives on morphosyntax*. Stanford, CA: CSLI Publications.

Wechsler, Stephen, and Zlatić, Larisa. 2000. A theory of agreement and its application to Serbo-Croatian. *Language*, **76**(4), 759–98.

2003. *The many faces of agreement*. Stanford, CA: CSLI Publications.

Zaenen, Annie, and Engdahl, Elisabet. 1994. Descriptive and theoretical syntax in the lexicon. Pages 181–212 of: Atkins, B. T. S., and Zampolli, Antonio (eds.), *Computational approaches to the lexicon*. Oxford: Oxford University Press.

Zaenen, Annie, Engdahl, Elisabet, and Maling, Joan M. 1981. Resumptive pronouns can be syntactically bound. *Linguistic Inquiry*, **12**, 679–82.

Zweigenbaum, Pierre. 1988. *Attributive adjectives, adjuncts, and cyclic f-structures in Lexical-Functional Grammar*. Tech. rept. Paris: Département Intelligence Artificielle et Médecine, Paris 6.

Zwicky, Arnold M. 1985. Heads. *Journal of Linguistics*, **21**, 1–30.

Index